PENGUIN BOOKS

THE TENTH PARALLEL

'Eliza Griswold's talent runs through this book like a blinding light.
Through her daring travel, quiet observation, empathy and gift for
language, she humanizes and clarifies conflicts in Africa
and Asia that are often neglected or misunderstood *The Tenth
Parallel* is both vitally important and 1   itten'
Steve Coll, author of *T*   *ars*

'The Tenth Pa   you
will ever read. E   of an
investigativ
Reza   *od*

'*The Tenth Parallel* traces the uneasy fault line of two great faiths,
which have so much bloody history between them. In exploring
the potent tensions that underlie so many of the conflicts of
the present age, Eliza Griswold gives us a rare look at how
complex and interwoven these two cultures actually are'
Lawrence Wright, author of *The Looming Tower*

'In this revolutionary work, Griswold . . . changes the way we think
about Christianity and Islam . . . She returns us to the most basic truth
of human existence: that the world and its people are interconnected'
Archbishop Desmond Tutu

'A deeply impressive achievement, which so often challenges our
common assumptions . . . It should be required reading for policy
makers, and for anyone interested in the spiritual dimensions of the
"clash of civilizations"' Philip Jenkins, author of *Jesus Wars*

'A very courageous and challenging account of the tensions
between Muslims and Christians that refuses to settle with any
damaging stereotypes, focusing instead on the extraordinary potential for
reconciliation and understanding in the lives of ordinary believers'
Rowan Williams

Eliza Griswold, a fellow at the New America Foundation, received both the first Robert I. Friedman Award for investigative reporting and a 2010 Rome Prize from the American Academy in Rome, and was a 2007 Nieman Fellow at Harvard University. Her journalism has appeared in *The Atlantic*, *The New Yorker*, *The New York Times Magazine*, and *Harper's Magazine*, among others. A collection of her poems, *Wideawake Field*, was published by FSG in 2007.

The Tenth Parallel

DISPATCHES FROM THE FAULTLINE
BETWEEN CHRISTIANITY AND ISLAM

Eliza Griswold

PENGUIN BOOKS

PENGUIN BOOKS

Published by the Penguin Group
Penguin Books Ltd, 80 Strand, London WC2R ORL, England
Penguin Group (USA) Inc., 375 Hudson Street, New York, New York 10014, USA
Penguin Group (Canada), 90 Eglinton Avenue East, Suite 700, Toronto, Ontario, Canada M4P 2Y3
(a division of Pearson Penguin Canada Inc.)
Penguin Ireland, 25 St Stephen's Green, Dublin 2, Ireland (a division of Penguin Books Ltd)
Penguin Group (Australia), 250 Camberwell Road, Camberwell, Victoria 3124, Australia
(a division of Pearson Australia Group Pty Ltd)
Penguin Books India Pvt Ltd, 11 Community Centre, Panchsheel Park, New Delhi – 110 017, India
Penguin Group (NZ), 67 Apollo Drive, Rosedale, Auckland 0632, New Zealand
(a division of Pearson New Zealand Ltd)
Penguin Books (South Africa) (Pty) Ltd, 24 Sturdee Avenue,
Rosebank, Johannesburg 2196, South Africa

Penguin Books Ltd, Registered Offices: 80 Strand, London WC2R ORL, England

www.penguin.com

First published in the United States of America by Farrar, Straus and Giroux 2010
First published in Great Britain by Allen Lane 2011
Published in Penguin Books 2012

1

Copyright © Eliza Griswold, 2010
Maps copyright © Jeffrey L. Ward, 2010

Printed in Great Britain by Clays Ltd, St Ives plc

978-0-241-95223-8

www.greenpenguin.co.uk

FOR PHOEBE AND FRANK GRISWOLD

For Anna Collier,

with warm regards,

E

Out beyond ideas of wrongdoing and rightdoing
there is a field. I'll meet you there.

—JELALUDDIN RUMI

A self-sufficient human being is subhuman. I have gifts that you do not have,
so consequently, I am unique—you have gifts that I do not have, so you are
unique. God has made us so that we will need each other . . .

—ARCHBISHOP DESMOND TUTU

I stopped asking such questions as
is he white or black
an anarchist or monarchist
fashionable or outmoded
ours or theirs
and I began to ask
what in him is of human being

and is he

—RYSZARD KAPUŚCIŃSKI

I believe in God, God. God, I believe in God.

—WILLIAM FAULKNER

CONTENTS

CONTENTS

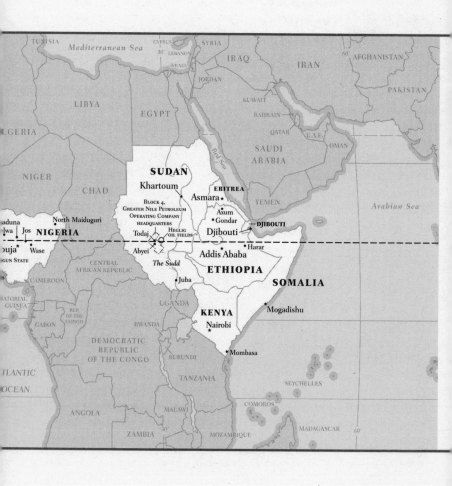

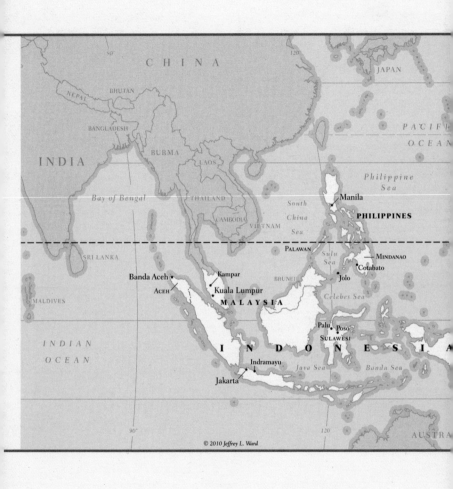
© 2010 Jeffrey L. Ward

THE TENTH PARALLEL

PROLOGUE

The chief was spending Easter Sunday in his hut, which smelled of stale smoke from a cooking fire and of something more glandular: panic. When the visitor from Washington ducked inside, the chief, a man in his mid-fifties named Nyol Paduot, rose stiff-kneed from a white plastic lawn chair. He had spent several days keeping watch against an approaching dust cloud kicked up by horsemen and Jeeps. It would mean his village of Todaj, teetering on the fraught and murky border between northern and southern Sudan, was under attack again. He was grouchy and unkempt: his eyes pouched, his salt-and-pepper beard scruffy, his waxy green-and-yellow shirt stained with the tide lines of dried sweat. He glowered at the American visitor, Roger Winter, whose bare legs poked out from khaki shorts. One leg bore the scar of a snakebite he had gotten not far away while helping to broker a peace on behalf of the United States. The 2005 deal was supposed to end nearly forty years of intermittent civil war between northern and southern Sudan, which had left two million people dead. In some places, the peace agreement had stanched the bloodshed, allowing the south to form a nascent government that described itself as "Christian-led." Under the terms of the deal, the north was supposed to make it attractive for the south to remain part of a unified Sudan by giving it a voice in the national government, and a fair share of oil revenues. But the north ignored most of the terms. The peace deal proved to mean nothing here on the boundary between the two Sudans, which jigs and jags like an EKG reading along the straight, flat latitude of the tenth parallel.

The tenth parallel is the horizontal band that rings the earth seven hundred miles north of the equator. If Africa is shaped like a rumpled sock, with South Africa at the toe and Somalia at the heel, then the tenth parallel runs across the ankle. Along the tenth parallel, in Sudan, and in most of inland Africa, two worlds collide: the mostly Muslim, Arab-influenced north meets a black African south inhabited by Christians and those who follow indigenous religions—which include those who venerate ancestors and the spirits of animals, land, and sky.[1] Thirty miles south (at a latitude of 9°43'59"), the village of Todaj marked the divide where these two rival worldviews, their dysfunctional governments and well-armed militaries, vied inch by inch for land. The village belonged to the south's largest ethnic group, the Ngok Dinka. But in 2008, when Roger Winter paid Nyol Paduot a visit, the north was threatening to send its soldiers and Arab militias to attack the village and lay claim to the underground river of light, sweet crude oil running beneath the chief's feet.

Oil was discovered in southern Sudan during the 1970s, and the struggle to control it is one of the long-running war's more recent causes. The fight in Sudan threatened to split Africa's largest country in two, and still does. In 2011, the south is scheduled to vote on whether it wants to remain part of the north or become its own country, made up of ten states that lie to the south of the tenth parallel and border Ethiopia, Kenya, Uganda, the Democratic Republic of Congo, the Central African Republic, and Chad. This looming split—which, if it happens, would likely occur largely along the tenth parallel—meant that Todaj and the nearby oil boomtown of Abyei, about ten miles south, were vitally important. Whichever side controlled them would control an estimated two billion barrels of oil.

Other than Paduot, and six elders gathered in his hut, the village appeared deserted. Prompted by gunfire and rumors of war, the five hundred families who lived there had fled south, terrified that Todaj was about to be wiped off the face of the earth. Their fear was well founded: three times in the previous twenty years, soldiers from the north had laid siege to Todaj, raping women and children, killing and carrying off young men, and burning to the ground the villagers' thatched huts and the Episcopal church made of hay.

It was the end of the dry season, and a breeze stirred the air over this colorless plot of parched earth, bare but for these empty dwellings and a few gaunt cows trawling for loose hay. The cows wandering hungrily around the village didn't belong to the people of Todaj, but to northern Arab nomads, the Misseriya, who, because of seasonal drought up north, came south at this time of year to graze their cattle. Paduot was afraid that when the rains began a few weeks later, and the nomads could return home to their own greener pastures, there would be nothing to keep the northern soldiers (cousins and sons of the nomads) from attacking Todaj.

"We know when they burn our village, they want the land," said the chief, a Ngok Dinka translator rendering his words into English. These patterns sounded like the ones unfolding less than fifty miles northwest, in the region of Darfur, because they were the same. Three decades ago, while Sudan's current president, Omar Hassan al-Bashir, was a military general stationed on this border, the Khartoum-based northern government perfected the methods of attack, using the paramilitary horsemen called the Janjawiid, whom it was now deploying in Darfur. Todaj faced this same threat, but other than Roger Winter, very few knew anything about the impending disaster. On BBC radio, Paduot heard much talk about Darfur. Although the same thing was happening here along the border, it rarely made international news. The two fronts had much in common, since all of Sudan's wars boil down to a central Khartoum-based cabal battling the people at the peripheries. The only differences between Darfur and Abyei, the chief explained, were religion and oil. In Darfur, there was no oil and both sides were Muslim, a confrontation he did not understand. "Why would Muslims fight against Muslims?" he asked aloud.

Here, the north had mounted its assaults in the name of jihad, or holy war, claiming that Islam and Arab culture should reign supreme in Sudan. Chief Paduot, who had survived several such conflagrations, had come to see Islam as a tool of oppression, one the northerners were using to erase his culture and undo his people's claim to the land and its oil.

"People hate Islam now," he said. Having stepped into the hut behind Winter, I glanced around to see if any of the elders was startled by the chief's remark. If they were, no sign of it crossed their faces, which showed only dread and exhaustion.

To defy the north, most of the villagers had been baptized as Episcopalians—they prayed daily, attended church on Sunday, and had cast off loose, long-sleeved Islamic dress in favor of short-sleeved Western-style button-down shirts, or brilliant batiks. For them, *Islam* was now simply a catchall term for the government, people, and policies of the north.

Race, like religion, was a rallying cry in this complicated war. The paler-skinned Arab northerners looked down on the darker-skinned people of the south, Paduot explained slowly. He seemed tired of giving tutorials to outsiders. What good were earnest, well-meaning people like us, who came with our water bottles and notebooks to record the details of a situation but could do nothing to stop it?

The divisions between north and south along the tenth parallel date back centuries, and colonial rule simply reinforced them. One hundred years earlier, the British colonialists who governed Sudan had virtually handed this swath of land south of the tenth parallel to the Roman Catholic Church. Daniel Comboni, a beloved nineteenth-century Italian missionary who was canonized as a saint in 2003, headed Catholic efforts in Central Africa with the expressed aim to "save Africa through Africans."[2] Under Comboni's direction, the Catholic Church ran all schools and hospitals (and forbade Protestant missionaries from proselytizing), until, in 1964, the northern government, employing Islam as a form of nationalism, expelled all missionaries from the country. African Christians—not Westerners—were left to lead the local church, which was then, as now, under fire from the north as an alien, infidel institution. This attitude has not changed, the local Catholic priest, Father Peter Suleiman, told me. "Every day we experience the misery of the south. You still hear the promise of death." And oil has made things worse. "The north believes that oil is a gift from God for the Muslim people," he said. Although the Catholic Church still held some sway along this border, Father Suleiman told me that an influx of more charismatic Protestant churches was gaining ground. In the village of Todaj, many of the villagers were convinced that they were still alive solely because they had prayed to Jesus Christ for protection.

Born into a family that prayed to ancestral gods, Chief Paduot became a nominal Muslim in order to gain admission to school (a practice begun by Christian missionaries and now emulated by Khartoum). Through a process of forced Islamization, the north had made it compulsory for people to declare themselves Muslims by saying the Shahada—"I bear witness that there is no god but God, and I bear witness that Mohammed is his messenger"—and adopting Muslim names in order to attend school, get a job, or avoid jail or violent death. In his forties, Paduot, chief by birth, decided that he wanted to leave Islam and become a Catholic. But the northern security forces threatened the local Catholic priest, one Father Marco, saying they would torture him if he baptized the chief. (They told Paduot they'd stone him if he became "a backslider from Islam.") He refrained from converting to Catholicism to safeguard his village from further trouble. "I kept Islam to protect my people," he said, but, to show his independence, he had returned to the indigenous practices of his youth—called the noble spiritual beliefs. Christians and Muslims alike disparaged the local indigenous religion on the ground that it didn't teach adherents to follow the one, true God. That was ignorance on their part, Paduot said. "We worship one Creator God, too, then smaller gods."

He had also married an Episcopalian. Now he led us out of the hut—its thick, round walls like a muddy mushroom stem—and pointed to a line of what looked like tiny corn-husk scarecrows along the roofs of his and other huts. "They are crosses," the chief said. Their frayed edges glowed in the afternoon's pewter light; they were symbols marking the beginning of the south, and visual reminders to anyone entering the village that it was a Christian place, the chief explained. Squinting into the overcast sky to look at them, I thought the threadbare totems were also bids for divine protection.

Yet the crosses seemed to be proving as ineffective as the chief's satellite phone, which hung by its power cord from two portable solar panels on the thatched roof of his hut. There was no one left for him to call for help. Though his cousin, Francis Deng, was serving as the United Nations Special Representative for the Prevention of Genocide, and though Paduot met regularly with local UN officials, representatives of the southern government, and visitors such as Roger Winter (a longtime head of the U.S. Committee for Refugees who had lobbied hard for the south in Washington and Khartoum), no one could do anything to stop the impending assault.

On the surface of this conflict, two groups, northern and southern, Muslim and Christian, were competing for land and water. Yet at a deeper level, the people were now pawns of their respective governments, and Paduot knew it.

He produced a worn map softened with use and pointed to three annotations in English: PUMP 1, PUMP 2, PUMP 3. These indicated the oil fields of the Greater Nile Petroleum Operating Company—a consortium of Chinese, Malaysian, Indian, and Sudanese interests operating in Sudan with the blessing of President Bashir. At the same time, Bashir was exhorting his holy soldiers, or Mujahideen—whom he called "the legitimate sons of the soil"—to re-up for jihad. Once again, he was making use of race and religion to safeguard oil interests before the country faced the impending split.

Some of his soldiers were stationed two hundred yards away, acting as sentries on the north-south border, the location of which was determined by whoever was strong enough to push it a few inches one way or another. Around their makeshift barracks, camps of nomads were springing up, as if preparing for war. Over the past few weeks, as Paduot looked on, the soldiers had received shipments of automatic rifles and rocket-propelled grenade launchers. If a full-scale rift between north and south occurred, it would begin right here with these weapons, Paduot warned. A village sentry came in and whispered in his ear. Abruptly, he stopped talking: soldiers were slouching against the hut's outside wall, listening to his every word.

In Africa, the space between the tenth parallel and the equator marks the end of the continent's arid north and the beginning of sub-Saharan jungle. Wind, other weather, and centuries of human migrations have brought the two religions to converge here. Christianity and Islam share a fifteen-hundred-year history in Africa. It began in 615 when Mohammed, his life at risk at home on the Arabian Peninsula, sent a dozen of his followers and family members to find refuge at the court of an African Christian king in Abyssinia (modern-day Ethiopia). Within a decade of Mohammed's death (in 632), the first Muslim armies landed in Africa, proceeding south from Egypt to today's Sudan. There they made a peace pact—the first of its kind—with the ancient Nubian Christian kingdoms along the Nile River. The pact lasted for six centuries. Then religious wars broke out. By 1504, the last of the Christian kingdoms in Sudan had fallen to Muslim armies.

From the seventh century to the twentieth, Muslim traders and missionaries carried Islam inland over the northernmost third of Africa, carving trade routes from the holy city of Mecca in Saudi Arabia to the West African kingdom of Timbuktu. Away from the coasts, crossing the landlocked region south of the tenth parallel proved difficult; the pale, grassy savanna thickened to bush, and the bush gave way to a mire of emerald swamp and jungle. Along the tenth parallel, the tsetse fly belt begins: and these blood-sucking insects, each the size of a housefly and carrying African trypanosomiasis (sleeping sickness),[3] virtually stopped Islam's southern spread.

To the east, five thousand miles off the African coast and over the Indian Ocean, natural forces also shaped the encounter of Christianity and Islam in the Southeast Asian nations of Indonesia, Malaysia, and the Philippines. The trade winds—high-pressure air currents that move steadily from either pole toward the equator—filled the sails of both Muslim and Christian merchants from the northern hemisphere beginning in the eighth century. These reliable winds propelled Christian and Muslim ships to the same islands, beaches, and ports, then returned them either to Europe or to the Arabian Peninsula, their ships heavy with cargoes of cinnamon and cloves.

The trade winds are part of the intertropical convergence zone, a weather system that moves to the north or south of the equator, depending on the season. In this zone, wind currents from the northern hemisphere run into those from the southern hemisphere. As the two cycles meet head-on, they generate cataclysmic storms. In Asia, these storms begin during monsoon season and generally spin west to Africa, where the most tempestuous of them move west off the African coast at Cape Verde, across the Atlantic Ocean, and become America's hurricanes. Within this band, Asia, Africa, and America are part of a single weather system.[4] (A dangerous year of monsoons in Asia and storms in Africa's catastrophe belt, for instance, can mean a disastrous year of hurricanes for the U.S. eastern seaboard.)

As the earth grows warmer, preexisting cycles of flooding and drought around the tenth parallel grow increasingly unpredictable, making it impossible for African nomads, most of whom are Muslims, and farmers (Christians, Muslims, and indigenous believers) to rely on centuries-old patterns of migration, planting, and harvesting. They must move into new territory to grow food and graze their livestock. Consequently, between the equator and the tenth parallel two groups with distinctly different cultures and cosmologies unavoidably face off against each other—as they do in the Sudanese village of Todaj.

Growing populations intensify these competitions. Due to the explosive growth of Christianity over the past fifty years, there are now 493 million Christians living south of the tenth parallel—nearly a fourth of the world's Christian population of 2 billion.[5] To the north live the majority of the continent's 367 million Muslims; they represent nearly one quarter of the world's 1.6 billion Muslims. These figures are an effective reminder that four out of five Muslims live outside the Middle East. Indonesia, with 240 million people, is the most populous Muslim country in the world. Malaysia is its tiny, rich neighbor; the Philippines, its larger, poorer one. Together, the three countries have a population of 250 million Muslims and 110 million Christians. Indonesia and Malaysia are predominantly

Muslim countries, with vocal Christian minorities. The Philippines—with a powerful Catholic majority (population 92 million) mostly to the north of the tenth parallel and a Muslim minority (population 5 million) to the south—is the opposite. It has been a strongly Christian country ever since Ferdinand Magellan planted a cross on an island hilltop there in 1521. Yet Islam, which arrived hundreds of years earlier, has remained a source of identity and rebellion in the south for the past five hundred years.

Africa's and Asia's populations are expanding, on average, faster than those in the rest of the world. While the global population of 6.8 billion people increases by 1.2 percent every year, in Asia the rate is 1.4 percent, and in Africa it doubles to 2.4 percent.[6] In this fragile zone where the two religions meet, the pressures wrought by growing numbers of people and an increasingly vulnerable environment are sharpening the tensions between Christians and Muslims over land, food, oil, and water, over practices and hardening worldviews.

The particular strain of religion that's growing the fastest also intensifies these problems. Christianity and Islam are in the throes of decades-long revolutions: reawakenings. Believers adopt outward signs of devotion—praying, eating, dressing, and other social customs—that call attention to the ways they differ from the unbelievers around them. Yet these movements are not simply about exhibiting devotion. They begin with a direct encounter with God.

For Sufis, who make up the majority of African Muslims, and for Pentecostals, who account for more than one quarter of African Christians, worship begins with ecstatic experience. Sufis follow a mystical strain of Islam that begins with inviting God into the human heart. Pentecostals urge their members to encounter the Holy Spirit viscerally, as Jesus's followers did during the feast of Pentecost when they spoke in tongues.

Such reawakenings demand an individual's total surrender, and promise, in return, an exclusive path to the one true God. "These movements aren't about converting to a better version of self," Lamin Sanneh, a theologian at Yale and the author of *Whose Religion Is Christianity?*, told me. "They are about converting to God." They say the believer can know God now in this life and forever in the next. In return, they expect the believer to proselytize—to gain new converts—from either among other religions or their own less ardent believers, which creates new frictions.

These movements are already reshaping Africa, Asia, and Latin America—the region we used to call *the third world*, or even *the developing world*. Nowadays, liberal and conservative Western analysts, and many of the region's inhabitants as well, use the term *Global South* instead. This somewhat clunky moniker is intended to cast off the legacy of the West, to challenge the assumption that the entire world is developing within a Western context. It is also meant to highlight a marked shift in demographics and influence among the world's Christians and Muslims. Today's typical Protestant is an African woman, not a white American man. In many of the weak states along the tenth parallel, the power of these religious movements is compounded by the fact that the "state" means very little here; governments are alien structures that offer their people almost nothing in the way of services or political rights. This lack is especially pronounced where present-day national borders began as nothing more than lines sketched onto colonial maps. Other kinds of identity, consequently, come to the fore: religion above everything—even race or ethnicity—becomes a means to safeguard individual and collective security in this world and the next one.

In many cases, then, gains for one side imply losses for the other. Revival provides not only a pattern for daily life but also a form of communal defense, bringing people together, giving them a shared goal or purpose, and inviting them to risk their lives in the pursuit of it. Often the end is liberation, and the means to liberation include martyrdom and holy war. With Islam, it is perhaps easier to understand how believers could see a return to religious law as undoing the corruption sown by colonialism. Yet in Christianity, too, religion has become a means of political emancipation, especially between the equator and the tenth parallel, where Christianity and Islam meet. Many Christians living in these states belong to non-Muslim ethnic minorities who share the experience of being enslaved by northern Muslims, and perceive themselves as living on Christianity's front line in the battle against Islamic domination. In Nigeria, Sudan, Indonesia, and the Philippines, and elsewhere, Christians have lost churches, homes, and family members to violent struggle. At the same time, they, like their Muslim adversaries, see the developed West as a godless place that has forsaken its Christian heritage.

I began investigating this faith-based fault line as a journalist in December 2003, when I traveled with Franklin Graham—Billy Graham's son, and head of a prosperous evangelical empire—to Khartoum, to meet his nemesis, President Omar Hassan al-Bashir, whose regime was waging the world's most violent modern jihad against Christians and Muslims alike in southern Sudan. Bashir was also beginning the genocidal campaign in Darfur. (In 2009, the International Criminal Court at The Hague issued an arrest warrant for Bashir for war crimes and crimes against humanity.) In Bashir's palace's sepulchral marble reception room, the two men argued pointedly over who would convert whom. Each adhered to a very different worldview: theirs were opposing fundamentalisms based on the belief that there was one—and only one—way to believe in God. At the same time, their religious politics spilled over into a fight between cultures, and represented the way in which the world's Muslims and the West have come to misunderstand each other. Being a witness to this conversation was like watching emissaries from two different civilizations square off over a plate of pistachios.

Soon afterward, I started to travel in the band between the equator and the tenth parallel. I visited places where the two religions often clash: Nigeria, Sudan, Somalia, and the Horn of Africa; Indonesia, Malaysia, and the Philippines. Over the past decade, there has been much theorizing about religion and politics, religion and poverty, conflicts and accommodation between Christianity and Islam. I wanted to see how Christianity and Islam are actually lived every day by huge numbers of vulnerable, marginal believers—individuals who are also part of the global story of poverty, development strategy, climate-change forecasts, and so on.

No theory of religious politics or religious violence in our time can possibly be complete without accounting for the four-fifths of Muslims who live outside the Middle East or for the swelling populations of evangelical Christians whose faith is bound up with their struggle for resources and survival. I wanted to go where such lives are actually led, where wars in the name of religion are not Internet media campaigns to "control a global narrative" but actual wars fought from village to village and street corner to street corner.

Most of all, I wanted to record the interwoven stories of those who inhabit this territory, and whose religious beliefs pattern their daily perseverance. Although it's easy to see Christianity and Islam as vast and static forces, they are perpetually in flux. Over time, each religion has shaped the other. Religion is dynamic and fluid. The most often overlooked fact of religious revivals, of the kind now unfolding between the equator and the tenth parallel, is that they give rise to divisions within the religions themselves. They are about a struggle over who speaks for God—a confrontation that takes place not simply between rival religions, but inside them. This is as true in the West as it is in the Global South. Religions, like the weather, link us to one another, whether we like it or not.

PART ONE

AFRICA

NIGERIA

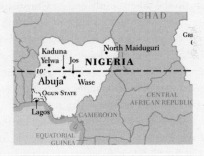

> *"Father, forgive them, for they do not know what they do."*
> —THE GOSPEL ACCORDING TO LUKE 23:34[1]

> *"Lord, forgive thy people, they do not know."*
> —SAHIH AL-BUKHARI, ISTITABE, 5

I

THE ROCK: ONE

Wase Rock is a double-humped crag that towers eight hundred feet above the green hills of Nigeria's Middle Belt. *Wase* ("wah-say") means "all-embracing" in Arabic, and it is one of Islam's ninety-nine names for God. Majestic and odd, the freestanding stone is smack in the center of the country, which, with 140 million people, is Africa's most populous. It is the largest in the world to be almost evenly split between Christians and Muslims. There are forty-five to fifty million members of each respective faith, but no exact figures, since the Nigerian government deemed questions about religion too dangerous to ask during the most recent census in 2006.[1] As in Sudan, fifteen hundred miles to the east, Nigeria's Muslims live predominantly in the desert north, and its Christians, to the swampy south. (There are some important exceptions, including the southwest, where the ethnic Yoruba have adopted both religions.) For the most part, Christianity and Islam meet in the Middle Belt, a two-hundred-mile-wide strip of fertile grassland that lies between the seventh and tenth parallels (from five hundred to seven hundred miles north of the equator) and runs from west to east across most of inland Africa.

This pale grassland belongs to the Sahel, which means "coast" in Arabic. The Sahel forms the coast of a great sand sea: the north's immense Sahara Desert. And the Middle Belt sits on a two-thousand-foot-high plateau of russet tableland; as the ground rises, the air freshens and cools. Depending on the season, the terrain ranges from bone-dry steppe to luxuriant green bush. On most days, a mild breeze blows down from the Middle Belt's knobby escarpments, over the savanna's glossy burr grass, and across a patchwork of small cassava and dairy farms, which produce milk that is an ambrosia of butter, honey, and sun.

The Middle Belt could be an earthly paradise, but it is not. I first arrived there in August 2006, to visit a local Muslim king called the Emir of Wase. As I approached Wase, the plateau became blistered with ruins. Almost every village had been burned to the ground, both the round thatched huts of the Christian farmers and the square mud houses that belonged to Muslim traders and herders. Since 2001, Nigeria's Middle Belt has been torn apart by violence between Christians and Muslims; tens of thousands of people have been killed in religious skirmishes. Almost all of these began over something other than religion—from local elections to fights over land, to mob violence that broke out between Muslims and Christians in reaction to America's invasion of Afghanistan in October 2001. Yet these small street fights, infused with deeper hatred, have often given way to massacres in churches, hospitals, and mosques. With each side determined to eradicate the other, the skirmishes have assumed the rhetoric of faith-based genocide; one Christian writer called

Nigeria's Muslims "cockroaches," a deliberate reminder of the 1994 Rwandan genocide.

Blessed with some of the world's richest oil reserves, Nigeria is sub-Saharan Africa's major petroleum producer. It is America's fifth-largest supplier of oil, a factor in the pronouncement by the U.S. assistant secretary of state Johnnie Carson that Nigeria is "undoubtedly the most important country in Sub-Saharan Africa."[2] But if Nigeria is one of the continent's wealthiest and most influential powers, it is also one of its most corrupt democracies. Since the end of military rule in 1999, politicians have reportedly embezzled between $4 billion and $8 billion annually.[3]

Despite the country's vast oil wealth, more than half of Nigerians live on less than one dollar a day, and four out of ten are unemployed. Being a citizen in Nigeria means next to nothing; in many regions, the state offers no electricity, water, or education. Instead, for access to everything from schooling to power lines, many Nigerians turn to religion. Being a Christian or a Muslim, belonging to the local church or mosque, and voting along religious lines has become the way to safeguard seemingly secular rights.

Nigeria's population is also growing at a rate of 2 percent a year—dramatically faster than the global average. This growth is particularly remarkable for Christians; high birth rates and aggressive evangelization over the past century have increased the number of believers from 176,000 to nearly 50 million. When it comes to religious competition, population is an undeniable asset. Due to these staggering numbers of new believers, many African Christians argue that, as the Middle Belt Anglican archbishop Benjamin Kwashi told me, "God has moved his work to Africa."

To visit the emir, I had borrowed a gold minivan that belonged to a one-armed pastor and an imam, former sworn enemies who had started an interfaith organization in the nearby city of Kaduna. Decals on the rear window read, "PEACE IS DIVINE." The minivan's driver was bald, barrel-chested, and in his mid-forties; Haruna Yakubu had formerly led Muslim gangs in Middle Belt clashes. Now he was seeking to deprogram the young men he had taught to fight in defense of their religion.

Wase lay on the far side of a river of the same name, and the only way to reach the tiny Muslim kingdom was to cross a narrow, one-lane concrete bridge. As we drove along the devastated floodplain toward Wase, some of the Christian farmers were beginning to rebuild. Tethered awkwardly outside the Christians' huts were muddy white cattle. Before the fighting, the farmers had hardly any cows; they belonged to the Muslim herders. The cattle were war booty.

When we reached the bridge, an orange truck was jackknifed across the lane, listing over the edge. A man in a Mylar suit and a matching peaked hat—like the tin man from *The Wizard of Oz*—pantomimed a traffic cop, but he was only playing at order. Cars were backed up behind the accident for several miles. The truck's heavy cab dangled off to the right and over the cataract rushing below, like a huge steel creature lowering its exhausted head for a drink. A market had sprung up: among the jam of people and cars, women sold peanuts and blackened corn from tin trays on their heads, the commerce of daily catastrophe. Radio chatter drifted from the open doors of trucks and cars. Nobody knew how long the wait would be—a week, maybe more. It would take a special winch to lift the truck, and it was days away. Until the winch arrived, all travel—to work, to the hospital, to buy clean water from the nearby town (Wase had none)—stopped dead. But the emir was not a man to be kept waiting, so we had to find a way across the bridge. Savvy Yakubu, the minivan's driver, quietly gathered a group of teenage boys hanging around—more than half of Nigeria's population is under eighteen—as I heaved open the van's sliding door and got out to walk. Somehow, the boys managed to lift our gold Toyota van, inch it around the jackknifed truck, and place it safely back onto the rickety bridge.

The emir's earthen castle stood atop a hill about five miles from Wase Rock. The clay forecourt swarmed with courtiers in billowing robes, and the clatter of hooves rang from the royal stable. On days like this one, when the emir was granting an audience, supplicants came from hundreds of miles away to ask his help with school fees or in solving disputes with neighbors. They waited in an octagonal two-story chamber, where a dozen members of the palace guard read the newspaper on the chilly floor. The king's advisor, or *waziri*, with a pink lace turban set on his head like a bicycle helmet, waited for the emir to summon his visitors, as his grandfather and great-grandfather had done before him. Most royal posts are hereditary, and the emir's bloodline has been a source of loyalty and honor since 1816, when his ancestor founded the kingdom at the base of Wase Rock.

This ancestor, a mysterious figure named Hasan, was a follower, a ji-hadi, of Nigeria's most famous Islamic reformer and a hero among African Muslims to this day: Uthman dan Fodio, a religious teacher and ethnic Fulani herder who launched a West African jihad in 1802 to purify Islam and promote the education of women. Dan Fodio, like most North African Muslims, was a Sufi. His was the first in a series of holy wars to rage across the center of the continent during the nineteenth century and into the early twentieth century. Most of these jihads began as religious rebellions within Islam, uprisings against African kings who the Sufi re-formers believed had corrupted the faith. Yet time and again, as Europe's Christian colonial powers arrived in Africa, these holy wars morphed into battles against the infidel West. These jihads, while largely forgotten, rep-resent some of the earliest and bloodiest confrontations of Islam with the West; they drove colonial policy toward Muslims not only in Africa but worldwide. They also laid the groundwork for Islam's opposition to the modern West.

By 1810, seventy-five years before the British would claim Nigeria as their protectorate, Dan Fodio's followers, called his flag bearers, had con-quered a large swath of West Africa as their own Islamic empire. The vanquished generally welcomed the flag bearers, who came riding south over the Sahel's high, pleasant plateau, on horses and camels and with Dan Fodio's pennant fluttering before them. When they neared the tenth parallel, the desert air moistened and the ground grew wetter. Here, the notorious tsetse fly belt began, and sleeping sickness killed off the jihadis' horses and camels, effectively halting their religion's southward advance. One of these jihadis, the emir's ancestor, established his kingdom on his favorite grazing land in the shadow of Wase Rock. For thirteen genera-tions, the emir's family has occupied this leaking keep. A place out of time, it feels more like an ancient oasis in Arabia than a palace in modern-day Nigeria; the only objects in the anteroom to signal the passage of two hundred years are the newspapers and a white plastic wall phone that buzzes when the emir is ready to hear petitions.

In his traditional dress of pistachio robes and a gauze turban that tucks under his nose and culminates in two wilting rabbit ears, the Emir of Wase is the only man allowed to wear shoes—gold-buckled loafers—in his castle. According to custom, his courtiers must sit barefoot on the floor below him. When I first met His Royal Highness Haruna Abdullahi, in 2006, however, he insisted I remain on his level, and sent his chief advisor to fetch my sneakers so we could speak as equals. Fine-boned and elegant, with dark skin and sharp features, the emir, like his ancestors, is an ethnic Fulani, and most of his people are still herders. An erudite man, he seemed bored in his clammy throne room and eager to set aside the usual supplications in order to discuss how his territory had been caught up in a religious conflagration.

For all his ancient trappings, the emir is a modern intellectual and a liberal religious scholar who traveled to Pennsylvania during the 1960s to study at the University of Pittsburgh, earning a doctoral degree in public administration. "I didn't tell anyone I was a prince in Pittsburgh," he said, laughing deeply. He sent a minion to a stack of old papers in the corner of the cold room to root out a copy of his dissertation, the title of which he could not remember and which the courtier never found. Instead, the courtier returned with a slim yellow booklet. Dropping his head, he fell to his knees and offered it to the emir. Together with a local Catholic bishop, the emir had compiled this collection of verses from the Christian Bible and the Quran to try to correct religious misunderstanding.

"These verses command believers to live together peacefully," he said, holding up the small pamphlet and setting it beside him on the antique couch that served as his throne. More than a decade earlier, when his father died at the age of 102, Abdullah had been working as a bank manager in the capital of Abuja. When he ascended the throne in 2001, the crisis had just begun, and from mosque loudspeakers and church pulpits, religious leaders on both sides were using the holy books to call for blood.

The emir, by his own count, had cared for between 350,000 and 400,000 Muslims, many of whom showed up at the palace gates and demanded his protection during the conflict. "I can't tell you how much money I spent on feeding all those people," he said. "Everyone who enters my domain, I have to account for before the Creator." For example, the jackknifed truck on the bridge—"If anyone falls off that bridge today, it's my responsibility," he said. This was his duty as a king, and what his Muslim name, Abdullahi—*abd*, "servant" or "slave," of Allah—commanded.

"Anytime people come to the palace, I have to open the door. I have no choice," he said. His voice was slightly muffled by gauze. Being a king was exhausting and expensive, and he could not afford to fix his own dripping roof. At the moment, there was a lull in the violence. On both sides, people had lost too much—land, livestock, and loved ones—to keep pummeling one another. No one could afford to keep fighting. This peace had been mandated by money, not mutual religious understanding, and the emir feared it would not last.

He picked up the yellow booklet beside him. In it, he had highlighted (in his native language of Hausa) the Quran's universal messages of coexistence for all of humankind, many of which were revealed to Mohammed early on in his life as God's messenger, when he was forty-something and a wealthy trader living in his Arabian hometown of Mecca.

"Religion is personal; it is in the mind," the emir said, smiling. "The books aren't written in straight language—you need not only to read but to understand." Tapping his college ring against the couch's edge, he relished these kinds of riddles, and seemed more at ease talking about the nature of power and the lessons that God had revealed to the Prophet Mohammed than discussing upcoming elections or the price of rice or the availability of drinking water.

"We know Jesus taught that if someone slaps you on the right cheek, turn to the left," he said ruefully. "We know that Mohammed was sacked from his village and stoned at Ta'if, but he quietly left for Medina." In 619, according to the Hadith, the reports of what the Prophet said and did during his lifetime,[4] Mohammed traveled to Ta'if, a mountainside town in Arabia about seventy miles southeast of the holy city of Mecca, to invite its people to become Muslims. Instead of welcoming him, the farmers stoned him and drove him, bleeding, out of town. Afterward, the archangel Gabriel—"Gibriel" in Arabic—came to the Prophet and asked him if he wanted revenge against Ta'if. Wiping blood from his face, the Prophet refused, saying, "Lord, forgive thy people, they do not know."[5] Mohammed knew about Jesus and his teachings; before his death, he instructed his followers to act as Jesus had, to be willing to die for their faith. Mohammed's words echo Jesus's plea from the cross: "Father, forgive them, for they do not know what they do" (Luke 23:34).

The emir made the point that if both of these men, beaten and bloodied—the incarnations of their respective faiths—asked God to forgive their aggressors, then who were today's religious leaders to advocate holy war? The two religions were deeply linked, the emir said, but leaders did not know of, or else had forgotten, their common bonds. The Quran also tells the story of the Virgin Mary giving birth alone beneath a date tree. When she returns in shame to her family's house, the newborn Jesus speaks: "God is my Lord and your Lord; so serve Him: that is a straight path" (19:36).[6]

Yet which was the right path: Christianity or Islam? Despite the emir's best intentions, this conflict over whose beliefs were sanctioned by God caught fire as soon as local Muslims and Christians began to see each other as objects of competition and obstacles to survival. And that came down to the economy. "People have no way to get jobs," the emir said. "Children are being taught not to go back to farms; they're not taught to survive practically, but to get white-collar jobs that don't exist." There are more than sixty million jobless Nigerian youth—including many of the boys who carried the minivan over the bridge—a ready army free to man the front lines in any religious conflict. Before elections, or at any opportune moment, the same corrupt politicians embezzling millions of dollars pay these youths to act as righteous and intimidating thugs. The first places destroyed in these battles are places of worship, then banks and cars—the symbols of worldly power to which these young people have no access.

"An educated idle mind can be dangerous," as the emir put it. This maxim could easily refer to the emir himself—trapped in his crumbling castle, his management degree rendered useless by a conflict for which he was not prepared. His grasp on power, however, was more complicated than it looked, and it was tied to the British colonial legacy. Following the Berlin Conference of 1885—known as the Scramble for Africa, when Europe's colonial powers met to divvy up the continent—much of the vast tract of "the Soudan," including the territories of contemporary Nigeria and Sudan, fell to the British. In these territories, Muslim North Africa met the "pagan" black African south. (On medieval Arab maps, this was the beginning of the "Land of the Blacks"—*Bilad-as-Sudan*—from which Sudan takes its name.) In Nigeria's Muslim north, the British faced some resistance from Dan Fodio's former jihadis, whom they managed to subdue by the early twentieth century. In Nigeria, the British were able to use the system of indirect rule that had proven so successful in India, and that meant bolstering the power of leaders such as Wase's emir.

Spread thin elsewhere by the demands of empire, the British left local leaders—such as the emir—in place to carry out their policies. The emir served as a buffer between the colonialists and the people. These were classic techniques of divide and conquer. Indirect rule also allowed the British to exercise power covertly and to turn Nigerian Muslims against one another. Many such leaders came to be seen as colonial agents, losing their religious legitimacy even as they amassed power and wealth. For the Emir of Wase, colonialism may have diminished his religious legitimacy, yet it had also increased the scope of his worldly power. This was exactly the kind of erosion of traditional authority that sent the citizens of the Middle Belt looking to new leaders, many of them claiming their authority from God.

Indirect rule also extended the emirs' control over other groups whom Islam had not managed to conquer. Chief among them were the hill tribes, the non-Muslim minorities who followed their own indigenous traditions, many venerating spirits as their neighbors did in Sudan. The hill tribes were warriors who faced a constant threat of being enslaved by their more powerful Muslim neighbors. Over centuries, they had fled to the high, dry escarpments of the Middle Belt to protect themselves from slave raiders. But British indirect rule made them the subjects of Muslim kings, such as the Emir of Wase, who sowed a legacy of hatred and mistrust that is still very much alive in the Middle Belt.

Over the past century, most of these non-Muslim minorities have converted to Christianity, many finding within it freedom from the legacy of Muslim oppression. A large number follow a new generation of Pentecostal preachers. Pentecostalism, like Islam, is growing faster worldwide than the global population (both religions at an estimated rate of almost 1.8 percent a year).[7] Its members try to encounter the Holy Spirit, as Jesus's disciples did on the feast of Pentecost, when the Holy Spirit descended on them. Because it is spirit-based, Pentecostalism grafts easily onto many indigenous cosmologies, and its practices—such as glossolalia (speaking in tongues) and ecstatic worship—are familiar to its new members. For Muslims who find Christianity's explosive growth threatening, the Pentecostal language of being saved by the Holy Spirit is especially difficult to fathom. The Trinity—Father, Son, and Holy Spirit—smacks of polytheism, or *shirk*; and the idea that God could father a son is blasphemy. Moreover, most Pentecostal pastors preach about overcoming your enemies, which, in Nigeria, has come to mean Muslims.

The emir found such Pentecostal preachers troubling, especially since most demanded believers' money for prayers. "The more you give, the closer you are to God!" he said skeptically. Since successful pastors can earn huge salaries, competition between them can be fierce, and in Nigeria this led them to fight one another. "The Pentecostals are dangerous because they preach against each other," he said. Churches split in two, with each new band of believers erecting a church of its own. In the eyes of those who did not recognize the pattern, the mushrooming of churches did not look like division, but growth. And their rivals' growth led to more Muslim fear, which led to more violence, the emir said. On it went, while the emir, in his castle, was powerless to stop the countryside from burning around him.

2

THE ROCK: TWO

The temperature drops in the shadow of Wase Rock. A butter-yellow stone church stands flanked by sturdy acacias and surrounded by a web of pebbled cow paths. The church marks the place where, in 1904, two early evangelical Christian missionaries, a thirty-year-old German named Herman Karl Wilhelm Kumm and his thirty-seven-year-old Irish wife, Lucy Kumm (née Guinness), built a handful of grass huts—a station for their new organization, Sudan United Mission. This was the first of fifty they hoped to build across the continent, along the border where Muslim North Africa ended and the Land of the Blacks began. They intended to stop Islam from spreading south among "the border pagans"[1]—the non-Muslims living along this fault line. By baptizing them as Christians, the Kumms would build a human bulwark against Islam's "winning" Africa.

"The *raison d'être* of this mission is to attempt to counteract the Mohammedan advance in Central Africa by winning the pagan tribes to the Christian religion," Kumm wrote his supporters in America and London. Not knowing Kumm's true aim, the Emir of Wase's great-grandfather even helped the missionary clear the land. The Kumms modeled their mission on that of David Livingstone, the Scottish Congregationalist missionary and explorer who had bushwhacked across Africa. He fought armed battles against Muslim slave raiders until, infected with malaria and crippled by chronic dysentery, he died in Zambia, in 1873. Livingstone's heart was buried under a mvula tree. His corpse—embalmed, wrapped in calico, canvas, and bark—was shipped to England and buried at Westminster Abbey, where his tombstone is inscribed: "Christianity, Commerce and Civilization."

Both Livingstone and the Kumms belonged to a burgeoning global religious movement—one that intended to reach the whole world with

the Gospel. It was rooted in evangelical Christianity, a broad-based movement that had begun in the sermons of early eighteenth-century British
and American preachers who called for a return to an egalitarian form of
faith uncorrupted by the secular forces of the day. The movement was
based on several core tenets that generally hold true today. First, preachers challenged their congregations to have a direct encounter with Jesus
Christ through scripture—not through the church and its rites. Each person had to decide to dedicate his or her life to Christ—and, in that decision, to be reborn, or "born again." Second, they averred that the words of
scripture were infallible, a term that implies different things for different
people. For some, it means that the Bible is literal, word-for-word truth;
for others, that the words of the New Testament are more generally inspired by God. Third, many saw it as their duty to reach new believers, a
project known as the Great Commission and rooted in Jesus's parting
command to his disciples: "Go therefore and make disciples of all nations,
baptizing them in the name of the Father and of the Son and of the Holy
Spirit" (Matthew 28:19). The evangelical movement, while strong in Britain, was especially popular in North America, and by the 1820s, most
American Protestants were calling themselves evangelicals. Today, one in
four American adults is an evangelical Christian, and for many, the basic
tenets established in the nineteenth century have not changed.[2]

During the nineteenth century, the advances of the industrial revolution—especially the steamship and telegraph—and the American Civil
War, made possible a theological revolution. The tenets of the evangelical
movement spread throughout the world. Many American evangelicals,
especially Yankees, had hoped that the Civil War would usher in a Kingdom of Heaven on Earth in the United States. Instead, the brash new
wealth of the Gilded Age turned Americans toward the Gospel of Wealth
as preached by Andrew Carnegie. Frustrated and disillusioned at home,
evangelicals turned their attention to reaching the rest of the world with
their message of salvation through Jesus Christ.

Some evangelicals believed that it was possible to accelerate Jesus's
return by reaching every single person on earth with this message from
the Gospel According to Matthew: "And this gospel of the kingdom will
be preached in all the world as a witness to all the nations, and then the
end will come" (24:14). The Great Commission is often misconstrued as
an imperative to convert the whole world. The underlying message is that
once the whole world hears the evangelical message, Jesus will return—

regardless of whether or not that message is accepted. To most, it's about offering an invitation, not getting an answer.

At the turn of the twentieth century, war, industrialization, and this new theology made evangelicals in America and Britain suddenly determined to "evangelize the world in this generation."[3] These were the words of the Reverend Arthur T. Pierson, a now largely forgotten Yankee evangelical who inspired a worldwide movement. As Pierson put it, "[A]ll should go and go to all." With his urging, the Young Men's Christian Association (YMCA), founded in London in 1844, launched the Student Volunteer Movement. Thousands of young men and women mobilized as missionaries to reach what they believed were the last blank spaces of the map with the Gospel. Preaching to the poor and focusing on building a "healthy mind, spirit and body,"[4] these clean-cut, educated young people led Bible study, built health clinics, and introduced organized sports. Their understanding that Christ was Lord offered more than a set of beliefs; it was the cornerstone of a whole way of life.

This worldview, with its emphasis on the language of light and darkness, good and evil, flourished in opposition to an enemy. Islam, many evangelicals believed, was their most formidable foe. The Kumms, for example, were concerned—correctly, it turned out—that the same innovations of the industrial revolution (the steamship and telegraph) that allowed Christian missionaries and explorers to spread the Gospel inland in Africa and Asia also encouraged the spread of Islam. More African Muslims were, for instance, going on hajj, the pilgrimage to the holy Saudi Arabian city of Mecca, spreading Islam more widely on their return home.

The nexus of this conflict lay along the tenth parallel. In June 1910, at the World Missionary Conference in Edinburgh, Scotland, twelve hundred Protestant missionaries gathered to chart the greatest crises Christianity was facing. (No Roman Catholics were invited.) The most pressing challenge to their faith—and to the world's future—many argued, was Islam. John Mott, the YMCA's founder, who spoke at the conference, wrote in his 1910 book, *The Decisive Hour of Christian Missions*:

> Two forces are contending for Africa—Christianity and Mohammedanism [Islam]. In many respects the more aggressive is Mohammedanism. It dominates Africa on its western half as far south as 10° N. latitude, and on its eastern half, as far south as 5° N. . . . If things continue as they are now tending, Africa may become a Mohammedan continent . . . Once re-

ceived, it is Christianity's most formidable enemy. It permits a laxity of morals, in some cases worse than that of heathendom. It sanctions polygamy. It breeds pride and arrogance, and thus hardens the heart against the Word of God.[5]

Karl Kumm, the ambitious German evangelist, also spoke at this watershed Edinburgh conference—the first of its kind to bring together more than a thousand Protestants from different denominations. He and his wife, Lucy, stood at the vanguard of this new movement to stop Islam. Lucy, the daughter of a famous Irish evangelical pastor, H. Grattan Guinness, was thirty-three when she and Karl were married on February 3, 1900, at the American Mission Church in Cairo. She was already a writer, and an accomplished evangelist in her own right. Well traveled in the world's roughest corners, she exemplified the power wielded by women missionaries at the beginning of the twentieth century. The evangelical movement, which began as a call to social justice, preached for women's equality at home and in the field, where women performed work as dangerous and unforgiving as that of men. Despite frail health, Lucy toiled among London's garment workers and went on to chronicle their plight and argue for their need of salvation in her book *Only a Factory Girl*. She had traveled among the world's Hindus in *Across India at the Dawn of the Twentieth Century*. Her books were not just religious tracts: they were calls for a new Christian world order based on equality and justice. Until the secular human rights movement began after World War II, Christian missionaries were the leading advocates for social change. Christian activists both liberal and conservative were hugely instrumental in bringing to light abuses such as slavery, and they are once again today. Along with her husband, Lucy Kumm turned her attention to fifty to eighty million souls whom she feared faced the threat of Muslim domination in what they, like so many others, called the Land of the Blacks. After reading her tracts, more than twenty young men—members of the YMCA's Student Volunteer Movement—set out for Sudan. Most contracted fever and died in the African mission field, which was called "the White Man's Graveyard."

The Kumms were only two of a number of missionaries in the Middle Belt at the time, and many were not particularly interested in competing with Islam. Doctors, teachers, and farmers, they brought with them the two *Bs*—Bible and bicycle—and offered practical solutions to problems of health, agriculture, and eventually education. Their work was the legacy of the mid-nineteenth-century mission strategist Henry Venn, who developed the "Three-Self" indigenous church. Each local community should be self-sustaining, self-governing, and self-propagating, he argued, and Christianity should empower people, offering a way out of oppression.

Kumm, though, was among those who took this to mean liberation from the looming threat of Islam, and he believed he could use people's loathing of their Muslim rulers to his advantage in converting them to Christianity. At first, however, he found that these so-called border pagans had little interest in his divine message. The formidable indigenous traditions that had led people to reject Islam for centuries now galvanized them against this new alien creed. Toiling at the base of the rock without converts, Kumm taught health, hygiene, and horticulture but did little converting. However, he needed money to keep the mission going, since Sudan United Mission, like many at the time, was not linked to any particular Protestant denomination.[6] Its success depended on Kumm's entrepreneurial spirit. To prove his plan could succeed, he needed converts. In his memoirs, he describes the watershed night in 1904, when, before leaving for a fund-raising trip in America, he summoned his local workers to the base of Wase Rock. "Boys," he said, "who would like before saying goodbye to me to accept Jesus as his personal savior?"[7]

No one answered, at first. Then his personal servant, Tom Alyana, a former slave, stepped forward and accepted Jesus as his Lord and Savior. Alyana would be the first of what now, a century later, have become millions of followers of Kumm's teachings. Soon after, Kumm and Lucy, now pregnant with their third child, traveled to America to raise money for their mission. In Northfield, Massachusetts, she began to miscarry. Refusing to go to the hospital until she had finished her book about Congo, *Our Slave State*, Lucy contracted a fever and died.

Heartbroken, Kumm returned to Nigeria to make a dangerous foray across the continent. Starting out at the base of Wase Rock in 1909, Kumm trekked east for more than one thousand miles, from the British territory of Nigeria, through French-occupied Chad, to British Sudan. Skirting the southern edge of Muslim North Africa, which he called "the Ultima Thule of Africa"—based on a term Greek explorers used for borders of the known world—he would travel along the tenth parallel investigating Islam's spread, and assessing prospective sites for his missionary forts. The trek was also a grueling public relations junket to raise money for his Sudan United Mission. Kumm's supporters sent him what they could, and he published their letters of encouragement in his newsletter, *The Light-bearer*. One devotee mailed him a pearl-mounted gold shirt stud and a note: "Perhaps the enclosed could be disposed of for a few shillings (it cost 11/-, and is practically new), it is all I have to give."[8] For the trek, Kumm took two hundred African porters and their families along with him, confident that he would convert them to Christianity during leisure hours. The party never stopped walking. Descending from the plateau at the beginning of the rainy season, the members of this bedraggled expedition soon faced a forced wade through the thick tree-lined corridors of gallery forests, and hacked their way through dense bush woven with webs of wet vines. As they traversed *chaur*, the deep, sandy ravines cut into open savanna, the party fell victim to flash floods. Kumm and his expedition basically swam across Africa.

"All these rivers," he wrote in despair, "terminate in one vast lake, between the 7th and 10th degree north [of the equator]."[9] He had hit the *sudd*—"barrier" in Arabic—the impenetrable swampland that begins along the tenth parallel and, like the tsetse fly, had helped to stop Islam from spreading south in Sudan. Kumm's oxen nearly drowned. His horses died of sleeping sickness. He watched his porters become "walking skeletons." Six had to be carried, and one died of starvation. At last he boarded a steamship, which chugged up the White Nile to the sand-swept colonial capital of Khartoum, where Kumm stopped before sailing back to England. At home in Britain, the popularity of missionaries and colonial adventurers was at its zenith. When Kumm landed at Dover on December 29, 1909, reporters from Reuters, *The Daily Telegraph*, *The Star*, and others waited for him on the dock. The next day's headline: "KUMM HAS COME BACK."

One hundred years later, the church Kumm planted at the base of Wase Rock, Church of Christ in Nigeria (COCIN), has hundreds of outposts in the Middle Belt. Most are small, zinc-roofed buildings that shine like dull nickels against the grassy plateau. And when religious violence breaks out in the region, the contemporary leaders of Kumm's church are often earliest into the fray.

I visited the gated compound of Kumm's church headquarters in Jos, the Middle Belt capital, in August 2006, within days of my visit to the Emir of Wase. The city's red roads were crammed with thousands of signboards—for churches, mosques, and miscellaneous religious organizations vying for customers. In one short stretch, I spied De Last Day Coffin Company, which competed for the attention of a passerby with signs for Living Faith Church and NASFAT, a Muslim tent revival in the vein of a Pentecostal church service. And that was only three. Within sixty seconds (I timed it) we passed Child Evangelical, Christ Resurrection, Apostolic Faith, Mount Olive, Grace Foundation, Christ Embassy, Assemblies of God, Divine Mercy Ministry, Jesus Foundation, World Impact Partners, Christ Pilgrims Welfare Board, Fountain of Praise, Every Night Is a Miracle Ministries, Family Restoration Gospel Ministry, Angels International College, Amazing Grace Private School, and the Great Commission.

At COCIN headquarters, a framed photograph of Karl Kumm hung from a nail in the main office. Here was the pale-eyed hero in profile. With the swept-back locks of a romantic poet, he fixed his gaze beyond the frame. I asked the church's information officer, whom I'll call Pastor J.,[10] if he knew what Kumm was supposed to be looking at.

He glanced at the picture and said he wasn't sure. But Kumm's prediction, the pastor added, had come true: the Middle Belt now stood as the last line of defense against Islam's domination of the country, the continent, and the world. As the pastor had written in one of his many books on the subject, *Shari'a: The Hidden Agenda*: "In a nutshell, the main objective and motive of the Muslims, is TO CRUSH THE CHRISTIANS SOCIALLY, POLITICALLY, AND ECONOMICALLY, OR CONVERT THEM BY FORCE TO ISLAM" (emphasis his).

Pastor J. belonged to one of the hill tribes, the non-Muslim ethnic groups that had fled to the plateau to protect themselves from Muslim raiders, and he carried the air of a wilderness prophet. "The moment they can crush Christianity here, the country will fall," he warned. A short, thickset man with bloodshot eyes, Pastor J. told me that the confrontation between Christianity and Islam foreshadowed Judgment Day. This was a matter of both scripture and geography, he pointed out. The Middle Belt's fault line was a microcosm of a global struggle—a long-standing threat to which the West was just waking up.

"I may sound like a prophet of doom, but I'm thankful for 9/11—if it had not happened, the United States would have been in the dark about the Muslim world," he said, reminding me that, as far as Christians in his congregation were concerned, Nigeria's religious crisis began "a few days before yours," on September 7, 2001. On that Friday, a Christian woman walked through a group of Muslims who were praying with their fore-heads to the ground outside a mosque full of worshippers. Her interrup-tion was immediately seen as an act of disrespect, and, within hours, Muslim and Christian mobs were attacking each other in the town of Jos.[11] Thousands on both sides were killed, but the world, distracted by events in New York City, paid little attention.

Some people believe that Christian militants sent the woman to walk through the middle of the mosque's Friday prayer—that the act was in-tended to incite violence. Later that day, in self-defense, said Pastor J., he killed a Muslim man with an axe. He felt no remorse. To him, being a Christian meant being a soldier for Christ. He said, "We teach our mem-bers to be alert and to defend themselves—if not, it would be suicide.

"I am ready to die for my faith. All we can do is to prepare our people for martyrdom. Remaining here to fight is the only solution," he added. He paged through the Bible lying open on his desk and fished a thick pair of glasses from his breast pocket to read the story of Jesus being struck by a Roman soldier before being crucified. In this story, Pastor J. said, Jesus never turns the other cheek. Instead, when the soldier slaps him, Jesus demands an explanation: "If I have spoken evil, bear witness of the evil; but if well, why do you strike Me?" (John 18:23). The pastor believed that Christians had the right to defend themselves. In order not to be crushed, Christians had to outpace Muslims by winning souls faster. He saw the Great Commission as not only a mandate to reach new believers with the Gospel but also a survival strategy.

More than Kumm's legacy, Pastor J.'s thinking reflected a global move-ment in Christianity and Islam. Both are in the midst of decades-long reli-gious reawakenings—global revivals that, like their namesakes in America and Britain during the seventeenth and eighteenth centuries, are calls to return to an idealized past. These revivals encompass a breadth of beliefs and points of view—from liberal to conservative. Some conservatives like Pastor J. consider themselves "fundamentalists." The name, which has become a catchword for both Christians and Muslims, comes from the title of twelve pamphlets, called "The Fundamentals," written in 1902 by evangelical leaders who formed the American Bible League to counter the threat that Darwin and modern science posed to their faith. The various authors, who argued that the Bible was God's inspired word, sent the pamphlets to three million readers between 1910 and 1915.[12] Since then, the word *fundamentalism* has been subject to a wide range of interpretations. Yet one hundred years ago, the term outlined what it still does today: a desire to return to a past when religion and its tenets were absolute. These theologies—driven by narratives of good pitted against evil—graft easily to competition over land and resources.

For Christians like Pastor J. who see themselves in theological and worldly conflict with believers of all other stripes, population growth helps to determine their survival. So do large numbers of believers. Religion grows stronger only if it can be practiced, Lamin Sanneh, a Gambian-born Roman Catholic who has written extensively about both Christianity and Islam, explained to me. If the church or the mosque is empty, there is no religion. "For both a Sufi leader and a Pentecostal preacher in Africa, this is a no-brainer," Sanneh said, and scripture supports this idea. God says to his people in Genesis, "Be fruitful and multiply," and many reawakened Christians see their duty to reproduce as a duty to God, as do Muslims. In the chapter of the Quran called "The Bee," God also commands Mohammed, "[Prophet] call [people] to the way of your Lord with wisdom and good teaching" (The Bee 16:125).[13] For both, the instruction is clear: by procreation and conversion, spread the faith.

3

THE FLOOD

When I returned to the Middle Belt in September 2007, the rainy season had begun. Low white mist shrouded the escarpments and burst open into midday deluges the likes of which I'd never seen. Sheets of blinding rain turned the red roads into cataracts. One morning, before the skies broke open, I walked around Jos searching for the thousands of religious advertisements I had seen along the roadside a year earlier. The local authorities had ordered them removed, I learned; they thought that so much signage intensified religious conflict. I stopped in one Internet café for a quart of vanilla yogurt and picked up a week-old local paper. Through the smudged newsprint I read that a flash flood in a nearby town had driven tens of thousands from their homes and killed scores of others. The death toll was unknown. The town, I read, was Wase.

I left Jos the next morning, in the same borrowed gold minivan with the bald and barrel-chested Haruna Yakubu at the wheel again. After a two-hour drive through a sea of brilliant, rain-fed grass, we reached the Wase River. The bridge was gone, and the gulley between the riverbanks swarmed with young men naked to the waist, flinging heavy white sacks of salt across their backs. They waded up to their chests through blood-colored water, reddened from runoff. On one bank, someone had lashed oil drums together to make small rafts. I left the van and climbed onto one, to be dragged across the river. Even on the open water, the air felt different; the mild breeze of a year earlier had turned to fetid stillness. As the waves hit the empty oil drums, it sounded like something was banging on them from below.

The Wase River had spilled over its bank one Friday in August, about three weeks earlier, and continued to rise. By early evening, the water was neck-high and still climbing. To escape the rising floodwaters, the several thousand people who lived in thirteen villages along the river began to hoist their babies into the trees. Children of one and two years old, who could hold on to branches, were hoisted up alone. Mothers climbed up with their infants. By nightfall, the elders estimated, altogether about two thousand babies were hanging from branches. They spent two days without food or water. Some were silent. Others cried from hunger. Below them, in the slick, black water, cows, goats, pigs, and a few human bodies floated past.

"All of our food is gone," Fakcit Alexander, one survivor, told me when I reached what had been her village after the water receded. She was in her early thirties but looked at least fifty. Her short hair was copper-colored from either mud or malnutrition, and her skin was ashen. She walked me around the wrecked village about a mile down the road from Wase Rock's two humps. The mud walls of a school still stood, but nothing else. The village had also lost all its corn, which had been just about ready for harvest. The cornstalks' height had hidden the flash flood's monstrous wave, so no one had time to run, Fakcit said. She led me to a fallen log in a clearing. I looked down and saw that she was barefoot. The flood had taken her shoes. The village gathered around her to listen as we talked. Two men were fixing a bicycle; the others were sipping from gourds filled with home brew. The only thing to do was drink, and they weaved around the village dazed with loss.

Like most of the communities at the edge of town, Fakcit's was Christian—a fact anyone could tell from the potent smell of sour mash fermenting in the sun nearby; most Nigerian Muslims do not drink alcohol. There were other traits that sometimes told Muslim from Christian. Fakcit belonged to one of the historically non-Muslim hill tribes, and although it was a generalization (and sometimes inaccurate), they tended to be shorter and broader than their rivals, the ethnic Fulanis, who looked taller and more angular, like the Emir of Wase. Many carried the spare air of nomads from the arid north, even though they had settled one hundred years ago.

In many of Nigeria's Muslim towns, Christians, like other outsiders, historically had to live outside the city walls, and in some cases they still do. The legacy of being an ethnic minority forced to the edge of town had embittered Fakcit. "The Muslims call us fools," she said. Three years earlier, a Muslim mob killed her father and burned this village to the ground. As the Christians sat gathered around a bicycle, two nomadic herdsmen—willowy Fulanis—walked quietly through the clearing and called greetings to the flood victims. As northern nomads, they were undoubtedly

Muslims, yet when I went to speak to them I noticed a curious marking on one man's face.

His tattooed cheek bore an indigo Coptic cross. I asked him about its origins; he shrugged and smiled. He did not remember receiving the mark as a child, nor did he know the symbol's history. Maybe his nomadic ancestors had once belonged to the ancient Christian kingdoms of Nubia, in northern Sudan. Maybe when the last of the Nubian kingdoms fell to Muslim armies in 1504, his kinsfolk converted to Islam. Maybe over the past five hundred years, his ancestors had migrated here to the southwest, two thousand miles from northern Sudan, bringing their cows and what they carried on their bodies: this symbol of their former faith.

Cross tattoo or no, he belonged to the Muslim herders who had come to blows with the Christians in the past several years. Despite Fakcit Alexander's grumbling, the flood seemed to have brought the two groups together—at least for the moment—or else there was simply nothing left to lose, nothing over which to fight. Although the flood had killed most of their cattle, the nomads' most pressing problem was water. For the past several years the land had become so desiccated that the herdsmen had begun to dig boreholes right at the edge of the river, where it was easiest to hit water—and most destructive to the bank. The farmers of Fakcit's village also planted corn right to the water's edge. Overfarming and overgrazing had destroyed the riverbank, so that when the flood came, the bank fell all the faster. This was one way in which human error compounded environmental pressures. Practically, the village was ruined, spent; but Fakcit and her fellow villagers were determined to stay.

"This place is our father's land," Fakcit said. "This place is our place." The flood brought with it plagues of insects and illness, including a malaria outbreak.[1] Each of Fakcit's eight children had contracted malaria from sleeping in the open air, even the baby; she pulled a warm, dozing lump from the cloth on her back. "They're covered with bites," she said, tugging the baby's small arm from the cotton folds so I could see the welts. His name was Cheldon, which means, "I am pleading for more from the Creator."

Two thousand babies in the trees—I pictured this as I stood with Fakcit beneath the harsh dazzle of the overcast sky. I pictured the babies later that night, when I was lying on a foam mattress in a cheap hotel nearby. I have pictured those babies again and again; they come up behind my eyes without bidding, in silhouette, like a woodcut, with an eggplant sky behind them, and greasy water licking at the tree trunks. Seen from a distance, the children would have clung to the limbs like strange fruit—the allusion inescapable—not swinging dead, but alive and grasping branches. According to the local Red Cross representative (one of the emir's courtiers, who carried a clipboard and kept track of the death toll) all of those babies survived. So far, according to the information he'd been able to gather, forty-seven adults had died, but numbers in Nigeria are usually speculative at best.

That afternoon I climbed the hill to the emir's castle for the last time, with a sudden, animal understanding of the difference high ground makes. Although he had been untouched by the flood, the emir was despondent; first the religious fighting, now the flood, and no time in between to re-cover. Only a few years earlier, he had gathered Muslims and Christians to pray for the end of a terrible drought. That kind of coming together was impossible now. What's more, there was no way to explain that this flood was a result of human action, the emir said, leaning his swaddled head against the fraying throne. Before I arrived he had been listening to a BBC radio program about the perils of the Sahel. "This flood is the first sign of climate change," he said. Yet his people believed such curses came only from God.

Of all seven continents, Africa is believed to be most affected by climate change. Poverty, overfarming, overgrazing, deforestation, and increasingly erratic weather patterns all contribute to the conservative prediction that, if the world's temperature rises as little as two degrees by 2100, as many as 250 million Africans will be left without adequate drinking water.[2] In Africa and Asia, the band along the tenth parallel is one of the most eco-logically precarious in the world. Here, the inexorable southward spread of North Africa's desert, which occurs in Nigeria at an estimated rate of between a quarter and a half mile each year,[3] meets unpredictable rains in the transition zone from Africa's dry north to its wet south.

Before satellite dishes and Skype, weather connected one continent to another. The intertropical convergence zone binds the northern and southern hemispheres by driving both of their high-pressure air currents toward the equator, where atmospheric pressure is lower. This system not only creates the trade winds but also carries carbon dioxide and other pollutants produced by the northern hemisphere toward the south. As these compounds travel south, they warm oceans and land, contributing to patterns of flooding and drought.

These equatorial patterns directly affect North America, too. Atlantic hurricanes, such as Katrina, are born in this zone. When the two collide, they form vortexes known as Hadley cells, which move clockwise until they sweep off Cape Verde. Most of these storms dissipate while passing through the doldrums, or "horse latitudes"—named for the practice of sailors in becalmed ships tossing their horses overboard to save precious drinking water. But some do not dissipate, and these eventually strike America's East Coast. This is the pattern Ernest Zebrowski, Jr., in *Perils of a Restless Planet: Scientific Perspectives on Natural Disasters*, calls the butterfly effect, borrowing the term from chaos theory. The tiniest change to the air currents in Nigeria—caused by a movement as minute as the beat of a butterfly's wings—may create chaos seven thousand miles away in North America.[4] A terrible flood season in the catastrophe zone can mean that the United States and Caribbean will face a horrific hurricane season.

The twin plagues of advancing desert (desertification) and flash flooding mean that for the first time in history there may be as many people fleeing from the weather as from war. By 2050, by one estimate, as many as one billion people will be displaced from their homes by environmental factors.[5] Every year, an average of ten million people are forced from their homes in the Sahel, according to Professor Norman Myers of Oxford University.[6] These numbers are speculative, and critics point out that it is difficult to determine why people move, and harder still to document such migrations. And no one knows for sure if the changing weather will lead to more or fewer insect-borne illnesses—malaria, yellow fever, dengue, and sleeping sickness. Scientists also disagree as to whether the rising temperature of the ocean, or of the land, will determine the weather's future, and whether floods or deserts will prevail.[7]

4

DROUGHT

From deluge to desert, there was no balance. In August 2007, I met Dr. Amin al-Amin, an ecologist in his forties and a member of a royal Muslim family from the north. He had started a nongovernmental organization called Nature Trust International, to address the perils of desertification in Nigeria and eight other West African countries. However, al-Amin (which means "the trusted one" in Arabic, one of Mohammed's nicknames) was not simply interested in the environmental aspects of the desert's southern spread; he was concerned with the ensuing social crisis as well.

"The line of latitude ten degrees to the north of the equator across Africa marks the beginning of a fragile ecosystem in terms of climate change, in terms of population growth, in terms of religious conflict," al-Amin told me. He thinks and speaks in terms of latitude, and referred to the tenth parallel as "latitude ten." As the Sahara Desert advances south and leaves former farms and grazing lands consumed by dunes, the northern Muslims must move south with their livestock to survive. Pushing south, the nomads enter settled areas and collide with farming communities, many of which are Christian. Such was the case in Sudan, and also in Nigeria, where for more than a decade al-Amin, along with other scientists, has studied the geographic coordinates of desertification, and the social problems between the two groups, which are fomented by a drastic lack of education and services.

Although the Middle Belt's high plateau is temperate, most of Nigeria is overwhelmingly hot, and even the late summer rainy season offers little relief. The air is just as warm as before, only wetter. On one smothering August afternoon, a few days after I had left the flood-devastated Wase, al-Amin picked me up in his green Mercedes SUV at a hotel in the Nigerian capital of Abuja—a boring, ordered city architecturally akin to Washington, D.C.—to show me firsthand how the dynamics of environmental migration were interwoven with religion. We were going to drive north of Abuja to visit a community of several hundred children who had migrated south about three hundred miles, from latitude fourteen. Their village to the north could no longer support their farms or grazing for their cows, so everyone was moving south, beginning with the children, al-Amin explained. He shouted over the air conditioner's full-tilt roar. The vehicle was a curious choice for an environmentalist, but not perhaps for the scion of one of Nigeria's Muslim royal families. "My great-grandfather was very close with Uthman dan Fodio," he said, invoking the name of the famous Sufi reformer and Nigerian hero. Al-Amin was wearing a fine-gauge white linen suit, through which he was sweating despite the air-conditioning. Driving made him nervous, he confessed, but he had given his chauffeur the day off so he could lead this tour himself.

We passed a seemingly endless procession of young boys trudging along the roadside carrying gnarled branches on their heads. "Look around. Do you see any trees?" al-Amin asked. For miles, the earth was crimson and treeless. (The boys must have walked for dozens of miles to find those few brittle branches.) Through the smeared window, it looked like a grainy image sent back to earth from a Mars probe. The ground had been stripped of most of its minerals. Thanks to the heat, the equatorial glare, and the punishing rainstorms, all that remained was the iron-rich laterite that reddened the tropical soil.

As we drove, al-Amin recounted a bloody confrontation he had recently had with a group of conservative Muslim scholars over the issue of desertification. According to the Maliki school of Islam—one of the four Sunni schools of Islamic jurisprudence and the one that most Nigerian Muslims follow—sin, not science, causes the desert's spread. Believing that it is his duty to dispel such misconceptions, al-Amin visits conservative schools, using his royal lineage to gain entry. He lectures scholars on the environmental causes of desertification, and explains that alcohol and fornication do not cause drought. As he puts it, the earth is growing warmer because of man, not God. Not long ago, during one such lecture, a conservative scholar leaped to his feet and told al-Amin to "quit talking nonsense." When al-Amin refused to back down, the audience began to pelt him with stones. With his left ear bleeding, he raced to his car. By the time he was locked safely inside, the crowd had shattered the SUV's windshield. Undaunted, al-Amin kept returning to the school, and finally convinced the students to take part in a reforestation pilot program.

"I like a bit of thrill," he said. He pulled off the capital's highway and into a warren of shanties slouching against a brick-colored boulder the size of a house. The street was almost empty except for a handful of teenage boys, none older than sixteen. The social problem that most concerned al-Amin involved the millions of itinerant Islamic students—boys between the ages of six and eighteen—whose families sent them to boarding schools for religious education.[1] Historically, these wandering students, called *al majiri* after the name of their schools, worked on their teachers' farms to pay for their educations. Al-Amin had attended one of these Islamic schools, once renowned for Quranic study. (By fifteen, students are supposed to be *hafez*, meaning they know the Quran by heart; "These days, instead, they are full-blown miscreants," al-Amin said.) Now they were changing—in part because of the weather. Due to desertification, the teachers, like everyone else, were forced to move south and leave their farms behind. The schools now clung to the edge of cities, like the capital, Abuja. With no more farms to feed the boys, the teachers sent them out to beg instead.

"It is a form of slavery," al-Amin said. "They need somewhere to stay and their teacher becomes their only protector. The children are victims because a natural disaster is taking place and it should be up to our government to solve it." But the government did nothing, and, instead, the teachers functioned like Fagins in a modern-day version of *Oliver Twist*. To educate fellow Muslims about this problem, Nature Trust International had staged a play about a religious teacher whom desertification forced off his farm and into corruption. It caused so much anger in northern Nigeria that the play was banned.

We searched for the community's leaders among the shanties, and found them sitting together in a lean-to (the only one with furniture and a thin carpet). After a few words of introduction in Hausa—I heard al-Amin drop Dan Fodio's name—we were ushered into the school. One hundred children under the age of eight were crammed into a single room. Teenage boys hung around outside. Most had metal begging bowls. "You know of any work?" one asked me. His only job, he explained, was to beg for the teacher in the nearby town. With no other education, soon these six-foot-tall, pimply

teenage boys would be too old—and too intimidating—for begging. They
were the same ready youth army about whom the emir had spoken—one
more reminder that four out of ten Nigerians are unemployed. We stayed
only briefly; it was almost dark, and al-Amin feared what might happen
when the sun set and the boys were accountable to no one.

Driving back to Abuja, we got stuck in a "go-slow"—a traffic jam. In
the middle of the highway, a large crowd had gathered around a boy of
about fourteen. He was fighting with an older, bigger man and both of
their faces were streaked with blood. Al-Amin pulled over and pushed
through the crowd to ask what was happening. The boy, it turned out, was
an itinerant Islamic student from the north. His parents had sent him
south to find a teacher (and a way to feed himself). "He has come from
latitude sixteen to try to find work," al-Amin shouted in my ear above the
fray, but the boy could not pay his one-dollar weekly rent on his bed, so
the landlord had beaten him, and the boy, in turn, had attacked the landlord with a razor blade. This kind of thing happened all the time, al-Amin
explained, pushing back out through the crowd's hot press and looking
down at the lap of his white suit. A splatter of blood had landed on the
linen and was drying from red to black.

5

THE TRIBULATION

Nigeria's troubles between Christians and Muslims began in the late 1960s, during the Biafran civil war, when Nigeria's southeast seceded under the banner of Christian emancipation from the Muslim north. The divisions intensified in the 1980s, when the first oil boom collapsed and the ensuing economic downturn led to widespread violence. But it was really the end of military rule in 1999 and the political free-for-all of weak democracy that ignited religious violence. Democracy, paradoxically, fueled the friction between Nigeria's Muslims and Christians. Elections are often violent, and people have voted along religious lines since democracy began.

Over the last decade, local and global events have fed the ongoing skirmishes—the 1999 and 2000 implementation of Islamic law in twelve of Nigeria's thirty-six states; the U.S. bombing of Afghanistan in 2001, during which Nigerian Muslims lashed out at local Christians as scapegoats for the West's attack on an Islamic country; and the 2002 Miss World pageant, when a local Christian reporter named Isioma Daniel angered the Muslim community by writing in one of Nigeria's newspapers that a beauty pageant was no cause for moral concern. "The Muslims thought it was immoral to bring 92 women to Nigeria to ask them to revel in vanity," she wrote in *This Day.* "What would Mohammed think? In all honesty, he would probably have chosen a wife from one of them." This comment, which millions felt smacked of blasphemy, inflamed Nigerian Muslims, and riots broke out on the streets, killing hundreds. In 2006, more riots, this time triggered by the Danish cartoons that depicted the Prophet Mohammed—an act many believe that Islam forbids—left at least sixteen people dead—more than anywhere else in the world.[1] In 2008, in the Middle Belt capital of Jos, several hundred Muslims and Christians were killed in clashes surrounding a local election. At least three hundred more died in Jos during 2009. Farther northeast, in the town of Maiduguri, a splinter group of *al majari* youth who called themselves Boko Haram ("Western Education Forbidden") launched local riots over what they vaguely saw as the rising tide of Western influence. Fighting spread to three other states and left seven hundred dead. By early 2010, hundreds more were killed in clashes between Christians and Muslims outside of Jos.

Two candidates stood on opposite sides of the barren soccer field as the people of Yelwa, a town of thirty thousand about an hour north of Wase, lined up to vote. For the past hundred years, Yelwa has been a mostly Muslim trading town. This May morning in 2002 was shaping up to be tense, as the town's Muslim traders milled between the field's iron goalposts. So did their historic enemies: the non-Muslim ethnic groups who were gaining in numbers and political power, and were now Christians. Most belonged to the church that Karl Kumm founded a century ago, the Church of Christ in Nigeria.

As the two groups waited in the heat to be counted, the meeting's tone soured. "You could feel the tension in the air," said Abdullahi Abdullahi, a fifty-five-year-old Muslim lawyer and community leader. A tall, angular man with a space between his two front teeth and shoulders hunched around his ears in perpetual apology, he was helping to direct the crowd that day. The gap in numbers, he said, was painfully easy to see.

"Let's face it, a Christian comes with his one wife; I come with my four. Who do you think has more people?" No one knows what happened first. Someone shouted *arna* ("infidel") at the Christians. Someone spat the word *jihadi* at the Muslims. Someone picked up a stone. Chaos ensued, as young people on each side began to throw rocks. The candidates ran for their lives, and mobs set fire to the surrounding houses. "That was the day ethnicity disappeared entirely and the conflict became just about religion," Abdullahi said.

Soon after, the Christians issued an edict that no Christian girl could be seen with a Muslim boy. "We had a problem of intermarriage," Pastor Sunday Wuyep, Abdullahi's community counterpart and the head of Kumm's church, told me when I first visited the town in 2006. "Just because our ladies are stupid and attracted to money," he sighed. Economics lay at the heart of the enmity between the two groups: as merchants and herders, the Muslims were much wealthier than the minority Christians. But Pastor Wuyep, like many others, felt that Muslims were trying to wipe out Christians by converting them through marriage. So he and the other elders decided to punish the women. "If a woman gets caught with a Muslim man," Wuyep said, "she must be forcibly brought back." The decree turned out to be a call to vigilante violence as both Christian and Muslim patrols took to the streets.

Mornings in Yelwa begin with prayer for both Muslims and Christians. One Tuesday morning in February 2004, seventy people were performing their morning devotions at Kumm's church. As the worshippers finished their prayers, they heard gunshots and a call from the loudspeakers of the mosque next door: "*Allahu Akhbar*, let us go for jihad." "We were terrified," Pastor Wuyep recalled. He had been standing outside the gate as the churchyard swarmed with strangers posing in fatigues as Nigerian soldiers. He stayed near the church gate, but many others fled toward the road behind the church. There, the men dressed as soldiers reassured them that they were safe and herded them back to the church. Then they opened fire.

Pastor Sunday Wuyep fled. The attackers—who were never identified—set the church on fire and killed everyone who tried to escape. They chased the head of the church, Pastor Sampson Bukar, to his house next door and ran him through with the long machetes that are called cutlasses in Nigeria. They set fire to the nursery school and the pastor's house. His burned Peugeot was still in the compound in 2006, though the church had been rebuilt and painted salmon pink. Boys were playing soccer, each wearing one shoe so that everyone could kick the ball. "Seven in my family were killed," Wuyep said in the churchyard. "We call them martyrs." He pointed to a mound of earth not far from where we were sitting. On top was a small wooden cross: it marked the mass grave for the seventy-eight people killed that day.

"This is about religious intolerance," he went on. "Our God is different than the Muslim God . . . If he were the same God, we wouldn't fight." For Pastor Wuyep, the clash was grounded in Christian scripture. "It's scriptural, this fight," he said. "The Bible says in Matthew 24, the time will come when they will pursue us in our churches." Wuyep and his followers, like many conservative Christians, believed that Jesus Christ would return to earth after one thousand years of bloodshed and war. This was the doctrine of premillennialism as foretold in Matthew 24. They believed the chaos of the Tribulation would precede the world's end and herald Christ's return. Because they believed they were living during last days, the Christians found meaning in their suffering, and in their own violence.

A few hundred yards down the road from the church is a cornfield, and in it a row of mounds: more mass graves. Green-and-white signs tally the piles of Muslims buried below: 110, 50, 65, 100, 55, 25, 60, 20, 40, 105. Two months after the church was razed, Christian men and boys surrounded Yelwa. Many were bare-chested; others wore shirts on which they had reportedly pinned white name tags from the Christian Association of Nigeria, an umbrella organization founded in the 1970s to give Christians a unified voice as strong as that of Muslims. Each tag had a number instead of a name: an identification code. They attacked the town. According to Human Rights Watch, 660 Muslims were massacred over the course of the next two days, including the patients in the al-Amin clinic. Twelve mosques and 300 houses went up in flames. Young girls were marched to a nearby Christian town and forced to eat pork and drink alcohol. Many were raped, and 50 were killed.[2]

Yelwa was still a ghost town in 2006. In block after burned-out block, people camped where their homes had stood. The road was lined with more than a dozen ruined mosques and churches, the rubble hidden by hip-high elephant grass and canary yellow morning glories climbing the old foundations. When I arrived at the home of Abdullahi Abdullahi, the Muslim human rights lawyer, his street was mostly deserted. He stooped on his way out of a low-ceilinged hut. Behind him, I could see the sour faces of a man and woman sitting on the floor by his desk. "Marital dispute," he said.

It was the rainy season, so I waited out the noon deluge in another small lean-to on his compound. Finally, Abdullahi ducked inside, a worn accordion file under his arm. His wife followed, carrying a pot of spaghetti, its steam rising against the cold, wet air. In the beginning, he explained, the conflict in Nigeria had nothing whatsoever to do with religion. "Let me give myself as a case study," Abdullahi said. He went to Christian mission schools and federal college, and never, as a Muslim, had any problem. "Throughout this period, I'd never seen religious segregation, because at that time the societal value system was intact. We were taught to respect each other's beliefs and customs." But as the population grew and resources shrank, people began to fight over who had come to Yelwa first, and who had arrived more recently as a "settler." Abdullahi held up an old sheet of newsprint on which an editorial's headline read, "We Are All Settlers!" Everyone who lived here came from somewhere else; everyone had settled.

Both sides had perpetrated atrocities, he admitted. "We could not control our own boys." Outside in the courtyard, three of the local "boys"—men, actually—sat against the hut shivering against the cold rain of the plateau in thin, well-pressed shirts. I wanted to know if they thought this was really about religion.

"Any Muslim struggling to protect himself is fighting in a jihad," Lawal, a thirty-nine-year-old headmaster, said. His cheeks were cut deep with three slashes; they looked like a cat's whiskers. He was wearing a purple shirt. "If someone attacks you, you have the right to defend yourself—call it jihad or whatever you want—but this was Christians attacking Muslims," he continued. He believed the Christians were plotting to eliminate the Muslims long before the church attack. "The Christians came in the sense of crusade. By the nature of the attack and the weapons they used, they attacked with a view to eliminating the Muslim community and leveling the town." Crusade, genocide—the goal was to eradicate a community, a people, a religion. Lawal lost everything: his family, his house, his cattle, his job as a headmaster. "There's no justice here; no one has been caught, punished, or arrested, so there's no security."

He leaned forward. "We want what belongs to us: the right to education, the right to practice my religion—"

Abdullahi raised his palm to clarify. No one was stopping Lawal from practicing his religion, Abdullahi explained, but the younger man wouldn't listen. In his mind, Islam was still under attack, and there was no dissuading him.

In 2004, after this spate of massacres, Nigeria declared a state of emergency. But, as the Emir of Wase had said, the fighting really stopped because it was too expensive for either side to continue. Whole communities lay in ruin. Cows, cars, farms, shops—all gone. Since then, Abdullahi has attempted to bring several cases to the government's attention, but as with the church massacre, the government has done little to investigate or to bring those involved to justice.

He handed me a folder with depositions from one such case and went outside. About twenty minutes later, Abdullahi returned with two young women, Hamamatu Danladi and Yasira Ibrahim, who had survived the incident detailed in the files. Danladi, rawboned and wrapped tightly in brown batik patterned with cowry shells, met my eye as she stood in the doorway; Ibrahim, with long, upturned lashes and a moon face, did not. Except for the fact that they had pulled the fabric over their heads to cover themselves, there was nothing about them to suggest they were Muslims. More often than not, my attempts to classify people according to skin color or height failed entirely. Abdullahi invited the women in, lowered his head, and left.

During the Christian attack, the two young women and others took shelter in an elder's guarded home. On the second day, the Christian militia arrived at the house. They were covered in red and blue paint and were wearing those numbered white name tags. The Christians first killed the guards, then chose from among the women. These two and others were marched toward the Christian village. "They were killing children on the road," Danladi said. Outside the elementary school, her abductor grabbed hold of two Muslim boys she knew, nine and ten years old. Along with other men, he took a machete to them until they were in pieces, then stuffed the pieces in a rubber tire and set it on fire.

When Danladi and Ibrahim reached their captors' village, they were forced to go against their faith by drinking alcohol, eating pork and dog meat. Although she was visibly pregnant, Danladi said that her abductor raped her for four days. After a month, the police fetched her and Ibrahim from the Christian village and took them to the camp where most of the town's Muslim residents had fled. There, the two young women were reunited with their husbands. They never discussed what happened in the bush.

"The Christians don't want us here because they don't like our religion," Danladi said. "Do you really think they took you because of your religion?" I asked. The women looked at each other. "In Islamic history, there are times when believers and nonbelievers have fought," Danladi said. "What happened here is part of this clash." After the clash, she explained, their leaders foretold of a time of poverty and suffering. "That's what's happening now." Soon, the world's end would arrive, and every person on earth would adopt the one true faith. "According to our *ulamas* [teachers], there is no way that the whole world will not be Muslim."

Later, I looked up Matthew 24, the verses that Pastor Wuyep had cited, in a soft-bound black leather copy of the King James Bible—a gift to me from the American evangelist Franklin Graham, after I traveled with him to Sudan in December 2003. Down the rice-paper page, where Jesus's words were printed in red to show that they were absolute and unerring, one verse caught my eye: "But woe to those who are pregnant and to those who are nursing babies in those days!" (Matthew 24:19). I thought of Hamamatu Danladi. After her rape, she told me, she didn't give birth for four more months, which meant she had carried her child for more than a year.

A year later, in August 2007, I returned to Yelwa to be sure I'd understood her story. This time, I carried along a digital recorder. It must have switched on in my pocket, because later that night, as I went through the audio files after the interview, I heard the sound of my flip-flops approaching her house, then her at the door gleeful, shouting in an unknown tongue. I treasure this recording: she sounds so joyful, in spite of the horror I had asked her to recall.

When we sat down to talk, I asked her to tell me again how long she had carried the baby in her womb. She repeated the story: she had carried him for more than a year. And even though he had spent more than a year inside her, he was born healthy. Maybe, she thought, he simply refused to come into this world during such tribulation.

At the time of the Yelwa massacre of Muslims in May 2004, Archbishop Peter Akinola was president of the Christian Association of Nigeria. He has since lost his bid for another term, but as head of the Anglican Church of Nigeria, he is still the leader of eighteen million Anglicans. He was also a colleague of my father's, Frank Griswold, when, from 1997 to 2006, he was the presiding bishop of the Episcopal Church, which has about two million members and is part of a larger network of churches called the Anglican Communion. Three years before I met Akinola, the diocese of New Hampshire had consecrated an open homosexual, the Right Reverend Gene V. Robinson, as bishop, an act without precedent in the Anglican Communion. This raised a hue and cry among Americans and Africans alike. Robinson's election was so contentious that my father—whose job it was, as presiding bishop, to consecrate new bishops—had to wear a bulletproof vest under his cassock at the service. The election also antagonized Archbishop Akinola, who saw in it more evidence that the profligate

West was willing to abandon its biblical faith and leave African Christians, already in peril among Muslims, to defend themselves against the sins of the West. Denouncing Gene Robinson's election as "satanic,"[3] Akinola suddenly stood at a distance from my father.

When I arrived in the capital of Abuja to see the archbishop, his office door was locked. Its complicated buzzing-in system was malfunctioning, and he was trapped inside. Finally, after several minutes, the buzzing stopped and I could hear a man behind the door rise and come across the floor. The archbishop, in a powder blue pantsuit and a darker blue crushed velvet hat, opened the door.

"My views on Islam are well known: I have nothing more to say," he said, eyeing me. I imagine what he saw was an American bishop's daughter. But he did have more to say. The fact is, I was asking about the threat Islam posed to Christianity, and this was the great question of his life. Once he began to answer, he grew expansive, even voluble, as he tried to pull the scales off the eyes of a Western reporter. Archbishop Akinola, who is sixty-six, is Yoruba, a member of an ethnic group from southwestern Nigeria, where Christians and Muslims coexist peacefully. But his understanding of Islam was forged by his experience in the north, where he watched the persecution of a Christian minority. He has repeatedly spoken critically about Islam and liberal Western Christians, and he was wary of my motives in asking him to comment. For Akinola, the relationship between liberal Protestants and Islam is straightforward: if Western Christians abandon conservative morals, then the global Church will be weakened in its struggle against Islam.

"When you have this attack on Christians in Yelwa, and there are no arrests, Christians become *dhimmi*, the status within Islam that allows Christians and Jews to be seen as second-class citizens. You are subject to the Muslims. You have no rights."

When I asked if the men wearing name tags that read, "Christian Association of Nigeria," had been sent to Yelwa before the massacre of Muslims, the archbishop grinned. "No comment," he said. "No Christian would pray for violence, but it would be utterly naïve to sweep this issue of Islam under the carpet." He went on: "I'm not out to combat anybody. I'm only doing what the Holy Spirit tells me to do. I'm living my faith, practicing and preaching that Jesus Christ is the one and only way to God, and they respect me for it. They know where we stand. I've said before: let no Muslim think they have the monopoly on violence."

Akinola was more interested in talking about the West than about Nigeria. "People are thinking that Islam is an issue in Africa and Asia, but you in the West are sitting on explosives," he said. "What Islam failed to accomplish by the sword in the eighth century, it's trying to do by immigration so that Muslims become citizens and demand their rights. A Muslim man has four wives; the wives have four or five children each. This is how they turned Christians into a minority in North Africa," he asserted.

The archbishop believed that he and his fellow Christians living at the periphery of Muslim North Africa knew the future that awaited the West. "The West has thrown God out, and Islam is filling that vacuum for you, and now your Christian heritage is being destroyed. You people are so afraid of being accused of being Islamophobic. Consequently everyone recedes and says nothing. Over the years, Christians have been so naïve— avoiding politics, economics, and the military because they're dirty business. The missionaries taught that. Dress in tatters. Wear your bedroom slippers. Be poor. But Christians are beginning to wake up to the fact that money isn't evil, the love of money is, and it isn't wrong to have some of it. Neither is politics."

6

MODERN SAINTS AND MARTYRS

Standing in his pajamas at the foot of the living room stairs, the seven-year-old boy struggled to remember his father's cell phone number. When he tipped his head up to me politely, I noticed that his mouth was scarred with white lines that looked like someone had sewn stitches through his lips. I was looking for his father, the Middle Belt's Anglican archbishop. Benjamin Kwashi came up repeatedly as both a victim of religious violence and, like his boss, Peter Akinola, as an outspoken critic of the liberal West. Apparently Kwashi had forgotten our appointment on this Saturday morning in July 2006. When I arrived at the locked gate, two ferocious dogs speckled with mange bared their yellow teeth and barked. I yelled for someone to call off the dogs, but there was no answer, so I darted past them, sprinted down the driveway, and pushed open the front door. It seemed at first that no one was home, until I heard a pair of small feet thump down the stairs.

The sound reminded me of my own feet on the back steps of a Philadelphia rectory twenty years earlier, in the days before people locked their doors in the suburbs. On Saturday mornings, with my parents out somewhere on church business, people would wander into the rectory looking for help. I was left, like this boy, to solve grown-up crises. I stood there, sorry I'd come, until the boy eventually remembered his father's number, his scarred mouth twisted into a lopsided smile.

"As a result of persecution, we have become more evangelistic," Archbishop Kwashi said. I found him at the church office, in shorts and a T-shirt, catching up on e-mail. "If you die in Christ, you go to heaven." On the bookshelf behind him: *The Purpose-Driven Life* and *Body by God: The Owner's Manual for Maximized Living*, a diet book created by missionary chiropractors planting churches around the world. Also *Modern Saints and Martyrs*, in which Baroness Caroline Cox, a seventy-three-year-old conservative British parliamentarian, writes about Kwashi. (Cox started Humanitarian Aid Relief Trust, or HART, which works on behalf of persecuted Christians worldwide. A baroness since the early eighties, when she was appointed to the House of Lords, Cox is a compelling and controversial figure who melds a hard-line Christian worldview with the language of human rights. She has spoken at Laura and George W. Bush's church in Midland, Texas, and has been criticized for perpetuating a misunderstanding of Sudan's war as a crusade against Christians. She has bought the freedom of an alleged 2,281 Sudanese slaves since the 1990s.)[1] All of these books on the archbishop's shelf were practical manuals for living according to a twenty-first-century life: from weight loss to career advancement to the necessary role of martyr.

About five months earlier, on February 13, 2006, while Bishop Kwashi was away in London, a group of Muslim men broke into his house, knocked his nineteen-year-old son unconscious, and blinded his wife. "They also broke my seven-year-old's mouth," he said, explaining the scars I had seen on the boy. "That's what we face every day. I've been running from Muslim persecution since I was a teenager."

This was why the archbishop kept attack dogs at his house. His son's experience and mine were nothing alike at all. To Kwashi, the violence against his family was evidence that Christians needed defending. His house and church in the Muslim north were also torched during the eighties—a direct result, he believed, of Christianity's growth among Muslims. "In Nigeria both sides are growing, and that growth engenders competition," he said. On one hand, it was a religious and political zero-sum game: gains for one side implied losses for the other. But for many, devoting one's life to God had little to do with self-interest. For men like Kwashi, believing even required a willingness to die. Behind him, a text screensaver slid across his computer's idling monitor: "For whoever desires to save his life shall lose it . . ." It was Matthew 16:25, a verse used as a call for contemporary martyrdom.

"For Christians, God has moved his work to Africa," he said.

Kwashi understood that Christians who had not felt Islam's pressure along this particular fault line might feel differently; he understood how his anger played into his conservative worldview, but that didn't change his opinion about what he saw as a global conflict playing out locally here in Nigeria.

"I have lost so many friends, and that makes me hang on to and sharpen my faith and believe even more strongly in my Bible and that it is true because I am being persecuted for it," he said. Scripture provided Kwashi a defense against Islam, as it had since missionaries arrived among the non-Muslim hill tribes two hundred years earlier. The Bible, along with guides to health and hygiene, also served as a practical guide to a new way of life—a syllabus. One popular slogan was "Our Faith and Our Farm." "Any shift away from the Bible is to strip me naked of my way to develop," Kwashi said. "I don't have the luxury of relativism that the West does."

Here was the split between the Global South and the West. Beginning in the sixties, Western mainline Protestants moved away from a strict interpretation of scripture. And as many Christians in Asia and Africa told it, over the past several decades the Westerners had left the job of spreading the Gospel to them. This shift, according to the bishop, is where America, in particular, went wrong.

"All the battles of the West are fought in Africa, from communism on," Kwashi said. Now, in the aftermath of the cold war, the proxy war between Islam and the West is playing itself out again in Africa. "The Islamic world wants to counter the Christian West. They don't understand that Christianity isn't the West. The Church is just a scapegoat for the West, and nobody wants to come to its help." What he saw as a chasm between frontline states such as Nigeria and the West was widening. African Christianity and most liberal Western traditions were at a stalemate over not just sexuality; gay bishops simply topped the growing catalog of moral and scriptural divergences between more progressive Western Christians and believers along the tenth parallel. "We are facing the threats of both America and Islam," he said.

7

THE GOD OF PROSPERITY

Democracy, as Nigerians told me repeatedly, is one numbers game; religion is another. Growing a church or a mosque can be a competitive business. To be viable in the twenty-first century, each has to prove that it can offer members something in response to their devotion—a phenomenon that is neither new nor limited to Nigeria. Yet Nigeria's religious marketplace is unique in that it's openly aggressive.

Church is no staid ritual in Nigeria; it is a carnival. One Friday night, I went to the Redeemed Christian Church of Christ at an all-night church ground with three hundred thousand other people. The figure is larger than the number of Quakers in America—the equivalent of an entire American denomination worshipping at the edge of Lagos. With no traffic, the church ground is an hour's drive from Lagos. The choir was a phalanx of thousands of young people sitting under a tent, and I wandered among them, swallowed by the rush of their voices. Most attendees would spend the night dozing in their chairs or buying peanuts and soda and tapes and T-shirts and a host of other amusements. The service started at eight. Around midnight, I left to face hours of traffic and the sizable risk of a carjacking by the bandits who freely roamed the highways, picking off tired churchgoers.

These huge services began during the oil boom of the 1970s, which brought a mass migration of people into cities looking for work. The boom's collapse also spurred the growth of the Pentecostal "gospel of prosperity," with its emphasis on good health and getting rich—or surviving a downturn—and of the African Initiated Churches, or AICs, which began about one hundred years ago, when several charismatic African prophets successfully converted tens of millions of people to Christianity. Today, AIC members account for one quarter of Africa's almost five hundred million Christians.

One bustling Pentecostal hub, Canaanland, the 565-acre headquarters of the Living Faith Church, has three banks, a bakery, and its own university, Covenant, the sister school of Oral Roberts University in Tulsa, Oklahoma. Canaanland is located about an hour and a half north of the city of Lagos, which, with an estimated population of twelve million, is projected to become the world's twelfth-largest city by 2020. With another three hundred thousand people worshipping at a single service at the Canaanland headquarters alone and three hundred branches across the country, Living Faith is one of Nigeria's megachurches, and the dapper bishop David Oyedepo is its prophet. The bishop, whose shaved pate glistens above deep-set eyes and dazzling teeth, never wanted to be a pastor: his interest was in escaping poverty, he told me. "When God made me a pastor, I wept. I hated poverty in the Church. How can the children of God live as rats?"

Bishop Oyedepo built Canaanland to preach the gospel of prosperity. As he said, "If God is truly a father, there is no father that wants his children to be beggars. He wants them to prosper." In the parking lot at Canaanland, beyond the massive complex of refreshingly clean toilets, flapping banners promise: "WHATSOEVER YOU ASK IN MY NAME, HE SHALL GIVE YOU" and "BY HIS STRIPES HE GIVES US BLESSINGS."

When it comes to gaining followers, Archbishop Akinola's Anglican Church is more threatened by the rise of Pentecostalism than by Islam. (This is one of the growing fissures between older and newer Christian groups that reveal deepening divides within Christianity.) Akinola finds its teachings suspect, since they are engendered by a focus on spirits and by the promise of worldly goods. Christianity means being willing to suffer and die for your beliefs, he argues. "When you preach prosperity and not suffering, any Christianity devoid of the cross is a pseudo-religion."

But Bishop Oyedepo's followers say that those who criticize don't understand what's happening in Africa. "There's a kind of revolution going on in Africa," said Prince Famous Izedonmi, a professor at Covenant University. I met him in the college cafeteria, where he overheard me asking my tour guide questions. The professor was a Muslim prince who converted to Christianity as a child to cure himself of migraine headaches. He was also the head of the university's Accounting and Taxation Department and director of its Center for Entrepreneurial Development Studies. "America tolerates God. Africa celebrates God. We're called 'the continent of darkness,' but that's when you appreciate the light. Jesus is the light."

When I asked how this came back to money, he clucked at me. "God isn't against wealth. Revelations talks about streets paved with gold. Look at how Jesus dressed." Since the soldiers cast lots for Christ's clothes, they were clearly expensive. In Canaanland, clothes matter: the pastors are flashily dressed and drive fast cars as a sign of God's favor. They draw their salaries from sizable weekly contributions. On Sundays at some Nigerian Pentecostal churches, armored bank trucks reportedly idle in church parking lots, and believers hand over cash, cell phones, and cars during the service—all in the belief that if they give to God, God will make them rich.

To see Pentecostalism as simply a get-rich-quick scheme is to miss its real relevance for Nigeria—and America. In many ways, Pentecostalism has updated Max Weber's Protestant work ethic for the twenty-first century. Pentecostals profess not to drink, gamble, or engage in extramarital sex, so all that formerly illicit energy and cash can go into either business or education. Covenant has been voted the best private university in Nigeria by Nigeria's National Universities Commission. Education is an essential element of the prosperity message; so is hard work. "Abraham was a workaholic," Professor Famous Izedonmi said. "He worked sixteen or seventeen hours a day."

During my first visit to Covenant in the summer of 2006, school was not in session, so I poked around the empty labs until I ran into a lone student, Mchenson Ugwu, twenty-two, studying mechanical engineering in hopes of getting a job in the oil industry. Ugwu was born again in 2004. "Once in a while I backslide and have to rededicate my life to Christ," he said. "That's how it works: backslide, rededicate." For him, salvation had very little to do with the next world; it was all about this one. "Because he owns everything here on Earth, if you make God your father, beginning and end, he'll keep you up. Our bishop is the perfect example. He tells us he hasn't been poor in twenty-five years, and God takes him from one level to the next."

Later, when the bishop was ready to meet me, I was led across his red shag carpet to a white fountain tinkling in the corner of his office. He wanted to define the Covenant curriculum, which was based on a term he'd coined: the Total Man concept. "The problem with the African man is that he sees himself as poor, and others see him as poor," the bishop said. He walked over to his desk and handed me a stack of his books—he's written sixty—including one of the bestsellers: *Understanding Financial Prosperity*. The cover features Nigerian banknotes, naira. The back cover reads, "I am not a preacher of prosperity, I am a Prophet. God spoke specifically to me while I was away in America for a meeting, 'Get down home and make My people rich!'"

When I returned to Canaanland in September 2007, the vice-provost arranged for me to meet the student council. Two dozen young men and women gathered behind U-shaped desks to answer questions about their faith and their school. They were so quiet and respectful it was more like facing a corporate board than a group of college kids. (In Pentecostal parlance, they called themselves kings and queens.) For a large number— and this was the student council—prosperity didn't mean just future success, it meant any future at all. Many had left other schools due to the scourge of gangs—called cults in Nigeria—which, as they told me in horrifying detail, frequently involved initiation rights of rape, theft, and murder. One student council member, who asked not to be named, claimed that he had broken into his math professor's home and watched in horror as a fellow cult member raped the professor's wife. Here, they were as safe from harm as they were from harming others.

The Christian gospel of prosperity is so powerful it has spawned a unique Nigerian phenomenon: an Islamic organization called Nasrul-Lahi-il-Fathi (NASFAT). The name comes from a verse in the eighth chapter of the Quran, "The Spoils of War," or al-Anfal, and it reads, "There is no help except from Allah." The kind of help NASFAT offers begins very much with this world. The organization is based on economic empowerment and prosperity, with an Islamic spin. Started with about a dozen members in the 1990s, NASFAT now has 1.2 million members in Nigeria and branches in twenty-five other countries. The organization has an entrepreneurship program, a clinic, a prison-outreach program, a task force to address HIV/AIDS, a travel agency, and a soft drink company called Nasmalt, whose profits go to the poor. It even offers a matchmaking service. NASFAT is not modeled after Islamic charities such as Egypt's Muslim Brotherhood, which provides Islamic-based social services to its clients and propagates a conservative form of Islam. It is the opposite: a way for Islam to engage with the West on its own terms. As splits within Christianity are shaping the future of the faith, so is splintering within Islam. Most conservatives loathe NASFAT and believe that this engagement with the secular world is *haram*, "forbidden," and distinctly un-Islamic. Yet faced with the encroachment of Christianity, NASFAT argues that the only way to survive in the religious marketplace is by playing the same game.

"We are competing for faithfuls," said NASFAT's executive secretary, Zikrullah Kunle Hassan, one blistering Sunday in September 2007. "Many people now want God. This is happening especially among the youth, that they feel they need to be committed to faith." Gesturing to the streets choked with more than a hundred thousand men and women in white as they came from a prayer service at the Lagos Secretariat Mosque, he explained that NASFAT meets on Sundays so that Muslims have something to do while Christians attend church. "The space on Sunday is usually not dominated by Islam, but other faiths and other values. But when our people come here, they come and drink from the fountain of Islam."

The prayer ground looked like a fairground—just like the Pentecostal churches did. Everyone among the throngs of thousands was clad in white, and except for the women's eyelet head scarves and the men's small white hats, there would have been no way to tell if this was a gathering of Christians or Muslims. Hawkers sold lemons from a wheelbarrow. Small booths offered those pretty, scalloped *hijabs*, embroidered with "NASFAT" in blue. Men sat on prayer mats eating rice, while women attended a lecture on ways to make money in keeping with Islam. NASFAT's primary mission is to reclaim those values the world sees as Western but that its members perceive as integral to the success of the global Islamic community, the *Ummah*. Foremost is education. "We know that the West is ahead today because of education," Hassan said. NASFAT has its own nursery, primary and secondary schools, and Fountain University. While many orthodox believers say that this new movement is *bidah*, "innovation," and therefore dangerously un-Islamic, NASFAT's adherents disagree, arguing that they are part of a charismatic Muslim movement that addresses social welfare—and is on its way to sweeping the world. This is a form of African Islam, again, born out of interface with the West, and also African Christianity. Unlike many conservative social welfare organizations, its aim is not to retreat into a seventh-century world, but to engage, engage, engage.

If the answer to every issue in life can be found in the Quran, Hassan said, then questions about how to survive and prosper must be addressed in the holy text. When conservative northern clerics kick up a fuss about NASFAT's growing presence in the communities, NASFAT reaches out to them with gestures such as involving community youth in business programs.

"To be honest, for us there's a competition of civilizations, there's a competition of values, and to me, the roots of the conflict are that we believe all civilizations have collapsed in the face of Western civilization," he said. "Communism collapsed. All other values collapsed. Islam remained resistant to Western civilization."

In order to survive, Islam has to address the contemporary needs of its people and compete with the Christian promise of prosperity. As one young member, who joined the organization to get a job through its business network, told me, "There's nothing you want to achieve that NASFAT can't help you get here in this country." He added, "Success, triumph, and glory are from the Creator."

"Prosperity gospel is more a symptom than the disease," said Father Matthew Hassan Kukah, the Roman Catholic author of *Religion, Politics and Power in Northern Nigeria*. In his view, Nigerians' resorting to religion to achieve prosperity is a natural response to their corrupt political landscape and the absence of any civil government. Again, when the nation fails, you turn to God. "*You* can buy a car and insure it," he continued. "You don't need a priest to pray over the car, to bless your house to keep robbers away . . . Here, there's no guarantee. God is being called upon to police a lot of areas of our lives."

Many Muslims share this point of view. Take the ongoing effort to implement Islamic law in northern Nigeria. Ideally, Islamic law is based on the tenets that God revealed to Mohammed, and that were later committed to paper by Mohammed's followers. Yet, over the centuries, four different schools of Islamic jurisprudence have interpreted what the Islamic code actually says. In other words, there's no such thing as a single form of Sharia. In Nigeria, on a practical level, Sharia, with its promise of local justice, seems to offer an end to the corruption that bedevils the people. And given that many Nigerians associate that corruption with the failure of Western-style democracy in Africa, "to reinstate the Sharia . . . is not only good religion, it is supremely sound politics," argues Murray Last, an emeritus professor at University College London. Not only has

Western-style democracy failed Nigeria, some Islamic leaders believe, but it also is a weapon the rapacious West uses to keep down developing nations.

Some have broadened this argument to include their suspicions that Western vaccines are a form of cultural subjugation—and of population control. For eight months during 2003 and 2004, many Nigerian Muslims believed the West was using the polio vaccine as a weapon against their religion. The northern state of Kano, among others, refused to allow the World Health Organization to vaccinate their children because they believed the vaccine would sterilize them. In August 2006, I met Dhetti Mohammad, a local Kano doctor who had led the ban. Dhetti, whose own children had been vaccinated years earlier, argued that because population was a source of strength among the world's Muslims, the West wanted to curb Islam's growth. The UN was designed to safeguard the West's global hegemony, he asserted, and that meant eliminating Muslims. To a Westerner like me, this seemed hysterical, and yet his argument mobilized tens of millions of people not to vaccinate their children. The campaign resulted in a devastating impact on the United Nations campaign to eradicate polio—cases of polio were diagnosed in nine African countries that had earlier been declared polio-free.

"In a developing world, people want to make other people slaves, second-class citizens—call it slavery, call it neocolonialism," Khalid Amiyu, a magnetic imam in his thirties, told me in 2006. Amiyu led prayers at a local mosque in the Middle Belt capital of Jos, and I met him at his home. "I've been an imam for twenty years. You think I can be a slave, I can be emasculated? No, no, I cannot! We are so obsessed with the white man. We think whatever he does is the solution for us. Maybe this democracy isn't right for us."

Islam, he argued, defends the greater good by fighting back against the destructive and corrupting power of the West, which, once again, Amiyu asserts, is undermining the power of Islam through a new imperialism. Amiyu lives in a small cement house in Jos—its windows barred and the path outside laced with blue rivulets of fresh sewage—in an all-Muslim ghetto about one hundred yards up a steep hill so slick it has its own name: *tudun fera*, or "peeled hill," because the earth has been slickened by people struggling up it. At the top of the hill, a group of Mormon missionaries have built a church hewn in polished stone.

"With the money those Christians have spent here, they could have cured malaria," Amiyu said. "Religion is losing its grip in the West, so they come to Africa and sow bigotry here." He added, "Why, if they accept that their own people don't want to be Christians, do they come here to convert Africa?" He led me through the house to the tap in an open courtyard and turned on the water: a thin yellow trickle. "We haven't had water in a week, and when it comes, it gives rashes." Because the neighborhood was a Muslim island in a larger Christian community, the government didn't attend to the Muslims' needs, Amiyu said. They had only occasional electricity, no sewage system, no clean water. But this local injustice reflected the global order's larger inequality. "When there is perceived injustice, the conflict will continue, and so far, there has been no justice at all."

Northern Nigeria has one of Africa's oldest and most devout Islamic communities, which was galvanized, like many others, in the 1980s by the global Islamic reawakening that followed the Iranian Revolution. In the eyes of many Muslims around the world, the Shah of Iran's 1979 overthrow initiated a moment of global Islamic resurgence. The shah's defeat was the West's defeat. Many Nigerian Muslims traveled to the Middle East to learn about their heritage. These revivals, however, quickly led to a growing debate over what it means to be a legitimate believer. Among Nigerian Muslims, as in other places, the pressures of religious renewal are creating splinters within Islam.

Beginning in the 1980s, many young Nigerian Muslims went to the Arab world to study, and returned preaching the tenets of a more conservative Islam; other students went to Iran, where they began to follow Shiite Islam. The Shia, who make up just over one-tenth of the world's Muslims—163 million—believe only the Prophet Mohammed's blood descendants can be Islam's legitimate rulers. In Nigeria, however, being Shia means mostly whatever you want it to. A group of young intellectuals (only a few of whom have studied in Iran), the Nigerian Shia hang posters of faraway firebrands, such as Ayatollah Khomeini and now Iraq's Muqtada al-Sadr, on their mud walls. To most of them, being Shia means being, above all, a revolutionary committed to social justice. In another context, they might be coffeehouse Marxists; in this one, they are determined to cast off class hierarchies and improve the quality of life in their communities. At least, these are the dreams they discuss when they sit around and talk, which, as jobless Nigerian men, they do quite a lot, over bottomless cups of weak tea.

The fragmenting ideologies among Nigerian Muslims sometimes turn violent. For decades now, different Islamic groups have competed for authority in the religious marketplace that dominates daily life. Predictably, the young, hard-line Sunnis and the self-described Shia often view one another as enemies. Both, however, also oppose the predominant Sufi traditions of most North Africans. Since Sufi practice is influenced from place to place by local traditions, this new generation of globalized Sunnis and Shias tend to view Sufi devotion as corrupted and "un-Islamic." Furthermore, Sufi brotherhoods are usually based on traditional class hierarchies, which the young Shia, who preach a radical social justice, vehemently oppose. From Sunni to Sufi to Shia, religious reawakening is further dividing Muslims in Nigeria.

Despite a huge outcry from local Christians and Western human rights groups, the implementation of Sharia, currently on the books in the northernmost third of Nigeria, has had very little practical impact. The criminal codes of the *hudud*, the harshest punishments allowed by Islamic law, have proven, for the most part, impossible to implement. This is perhaps the greatest lesson: that people will idealize religious law until they have experienced the limits of its application. Northern Nigerians have now seen that Sharia has not stanched the corruption they face every day. In fact, many of the politicians who backed Islamic law have been linked to massive corruption; these include its biggest advocate, the former governor of Zamfara state, who is rumored to have paid a man to let the state amputate his hand.

8

"RACES AND TRIBES"

"When the West sneezes, Africa catches a cold." I first heard this expression from a Nigerian pastor named James Movel Wuye, who works alongside his former mortal enemy, Imam Muhammed Nurayn Ashafa, to bring about a change of consciousness in the way Nigeria's Muslims and Christians view one another. During the eighties and nineties, the two leaders taught thousands of young people to kill, and now they "reprogram" them to tolerate each other's differences. *Tolerance* is a word of which both are wary, since to them, it smacks of a moral relativism to which they do not subscribe. To them, it suggests they should tolerate heresy and falsehood. Each strictly adheres to the tenets of his respective faith and unabashedly calls himself a fundamentalist. The imam's followers lopped off the pastor's arm with a machete more than a decade ago. Now they are partners in an effort to foster amity among the Nigerian youth they once taught to fight in the name of their respective religions. The reason, first and foremost, is to ensure their mutual survival, since fighting has cost each community so much.

The two men travel to religious conflict zones all over the world—they have visited the World Trade Center site together several times—but they still live in the Nigerian city of Kaduna, which means "crocodile" and is named for the river that runs through its center, dividing north and south. The tenth parallel also runs through the town, which is in many ways a microcosm of Nigeria: its population of one and a half million people is split in half between Muslims and Christians. The Muslim neighborhoods—nicknamed Baghdad and Afghanistan—are on the north side of town. The Christian ones—called Haifa, Jerusalem, and, inexplicably, Television—are on the south side. The inhabitants name the neighborhoods themselves. It is one more way to claim a place in a global religious order. Over the past twenty years, many of the city's churches and mosques have been burned down, and thousands of residents have been killed.

When I first arrived in downtown Kaduna in 2006, I climbed five flights of stairs in a nondescript office building—the elevator did not work, as there was no electricity that day—to track down their Christian-Muslim Interfaith Mediation Centre. Outside, a small plastic plaque read, "Peace Hall." Inside, Pastor James, a middle-aged man less than five and a half feet tall, had a terrible cold. Before he blew his nose, he wrapped toilet tissue around his bare right forearm, which did not move. It was made of hard plastic.

The pastor belongs to an ethnic minority called Gbagyi—some of Karl Kumm's "border pagans." Before they became Christians, they were ab-original warriors who fought off Hausa Muslim slave raiders. The arrival of the British actually made things worse, as indirect rule strengthened Muslim dominion over the pastor's people—much as Karl Kumm and other missionaries had feared it would.

"They were merciless, the Muslims who were ruling over us," the pas-tor said. His people still call the Hausa Muslims *ajei*, which means "those who trouble us." Pastor James grew up in a military barracks—his father was a soldier—and when he and the other barracks boys played war, their imagined enemies were their Hausa oppressors. As a teenager, Pastor James smoked cigarettes and wooed a long list of girlfriends. He also joined the Christian Association of Nigeria and, at twenty-seven, became general secretary of its Youth Wing. In 1987, the Middle Belt exploded. When fighting between Christians and Muslims reached Kaduna, Pastor James became the leader of the Christian militia. "We took an oath of secrecy," he said. "We carried pictures of those who had been killed. We were martyrs: we felt that we were dying in defense of the Church." The war, like the faith itself, became a struggle for liberation.

"I used to say, 'We've been beaten on both cheeks, there's no other cheek to turn,'" he said, teaching others to justify bloodshed by relying on the literal, inspired word of scripture. Once it was the call to violence couched in self-defense. "I used Luke 22:36—as Jesus said to the disci-ples the night before his crucifixion, 'And if you don't have a sword, sell your cloak and buy one.'" When the pastor was thirty-two, a fight broke out between Christians and Muslims over control of a market. "That day, we were outnumbered," he said. "Twenty of my friends were killed. I passed out, so I don't know exactly what happened." When he woke up, his right arm was gone, sliced off with a machete.

To understand Kaduna's faith-based battle lines, I had to see them, Pastor James said, so he summoned an employee. This was the first time I met Haruna Yakubu, the former Islamic militant who now works as the center's youth coordinator, and who would drive me around the Middle Belt in the minivan. That first afternoon, Yakubu drove me through the former colonial city, where neem trees line the old roads like ghosts of the bygone British. The colonial polo fields were worn bare but still in use. Mostly wealthy Muslim horsemen play there—others do aerobics in the bleachers. American-style fitness, its own imprint of empire, has also arrived.

Yakubu first took me to see the concrete skeleton of the fire-ravaged Alafia Oluwa Baptist Church. "The Baptists want to sell it," he said, as we climbed out of the car. The cross and spire had been sheared off, but the walls and heavy concrete Romanesque arches were still standing. They now enclosed a large grassy field; a cow was tethered to a nearby tree. I walked toward the narthex, but Yakubu stopped me. It stank of human shit. "The locals have turned it into a toilet," he said, uncomfortably. On the wall, through a hole blasted into the cement, I could see someone had painted a picture of a naked woman, a penis with "Pastor S" written on it pointed between her spread legs. "We're trying to convince the Baptists to come back, but they don't want to." In 2007, the Christians sold the church to the Muslims after all. When Yakubu and I passed by the next year, the word *masalaci*, which means "mosque," had been spray-painted across it in red.

We drove in silence through the neighborhood known as Afghanistan. Yakubu said, "Our religious leaders are some of our most dangerous people. They preach that they want us to go back to Medina, but we can't go back to Medina." Here was a contemporary struggle for Islam's soul: whether believers should cling most tightly to their history in Medina, the city from which believers battled for their right to self-determination, or whether God's message to Mohammed in Mecca—more inclusive and universal—reflected the future of the faith.

"Even the Prophet lived with Christians; why can't we? If we call ourselves true Muslims, why can't we do that?" Yakubu said. Along the road, red-eyed boys sold jerry cans of petrol. Although Nigeria is flooded with oil, corruption and mismanagement force the country to import much of its gasoline. During price hikes and shortages, these young hawkers appear by the roadside; their gas cans become weapons.

Pastor James's former enemy, Imam Muhammed Nurayn Ashafa, lives on the Muslim side of the river. One Friday morning before afternoon prayer, I went to visit him at home. By the time I arrived, he had already resolved three neighborhood disputes. Two smiling old men in dark glasses sat on his green sectional couch. They were blind, and Ashafa had started a foundation to help them. His two young wives, Fatima and Aisha—both named for the Prophet's wives—served tea on top of a tin canister. The windows were shut, and the green-and-white striped curtains drawn in purdah. On one closed door, a bumper sticker read, "Combat AIDS with Shari'a." The method was clear: abstinence. The imam and the pastor share the same conservative moral values, which has also helped them to find common ground. Ashafa, tall and narrow, his beard grizzled, grew up equally as steeped in the history of his people. He comes from a long line of Muslim scholars who were powerful under the caliphate of Uthman dan Fodio, and his story, too, is a tale of oppression and reaction to oppression.

"My family had, all its life, struggled against colonialists and missionaries because they watched the colonialists bring Christianity into the hinterlands. I grew up hearing stories of how our land was stolen and our people were crushed." When Ashafa was a boy, since missionaries ran the local school, his father refused to let him go. "Missionaries are evil," he told his son. But Ashafa's uncle talked his father into it, saying, "Let the boy go to school. Don't you trust your God?"

At mission school, Ashafa won the prize for best Bible student. (He had a gift for memorization.) After school, with his slingshot, he flung stones at women showing their bare arms or backs in the streets. When the religious crisis hit Kaduna in 1987, he became the equivalent of Pastor James on the Muslim side.

"We planted the seed of genocide, and we used the scripture to do that," Ashafa said. "In Islam, you must fight in defense of any women, children, or old people—Muslim or not—so, as a leader, you create a scenario where this is the only interpretation," he explained. His mentor, a Sufi hermit, tried to warn the young man away from violence, telling

Ashafa, "You will not cross the ocean with hate in your heart." In 1992, Christian militiamen stabbed the hermit to death and threw his body down a well. Ashafa vowed to kill Pastor James, and revenge became his only mission, until one Friday, his local imam gave a sermon on the story of the Prophet Mohammed's journey to the Arabian town of Ta'if. When Ashafa heard that the Prophet said to the angel Gabriel, "My Lord, forgive my people; they do not know what they are doing," he wept. "The imam was talking directly to me," he said. He knew he had to forgive Pastor James. He went to visit the pastor's sick mother in the hospital, and although Pastor James remained leery, the two men began to work together, talking to the communities they'd formerly incited to violence, bringing the young people together to speak to one another, working out an early-warning system so that local religious leaders from different sides called one another when they heard rumors such as "they're killing our brothers across town."

One of Ashafa's greatest challenges is to manage Kaduna's Muslim groups when they clash over methods of devotion. Sufi mystics gather to pray and sometimes play music: half chant, half steel drum, amplified, in the streets. (They're hired to come sing outside a house when a baby is born, for instance.) Sunni hard-liners oppose the Sufi majority as un-Islamic, and claim that these rituals are influenced by African tribalism, not traditional faith. Everyone fears the self-proclaimed Shia, who, thanks in part to Hezbollah's popular satellite TV station, have sharpened their revolutionary sensibilities over the past few years. These religious rifts in Kaduna are local and global; many mirror the tensions of the larger Islamic world. The imam tries to stay neutral, but is frequently accused of being a sellout because he associates with Christians. He identifies himself very much as a fundamentalist and sees himself as one who emulates Mohammed. Although he and Pastor James don't discuss it, he also proselytizes among Christians. "I want James to die as a Muslim, and he wants me to die as a Christian. My Islam is proselytizing. It's about bringing the whole world to Islam."

Sometimes their human differences creep into their religious missions. "Ashafa carries the psychological mark. I carry the physical and psychological mark," Pastor James told me. "He talks so much. I'm a little miserly with words. So when he uses his energy like that, he sleeps very deeply.

There were instances where we shared a room. He's a very heavy sleeper. You can actually take the pillow off his head and he will just go back to sleep. More than once, several times, I was tempted to use the pillow to suffocate him. But this restraining force of the deepness of my faith comes ringing through my ears."

James's transformation came in the mid-nineties, at a Christian conference in Nigeria sponsored by Pat Robertson, one of the most vocally anti-Muslim preachers in the world. A fellow pastor pulled James aside and said, in almost the same words as the Sufi hermit, "You can't preach Jesus with hate in your heart." James said, "That was my real turning point. I came back totally deprogrammed. I know Pat Robertson might have had another agenda, but I was truly changed." At one of Kaduna's local television stations, James hosts a TV show about Jesus Christ in Hausa, the language of local Muslims. The station broadcasts both Muslim and Christian programs. When I visited, the studio was little more than a plywood shed, with two oilcloth backdrops hanging on the wall. One was of Mecca lit up at night, and all white except for the black stone *kaaba* in the center. On the other, an airbrushed image of a luscious desert island shimmered. This was the Christian backdrop—a different version of earthly paradise. James took his seat in front of a palm tree and opened the Bible. It was after ten at night, and as he preached, his wife, Elizabeth, nodded off on the other side of the shed, in front of Mecca. I marveled at James's devotion and thought of the people—some of whom would be Muslims—watching him on their crackling, generator-powered television sets for miles around.

For James and Ashafa, their "deprogramming efforts" include reading scripture aloud with former fighters. At first, I did not believe that such a simple practice could actually work. As an outsider, I doubted that words on the page, no matter the color, could make a substantive difference as to how people viewed one another. But along the tenth parallel, the Bible and the Quran play an integral part in peoples' daily lives. Scripture often provides a more practical rule of law than the government does. It lays out a social and moral code for human interaction. It gives meaning to suffering and poverty. It offers a group identity through which followers can secure their worldly needs, and, finally, find some certainty about the hereafter, about Providence.

Yet time and again people's professions of their beliefs, like James and Ashafa's work with former militants, baffled me. They were ultimately mysterious, and could not be explained away by self-interest, or anything else of this world. As Barbara Cooper, who began her career as a Marxist historian and is the author of *Evangelical Christians in the Muslim Sahel*, put it to me simply, "Faith is the X factor."

The imam and the pastor now travel the world telling their story. I caught up with them in New York before Thanksgiving 2006, and they wanted to return to Ground Zero, where they had been in 2003 after receiving another peace award. We took an elevator into the pit where the base of Tower Two had been.

"What a tremendous act of ego," the imam said, as he peered through wire mesh into the wreckage. "Ask him where the cross is," he instructed me, pointing to a policeman standing nearby. I had not been back to the site since reporting there in September 2001, and had no idea what he meant.

"What cross?" I asked.

"The *cross*, the iron cross," he said. "He'll know what I mean."

I spoke to the policeman, and we took the escalator back up to the street and walked north two blocks until we reached the two sections of broken girder welded into the form of a thirty-foot cross. "God bless our fallen brothers" had been scratched into the steel many times over. For a few moments, no one said anything.

"It symbolizes that God is with the American people," the imam said, "and that the American people have to return to God."

"Where did you hear that?" I asked. "Last time I was here a young guy told me that," he said, watching me reach for my notebook. "No, not a young guy, say, an elder." He looked up at the cross. "Just say 'an anonymous American citizen.'"

The imam loved his stories, and both men were aware—especially here in the rich belly of America—that their calling was also their business. This was not the case in Nigeria, where they worked tirelessly to quell fights between neighbors and families without any chance of gain. I had watched the pastor puzzle for hours over how to distribute an environmentally friendly stove that burned almost no wood. (Buying wood currently costs as much as one dollar a day in the deforested north, so the stoves, as well as being environmentally sound, would save people money, and potentially keep them from fighting over land.) Dealing with the stoves was just as important as dealing with scripture. The pastor and the imam also understood too well how a fight between the neighborhoods Baghdad and Jerusalem over electricity could quickly envelop the city, or the country. In Nigeria, they were saints; here . . . well, here they seemed like businessmen. So what—weren't they, too, allowed to have more than one identity?

I hailed a yellow cab and we all piled in. As the taxi rattled over the cobbled streets of lower Manhattan, the pastor and the imam traded verses from the Bible and the Quran, competing good-naturedly for my attention. However, this was no parlor game: it was their most earnest attempt to understand each other, since scripture, more than any other element, determined who each man was. God created people poles apart, Ashafa mused, so that, through contrast, they could understand each other. At least that's what the Quran says; he quoted: "People, We created you all from a single man and woman, and made you into races and tribes so that you should recognize one another" (The Private Rooms 49:13). "The Bible says almost the same thing," Pastor James interrupted, citing Acts 17:26: "From one man he made every nation of men, that they should inhabit the whole earth . . ." This, Pastor James clarified, did not mean that all religions were the same, as liberal Westerners tried to assert. Mutual understanding could not mean denying exclusive salvation. "Jesus said, 'I am the way and the truth and the life,'" he repeated. For both these men, homosexuality was anathema. "We see same-sex marriages in the United States as signs of end times: it's Sodom and Gomorrah," James told me. "But I also want to say you can believe what you want to believe. We have to find a space for coexistence."

SUDAN

*I am the way, the truth, and the life. No one comes to the
Father except through me.*
—THE GOSPEL ACCORDING TO JOHN 14:6

*If anyone seeks a religion other than complete devotion to
God [Islam],[1] it will not be accepted from him: he will be
one of the losers in the Hereafter.*
—THE QURAN, THE FAMILY OF ʿIMRAN 3:85

9

IN THE BEGINNING

Philosophers and cartographers began to orient
themselves by drawing imaginary lines around the
earth in the third century BCE. Latitude, the horizontal lines that ring the globe—not the vertical

measure of longitude[1]—was the first such scale. Early philosophers divided the earth into five horizontal bands: there were two frigid zones, one at either pole; two temperate zones, between the poles and the tropics; and near the equator, the Torrid Zone. Since their inception, latitudes have carried social and moral connotations, and cartographers have used them to separate one "type" of human from another. For more than two thousand years, the tenth parallel has served as such a dividing line; in its history begins the contemporary contest between Islam and the West.

The tenth parallel falls within the Torrid Zone—between the Tropic of Cancer and the Tropic of Capricorn (from a latitude of 23°26'22" north to a latitude of 23°26'22" south). In the third century BCE, although he had never been there, Aristotle defined this region as a heat-blasted badland rich in resources—gold, ivory, cinnamon—yet inhabited by dangerous monsters scorched black by the tropical sun. "Yet we know the whole breadth of the region we dwell in up to the uninhabited parts," he wrote in his text on the subject, *Meteorologica*, "in one direction no one lives because of the cold, in the other because of the heat."[2] From Aristotle to the twelfth-century Arab philosopher and scientist known as Averroës,[3] to the twentieth century, astronomers and cartographers have drawn maps to reflect their sense of geographic and racial superiority. Hebrew scripture reinforced this divide from the first century onward, when Philo, a Jewish scholar from Alexandria, Egypt, argued that the people who lived in the Torrid Zone descended from Noah's accursed grandsons, the sons of Ham.[4] This malediction occurs in the Book of Genesis, when a drunken Noah awakes in his tent to learn that his youngest son has peered at his nakedness. Noah curses his son, saying he will be "a servant of servants" (Genesis 9:25). As Philo and other ancient philosophers interpreted it, God afflicted the sons of Ham, who lived in the Torrid Zone, with the double hex of both slavery and blackness.

On medieval Arabic maps, the tenth parallel marked the northern boundary of the territory called Bilad-as-Sudan, the Land of the Blacks, a land beyond Islam's reach,[5] which was believed to have little or no culture (despite the African kingdoms that flourished there), but a multitude of resources: gold, salt, ivory, and human slaves. In Greek mythology, *Aethiopia* means "the land of burnt faces" and refers not to the modern-day country of Ethiopia, but more often to sub-Saharan Africa—another forsaken place of "backward" peoples. In his *Metamorphoses*, the Roman writer Ovid, born in 43 BCE, recounts the story of blackness caused by heat so extreme, it boiled human blood and rendered North Africa a desert.[6] As late as a hundred years ago, British and American mapmakers labeled the vast tracts lying to the south of the tenth parallel "Negroland,"[7] tacitly writing off millions of people and thousands of years of culture and history. Many of the names of contemporary African nations along this line—Guinea, Nigeria, Ethiopia, and Somalia—in some way mean "black."

When Columbus first set sail, Europeans believed it was impossible to travel to the Torrid Zone and return safely. Yet Columbus, who undertook his voyage in part to spread the "Holy Faith"[8] of Christianity, discovered territories in the Torrid Zone that were far more temperate and irenic than philosophers had imagined.[9] Nevertheless, he concluded that the sun-blackened people he met were innately childlike and savage, and prone to consuming human flesh. (It was Columbus who coined the word *cannibalism*, after mishearing one indigenous group defame their enemies, the "Canibes" or, more probably, "Caribs," as flesh-eating monsters.) His observations helped justify enslaving the peoples of these lower latitudes in the service of empire.

Many African Christians believe that the Bible came to the continent straight from Jerusalem through the conversion of a eunuch—a castrated slave—in the year 37.[10] According to 8:26–38 of the Acts of the Apostles, a book in the Christian Bible that chronicles the doings of Jesus's followers after his death and resurrection, this unnamed eunuch was a high-ranking and literate servant who oversaw the treasury of the Kandake, a queen of Sudan. He traveled from Sudan, which lay within the Roman Empire, to Jerusalem on business, and one day he went by chariot from Jerusalem to Gaza, reading aloud along the way. On the road he passed an early Greek evangelist named Philip, who overheard his reading: "Who can describe his generation? For his life is taken away from the earth." Philip recognized this passage from the Book of Isaiah (53:8). The eunuch was reading from the Hebrew scriptures, which predate Jesus's birth; the passage in Isaiah is one that the first Christians believed foreshadowed their savior's life and death. Philip ran into the road, as the Holy Spirit prompted him to, and asked, "Do you understand what you are reading?" "How can I," the eunuch replied, "unless someone explains it to me?" He invited Philip into the chariot, where Philip shared the gospel's *evange-*

lion, or "good news"—that this ancient prophecy had been fulfilled in Jesus, and the time had come to follow his teachings. Then he baptized the eunuch as a follower of Jesus in a roadside river.

The eunuch, as tradition has it, then returned to Africa, where he became "the first evangelizer of Sudan,"[11] preaching in secret and under penalty of death the way most of Jesus's early followers did. Under the Roman Empire, the practice of Christianity was punishable by death until 313, when the Roman emperor Constantine officially legalized it. By the end of the century, Christianity became the creed of the Holy Roman Empire. But the first three centuries of Christian history are rife with stories of the suffering and martyrdom of Jesus's first followers, who were thrown to lions, torn apart by wild dogs, or subjected to other excruciating deaths. For many Christians along the tenth parallel, these early stories inform their view of Islam and the secular West as modern-day oppressors.

Christianity's nearly two-thousand-year history in Africa is a story of splits and schisms, of crusades and excommunications. In Africa, as in other places, Christians have come under greater pressure from other Christians than from any outside force, including Islam. In Egypt, it was in part Christians' fear of their fellow Christians that made Jesus's followers amenable early on to Muslim rule. The first Muslim armies arrived during the decade following the Prophet Mohammed's death in 632. Orphaned soon after he was born (in 570), Mohammed grew up in the bustling Arabian trading town of Mecca. According to his early biographers, Mohammed's charisma and commercial acumen earned him the name "Al-Amin," the trusted one.[12] During the sixth century, his tribe, the Qureysh, was growing rich from the burgeoning Arabian trade routes, as luxury goods—ivory, spices, medicine, and slaves—were now traveling north from the Land of the Blacks through the desert. The once-nomadic Arabs, who prayed to a number of gods, were settling down to make their fortunes. By the age of forty, Mohammed was married to an older, wealthy widow named Khadijah, to whom he would turn, terrified, when God began to speak to him in a cave on Mount Hira.

As he began to preach about the one, single God—as God had commanded him to—he drew followers mostly from among the poor and the powerless, much as Jesus had done. He also created enemies among the wealthy Qureysh. In 622, thirteen years after his first revelation, he fled in secret from his hometown of Mecca to the city of Yathrib and renamed it Medina, "the city of the Prophet." During this first flight—or *hijra*—the Prophet, as he was now called, entrusted his family to the care of an East African king—the Christian ruler of the ancient kingdom of Abyssinia, which lies in today's Ethiopia and Eritrea. Mohammed didn't seek safety for those he loved on the Arabian Peninsula, but across the Red Sea, in the court of a Christian king. So Islam reached Africa during the Prophet's lifetime by way of a Christian. This was not under the standard of a conquering army, but through a shared belief in the oneness of God, and the mutual understanding and trust born of that fundamental principle.

In his new home in the city of Medina on the Arabian Peninsula, Mohammed became the political ruler, the religious leader, and the military commander of the first Islamic state. His movement grew so powerful that eventually he returned to Mecca and reclaimed the capital city without a fight. At the time of his death in 632, his followers dominated the Arabian Peninsula. As they conquered tribe after Arabian tribe, they required their new subjects to submit to the Islamic faith. Within ten years of Mohammed's death, Muslim horsemen sailed from the Arabian Peninsula to Africa and landed in Egypt.

Egypt, then a province in the eastern Roman Empire, was predominantly Christian at the time. The province fell quickly to the Muslim armies, since an internal fight had splintered Jesus's followers. Egypt's Christians, now known as Copts, were isolated from the rest of the Christian world. They had lost a theological debate against the larger Christian world of dyophysites who believed that Jesus had two different natures: both human and divine. The Egyptians were monophysites: they believed that Jesus had a single nature, which was both divine and human at once. This seemingly arcane division grew so heated that it came to define one of the most important early splits inside Christianity. Egypt's Christians, having lost this battle, were now vulnerable to persecution by fellow believers. By accepting Muslim rule, they were granted a measure of safety. Egypt, at the time, also was substantially weakened by war against the Persians, and could not hold off the invading Muslims. As *dhimmi*, or non-Muslims, all of Egypt's Christians gained the status of protected people living under Islamic rule.[13] Like Jews, also fellow people of the Book (in Arabic, *ahl-al-kitab*) who believed in one God, they were not full and equal citizens. Dhimmi were socially subservient to Muslims and had to pay the *jizya*, or protection tax, in lieu of military service. For decades, Muslims did not even enter the cities; they built their forts outside of Christian settlements, and it took more than fifty years for them to build a large mosque in Egypt. Conquest did not mean conversion, and the two religions, while stratified, lived side by side.

By the middle of the seventh century, the conquering Muslim armies drove farther south along the Nile River until they reached Nubia, the ancient Christian kingdoms in Sudan where the fabled royal eunuch had lived. The women and men of Nubia were expert archers, able to put out 150 Arab eyes in one day.[14] With bow and arrow, they protected their land—called Ta Sety, or "the Land of the Bow"—from the advance of the Muslim armies until 652, when Christian and Muslim rulers agreed to the terms of the first lasting peace treaty in Sudan.

No written versions of the treaty—called the baqt—have survived, and most accounts of it were passed down orally through the Arab chieftains who negotiated it alongside the Coptic kings of Nubia. And yet the ensuing peace lasted for more than six hundred years, making the baqt one of the most effective treaties in history. It proved to be a peace between equals. Each year, the Coptic Christians—who had traded in slaves long before Islam arrived—sent 360 slaves to the Muslims, along with ostrich eggs and feathers used for decoration. The Muslims, in turn, delivered 1,300 kanyr of wine (about two liters each, four bottles per slave) to the Christians of Nubia. As Richard Lobban, who teaches Sudanese history at the Naval War College in Newport, Rhode Island, points out, this exchange foreshadows the Atlantic slave trade: liquor from the north traveled south, in return for raw goods and slaves.

It was also worldly competition—over territory, trade routes, and spices—that brought the peace between Christianity and Islam to an end. From the eleventh to the sixteenth centuries, the Christian West led a series of crusades against Islam. In truth, Muslims were more concerned with the threats from other Muslims, including those from the Mongol kingdom to the east. Although the crusades did not reach into Nubia, existing letters show that European crusaders did try to win Nubian support for their campaigns.[15] The Muslims feared that the Nubians would take up arms against them, and easily defeated the last of the weakened Nubian kingdoms in 1504.

Except for a few telling symbols—crucifix tattoos, crosses carved into lintels[16]—Christianity was all but effaced from Sudan for the next three hundred years. Instead, Islam spread over the northern part of the continent as trading posts served as hubs in a network of Islamic conversion. Most North Africans became Sufis and belonged to different brotherhoods—*tariqas*, meaning "the way"—each having a slightly different way to pray. By the thirteenth century, their trade routes ran across the Sahara Desert from Mecca to Timbuktu as traders traveled to and from Arabia on the hajj. Through the lingua franca of Arabic, Islam wove together disparate cultures and kingdoms across North Africa.

With Islam firmly planted in the northern third of Africa (stretching as far south inland as the tenth parallel), Christianity returned to the continent largely during the nineteenth century, after a three-hundred-year absence. Its unfolding encounter with Islam—largely along this fault line—has come to define, over time, a larger struggle between Christian and Muslim revivals, modern movements that cast back to the past for their authenticity and power. The convergence of these movements, both religious and political, defines our historical moment, and it begins in Sudan.

During the nineteenth century, Christianity served as the spiritual engine of the European colonial enterprise's three Cs: "Christianity, commerce and civilization," the words carved on David Livingstone's tombstone. As evangelical missionaries targeted the border pagans who lived along the tenth parallel, secular industrialists also took note of the line, because the tenth parallel marked the geographic beginning of the scourge of sleeping sickness. One civil engineer, M. W. Wiseman, proposed building a grand transcontinental railroad across the continent of Africa here. "The limit of a camel's usefulness is passed at the tenth parallel," *The New York Times* reported in a story (August 23, 1891) about Wiseman's proposed project, and "south of that line the camel dies."[17] But the project faltered; Wiseman's critics pointed out that the labor his railroad would require was exactly the kind imperialists and missionaries were trying to stamp out: slavery.

Abolishing slavery served as the clarion call of the nineteenth-century evangelical movement, with its roots in social justice, including workers' and women's rights. When evangelical Christian missionaries arrived in Khartoum during the 1870s, the slave trade was booming. At the time, Sudan fell within the Ottoman Empire, and Turks and their Egyptian proxies governed Sudan. Like their predecessors, the Turks and Egyptians raided the south—the Land of the Blacks—for the familiar booty of gold, ivory, and slaves. They made no secret of setting Sudan's territorial boundaries according to these appetites. Maintaining empires cost money. The Egyptian khedive Mohammad Ali Pasha bankrupted Egypt and settled his debts by handing the British control of the Suez Canal in 1873. He wrote to his sons on a slave-raiding mission to the south: "Show me your zeal . . . have no fears, go everywhere, attack, strike, grab."[18] The majority of Sudanese blacks were enslaved by a small group of Arabs, and each year, slavers shipped eighty thousand to one hundred thousand human beings north, where they were pressed into service as soldiers, *jihadiqeen*, in the Ottoman armies. Appalled by the teeming human markets, the newly arrived missionaries pressed the colonial authorities to end the slave trade. Although the British did officially ban slavery in 1877, Egyptian slaveholders effectively ignored this prohibition, freeing their slaves only to reconscript them into the Ottoman army. By 1884, the competition for Africa among rival European powers had grown so fierce that at Portugal's urging, the German chancellor Otto von Bismarck invited representatives of Austria-Hungary, Belgium, Denmark, France, Portugal, Russia, Spain, Sweden-Norway (governed as one until 1905), and the United Kingdom to Berlin to carve up the continent peaceably, lest a full-on war for Africa break out. At this, the Berlin Conference of 1885—the "Scramble for Africa"—evangelists were key figures in the bargaining. Although the colonial officers and industrial scions were enthralled by Africa's vast untapped resources, the missionaries had the scramble for souls in mind, and were granted, like explorers and scientists, "especial protection"[19] to traverse new territories under the sheltering flags of their respective empires.

Many American and British evangelicals headed for the English-speaking territories of the British protectorates in Nigeria and Sudan. The tenth parallel, and its division between Islam and the border pagans—most of whom belong today to Africa's swelling ranks of Christians—ran across both territories. Soon, the British would draw a line across one million square miles along the tenth parallel, and deepen the natural divide that already separated two worlds.

FAITH AND FOREIGN POLICY

The casualty ward of Khartoum's Ahmed Gasim Children's Hospital was strung with fake red flowers for the Muslim holy month of Ramadan. It steamed with the press of bodies and the glare of TV lights. The Reverend Franklin Graham murmured a prayer over four-month-old Shirain, who was dying of a congenital heart defect. The child was smaller than his outstretched hand, and she lay swaddled and inert on a pus-stained cot. Her gray eyelids, like moth wings, stayed closed and still as flashbulbs flooded the cot she shared with her mother, Nada, a woman of twenty-eight. Graham, in a blue wool blazer and cowboy boots, was sweating.

In December 2003, Franklin Graham was already one of America's most powerful evangelical leaders. At fifty-seven, he was also the eldest son of Billy Graham. Known as the personal pastor to George W. Bush, Graham was poised to inherit his father's $200-million-a-year organization, the Billy Graham Evangelistic Association,[1] and he already ran one of his own, Samaritan's Purse, a $175-million-a-year worldwide evangelical Christian relief and development organization founded in 1970.[2] For more than two decades, Franklin Graham had provided relief and medical aid in southern Sudan, but this was his first trip to the northern capital of Khartoum. Graham, a bush pilot who had flown his own Gulfstream to Sudan, was going to meet his enemy, President Bashir, a man he had called "just as evil as Saddam Hussein."[3] In the late fall of 2003, that simile had particular weight, since America was soon to invade Hussein's Iraq, and had already deposed the Taliban regime in Afghanistan. President Omar Hassan al-Bashir, a former general who had seized power in a 1989 military coup and then declared a jihad against the south, had already begun to wage attacks against the Fur people to the west, in the formerly independent kingdom of Darfur, but in Khartoum, word of the unfolding genocide was little more than whispered.[4]

Yet Graham had come to Khartoum at Bashir's invitation; the Sudanese regime was trying to curry favor with Washington and thus avoid being the next Muslim country America attacked. Bashir was also hoping to persuade the United States to lift the economic sanctions that had been put in place in 1998, after Al Qaeda operatives blew up American embassies in Kenya and Tanzania on orders from Osama bin Laden, whom Sudan had been sheltering since 1991.

Graham had own his reasons to come to Khartoum, and some of them lay in the ward of this hospital. With its coppery sting of blood and bleach, the air made Graham's eyes water. "There is an opening in her heart," Nada said, peering wearily at her daughter. The strain of staying alive had wizened the baby's features. Although the operation that could save her life was a simple one, it was not available in Sudan. Shirain would live for one more month, maybe two, the hospital's director, Dr. Muzackir A. Monim, told us. He followed Graham's entourage around the ward as they placed taped-up Nike and Payless ShoeSource boxes on each of the fifteen cots. The boxes were part of Operation Christmas Child, one of Graham's efforts at worldwide evangelization. People in America and Britain pack the boxes with toothbrushes, socks, toys, and sometimes Bibles, and place handwritten letters inside. I read one from a ten-year-old in Brooklyn: *I hope you like your gifts in the shoebox. You can think of the gifts as a blessing from Jesus Christ. Do you know Jesus Christ as your Lord and Savior? I hope we are both similar in many ways.* In 2003, Operation Christmas Child delivered six million gift-packed shoe boxes around the world, sixty-six thousand of which arrived in Khartoum.

Graham placed a box on Nada and Shirain's cot, along with a pamphlet called "The Greatest Gift of All." He moved on to another patient—a three-month-old boy named Osama—as Nada rifled through her box, pulling out a roll of pink chewing gum called Bubble Tape, a stuffed rabbit, and a book of Bible stories. She stroked the bunny distractedly and opened the pamphlet, which began: *Dear God, I know I'm a sinner. I made the wrong choices and did bad things. I'm sorry. Please forgive me. I know your Son, Jesus, died for my sins and I believe you raised him from the dead. I want Jesus to be my Lord.*

Squatting next to the bed, I asked Nada what the book was about. "Jesus," she said. "This book talks about Jesus and what your soul is." The patients and parents in the hospital were Muslims, and for Graham, reaching them with the Gospel's good news was imperative. Whether they chose to accept the invitation was up to them.

Graham formed his controversial views of Islam here in Sudan. In November 2001—two months after the September 11 attacks—during a chapel dedication in North Carolina, Graham had famously declared, "We're not attacking Islam, but Islam has attacked us. The god of Islam is not the same God. It's a different god, and I believe it is a very wicked and evil religion."[5] Although these comments had led Graham to be vilified by Muslims worldwide, President George W. Bush had invited him to lead the 2003 Good Friday service at the Pentagon anyway. Graham had asked to be photographed with the Pentagon's Muslim employees following the service, but they refused. Now he had arrived in Khartoum to ask for permission to evangelize among Sudan's northern Muslims; and I, traveling with him, had come along to ask how evangelicals had come to play such a large role in American foreign policy.

The answer lies in the life of Billy Graham, and now in that of his son Franklin. Both men have made religious liberty one of the most pressing human rights issues in U.S. foreign policy. With his 1950s cold war crusades, Billy Graham sought to mobilize the enormous potential of American Christians to oppose what he saw as the evils of communism—principally its denial of God's existence and the horrific treatment that Christians received inside the Soviet Union. Graham's struggle helped marshal American resistance to the Soviet Union's propaganda efforts in the developing world. It also helped heal a rift that had been tearing the evangelical community apart.

In the early twentieth century, the scientific method and the theory of evolution challenged evangelical beliefs about the nature of creation (that God had made the world in six days, for example). Some evangelicals responded by turning inward, especially in the American South, and rejecting modernity altogether. Beginning in the 1920s, these self-proclaimed "fundamentalists" retreated from the secular world and split off from the broader evangelical movement. In the 1950s, young Billy Graham challenged them in their isolation, while affirming basic evangelical tenets: that believers must choose to give their lives to Jesus Christ, and that scripture was infallible. Yet he also refocused American evangelicals' energy outward, by turning their attention to the mandate of the Great Commission: to spread the Gospel to the entire world. Under his leadership, the popular evangelical advance of the late nineteenth century began to repeat itself. Once again, the movement flourished in opposition to a common enemy (that time, Islam; this time, atheistic communism). Using the American Jewish lobby's efforts on behalf of Soviet Jews as their model, Graham and his followers ceaselessly lobbied Congress on behalf of Soviet Christians—both evangelical and Orthodox—who were being persecuted in the USSR.[6] Franklin Graham took up his father's charge on such proxy battlefields as Angola and Nicaragua, where, in 1986, he trained 250 Contra rebels to be chaplains.

Franklin Graham relishes the most adventurous—and dangerous—edge of evangelism and relief work. A self-styled evangelical gunslinger, he occasionally wears a .38-caliber pistol strapped to his ankle. Physically, Franklin shares his father's avian attributes: the crown of stiff hair, the aquiline nose, and the startling blue eyes. Yet the younger Graham is much less of a political dove than his father. Billy Graham was a vocal supporter of civil rights and advocated strongly for nuclear nonproliferation; he called himself "God's ambassador," a big-tent term that emphasized his appeal among Protestants, Catholics, and Jews alike. Franklin Graham, lining up alongside the emerging powers of Jerry Falwell and Pat Robertson, called himself the ambassador to Jesus Christ, which emphasized the exclusionary nature of his faith.

Growing up Graham wasn't easy, Franklin says. Until he was twenty-two, he slouched in his father's shadow. He smoked, drank, dropped out of Stony Brook, a Christian boarding school on Long Island, and got kicked out of a technical college in Texas for keeping a girl out past curfew. None of this pleased Billy. During a walk on a North Carolina beach one day, he told Franklin, "You've got to accept Jesus Christ or reject him."[7] Salvation, for Billy Graham, was a black-and-white issue. Franklin, like everyone else, had to choose his soul's future. Not long after, in 1974, in a Jerusalem hotel room, Franklin threw out his cigarettes and offered himself to the Lord.

He focused on the most hot-button issues—where the American military, foreign policy, and his evangelical aims overlapped. After the first Gulf War, he sent thousands of Arabic Bibles and Christian tracts to Saudi Arabia as part of what he called Operation Desert Save. The influx of

Bibles enraged General Norman Schwarzkopf, who feared the Bibles would confirm their Saudi hosts' suspicions that the U.S. military was on a secret mission to evangelize. The general had an aide call Graham, who recounts the following phone conversation. The aide—an anonymous colonel—told Graham to stop sending Bibles. Then the colonel confessed that he, too, was an evangelical Christian, but he was "under orders." "So am I, sir," Graham responded, "orders from the King of Kings and Lord of Lords."[8] The Bibles were taken away. Graham, however, was undeterred: in no time at all, he would help lead a new revival.

In 1991, when the cold war ended with the dissolution of the Soviet Union, the evangelical lobby's interest in U.S. foreign policy did not. In the power vacuum left behind, Franklin Graham stood at the vanguard of a new movement, one that would once again pit evangelical Christians against the emerging power of militant Islam. Nowhere was this cast in sharper relief than along the tenth parallel in Sudan, where news of the Islamic regime's persecution of Christians in the 1990s supported this view. American evangelicals—including Franklin Graham—were watching firsthand. Evangelical Christianity had deep roots in southern Sudan, dating back to the missionaries who had preached there during British rule. Although Christians made up only a minority of the population, they formed a strong presence on the ground in churches, hospitals, refugee camps. This gave American evangelicals back home unparalleled access and information about the war. In response, Bashir targeted their outposts. On March 2, 2000, his regime bombed Graham's hospital in Lui—the largest in southern Sudan—for the first of two times.

Beyond Sudan, other Muslim countries were hardening their stance against the West, and against Christianity. For decades, Muslim countries had been growing alarmed by the West's economic and political dominance. The 1948 Universal Declaration of Human Rights (UDHR), drafted in the wake of the Holocaust by a committee including Eleanor Roosevelt and the French Catholic theologian Jacques Maritain, had appeared to many Muslims as a secret tool for backdoor evangelization, and so an affront to their faith. In 1990, representatives of forty-five Muslim countries signed the Cairo Declaration on Human Rights in Islam. The concept of universal rights—the precursor to human rights—the Cairo signatories argued, was encoded with a Judeo-Christian value system, beginning with the emphasis on the individual over the community, as well as questions about personal freedoms and rights. In response, Muslim countries rallied to protect their societies from the incursion of such values. Ostensibly, to defend their faith and culture, they provided a code for ethical human behavior governed exclusively by Islamic law—not nations or individuals. Criminal law, women's rights, and labor law—all were to be determined exclusively according to Islamic law.[9] Since there is no single way to interpret Islamic law, this leaves the countries that signed the Cairo Declaration open to interpreting Sharia as they see fit.

For many evangelicals, the Cairo Declaration was a shot across the bow—largely ignored by the secular press but followed intently by those concerned with the state of Christianity in the world at large. In 1995, Michael Horowitz, a Jewish activist and a neoconservative who had served as general counsel for the Office of Management and Budget under the Reagan administration, published a now famous opinion piece in *The Wall Street Journal* with the headline "New Intolerance Between Crescent and Cross."[10] Evangelicals, he wrote, were the victims of a rising tide of Islamic persecution. To him, this development was the beginning of a new holocaust, and evangelicals were the "Jews of the 21st century."

The evangelical lobby, with its cold war experience and Washington contacts, turned its attention to protecting Christians in frontline states against Islamic persecution. In 1998, the lobby had its first real sweeping political success when Congress passed the International Religious Freedom Act (IRFA), which sought to protect an individual's right to choose and freely practice his religion around the world, as guaranteed by Article 18 of the Universal Declaration of Human Rights.[11] The bill passed unanimously in both the House of Representatives and the Senate at a time when Congress was deeply divided over the impeachment of President Clinton. Its sweeping success would make religion a leading aspect of human rights in the twenty-first century. Religious freedom defied the traditional lines between liberals and conservatives and gathered support across the political spectrum: the bill had the backing of such unlikely political bedfellows as former Republican senator John Ashcroft, a conservative evangelical who focused on stopping the persecution of Christians; and then senator Joseph R. Biden, Jr., a Roman Catholic who lauded religious freedom as an aspect of U.S. foreign policy. Other powerful political champions included Senators Joseph Lieberman, Nancy Pelosi, Frank Wolf, and Sam Brownback, to name a few. Evangelicals also found unusual partners in a new, broad-based coalition of allies all equally appalled by the war in Sudan, including the Congressional Black Caucus and the broader human rights lobby. IRFA would be the first of many such joint campaigns.[12] An Office of International Religious Freedom opened at the State Department with its own ambassador-at-large, an independent budget, and a mandate to monitor freedom of religion abroad. A new age of Christian activism, which included Jews, Muslims, Tibetan Buddhists, and Iranian Baha'is among its ranks, had begun.

The IRFA has little legal force abroad. Its real value is to function as a restraint on the U.S. government, making sure that the current administration honors religious freedom (or at least pays it lip service) in diplomacy. It requires that the United States evaluate countries on the basis of religious freedom, compile an annual report, and take action against the worst offenders, ideally in the form of sanctions.[13] Although the IRFA has been widely praised at home, where religious freedom is an easy issue to rally around, it prompted concern in some Muslim countries, which fear that Christians are attempting clandestine evangelization through American foreign policy. In 2001, when three members of the U.S. Commission on International Religious Freedom (another office spawned by the IRFA) visited Cairo to prepare a report on Egypt's treatment of its minority Christian population, the Copts, the Egyptians stonewalled them.[14] Only a very small handful of officials would even meet with them. As a representative of the Middle East Council of Churches in Beirut (which has the Coptic Church in Egypt as a member) put it plainly, American evangelical engagement in politics evokes "memories of the Crusades" and is viewed as "a new invasion of American foreign policy and some evangelical groups who want to convert Muslims."[15]

Many African Christians and the Americans watching close at hand were coming to believe they were on the front line of a new global conflict, and their counterparts in Washington thought likewise. Once again, to them, Africa served as the knife-edge of global evangelization and the front line for a defense of the Christian faith. A century earlier, the technological advances of the industrial revolution had allowed many evangelical missionaries to spread their message all over the world. Now computers, spreadsheets, and statistical modeling programs allowed them to identify the last "unreached" people, analyze them against the broader population, predict changes in population and culture over time, and devise a high-tech strategy for evangelization. Once again, the push for the Gospel and the drive for human development went hand in hand.

In 1990, the Brazilian evangelist Luis Bush—a former business analyst at Arthur Andersen in Chicago—devised a map showing the locations of the people whom he called "the neediest people on earth." By this he meant both those who had never heard of Christianity ("the spiritually poorest of the poor") and those struggling to survive ("the financially poorest of the poor"). Using United Nations statistics on population, poverty, and religious affiliation, he employed a cutting-edge geographic information system (GIS) computer program at the San Jose office of a secular company called Strategic Mapping Inc. to create "the 10/40 Window," which served to illustrate an evangelical strategy for proselytizing to the entire world.

The 10/40 Window is a twenty-seven-thousand-square-mile red rectangle whose southern edge is the tenth parallel (running through Sudan, Nigeria, and the Philippines), and whose northern edge is the fortieth, (passing through Portugal, Afghanistan, and North Korea.) The Window (also known as the "the Window of Opportunity" and "the Resistant Belt") is home to 2.7 billion people, almost half the world's population: 900 million Muslims, 400 million Buddhists, and 600 million Hindus. Eight out of ten of those people live on less than $500 a year. Most important to the proselytizers, only 3 out of 100 are born-again Christians.[16]

The red rectangle, the catchy name, the round numbers—the 10/40 Window was a brilliant visual strategy. It was also statistically accurate. By joining spiritual need to material need, and representing the two together in the graphics of a secular newsmagazine or foundation report, it captured the new evangelical approach in a stroke. Luis Bush told me that when he saw the map come up on the computer screen in the San Jose office, he collapsed facedown on the floor and thanked God for its clarity. Not long afterward, he presented the 10/40 Window at a Billy Graham Conference in the Philippines—a majority Christian country divided along the tenth parallel between a Catholic north and mostly Muslim south. Along it, some Christian observers feared a "domino effect." "If the line falls to Islamic domination through civil war or constitutional coup," wrote Elizabeth Kendal, an evangelical reporter and blogger, "it will destabilize all of West Africa along that ethnic religious fault line that runs from the Sierra Leone/Liberia border in West Africa, east through Ivory Coast, Ghana, Togo, Benin, Nigeria, southern Chad, central Sudan, to Asmara, Eritrea on the Red Sea."[17]

In the early 2000s, as news of the 10/40 Window reached the Internet, it caught the attention not only of like-minded evangelical activists but also of conservative Muslims, who saw it as one more component in the Christian West's scheme to convert the world's Muslims. This was no small thing; in my reporting, from Nigeria to Indonesia, I have heard Muslims rail against the 10/40 strategy again and again. In their view, evangelism and neocolonialism go hand in hand, two aspects of a global effort to curb Islam's power by converting Muslims to Christianity. As Amir Abdullah, one such thinker, wrote in the Australian revivalist magazine *Nida'ul Islam*: "Like a cancerous growth, we are seeing Christians gain a foothold in the lands of the believers. The first time these crusading forces came with swords and suits of armor, this time they arrive with credit cards and million-dollar aid cheques. To the modern crusaders of the Christian missions it is exactly what China is to the Coca-Cola Company—one billion people just dying to hear the message."[18]

Khartoum lies within the 10/40 Window, and although Samaritan's Purse stresses that the organization works *wherever* there's need, while I was traveling with Graham in December 2003, one of his longtime employees, Barry Hall, told me, "We are now 10/40 Window–focused, especially since the war on terror began opening so many doors for the Lord in Afghanistan." This conflation of war with "opening doors" has disturbed some observers. In it many see a desire to take advantage of suffering among the world's poor in order to advance the evangelical Christian theology.

"I would never take advantage of them for personal gain," Graham wrote in his book *Rebel with a Cause*. "But you better believe I will take advantage of each and every opportunity to reach them with the gospel message that can save them from the flames of hell."[19] Later, Graham's colleague Dr. Richard Furman, the head of World Medical Mission, the medical arm of Graham's organization, told me that in one of Samaritan's Purse's African hospitals, the doctors will draw a plus or minus sign on a patient's chart to indicate whether he is an evangelical Christian. If not, his operation may be postponed until someone shares the Gospel with him, lest he die without an opportunity for salvation.

"The main thrust is on telling them about Jesus Christ, not getting the operation done," Furman said. The drive to make the Gospel heard—not to make converts—is Graham's mission. Samaritan's Purse also does some of the most effective relief work in the world, Christian or otherwise. An operation of 450 employees worldwide, the group is especially known for its work in the Balkans. "In Kosovo, we put thirteen thousand people under a roof before that first winter," Barry Hall told me. "Go ask those folks, 'Was anything required of you—to take a Bible or make a decision for Christ?' and they'll tell you no."

The day after Graham's visit to Ahmed Gasim Children's Hospital, I returned on my own, hoping to speak with Nada. She was staying on the grounds with her husband, Youssif, until Shirain died. I found the two of them sitting on Shirain's cot. Had the "Greatest Gift of All" pamphlet made her consider converting from Islam? "No," she said, shaking her head and smiling at the question. Youssif added, "A Christian will bring a Bible, and a Muslim, a Quran. But it won't change our religion at all—everyone has his own faith." Nada added that when Muslim missionaries visited the hospital, they brought blankets. "It's only natural that they give us something, because they want something in return."

Across the blanched stone courtyard, the hospital's director, Dr. Monim, was sitting at a desk in a plain, beaten-up office. It was early, but the day's desert heat made the air leaden. "This work is exhausting and depressing," he said. The hospital had no intensive care unit, no postnatal facilities, and no X-ray gear. It was the only pediatric hospital for a million square miles. The minister of humanitarian affairs had grumbled about Graham's distributing "The Greatest Gift of All," Dr. Monim said, but the government provided the nonprofit hospital with little aid. "We'll take what we're given," he said. "Mr. Franklin can do whatever he wants." Within the next few years, Samaritan's Purse would transform the hospital into a state-of-the-art intensive-care facility—with ventilators and heart and lung monitors. On February 22, 2007, former senator Bill Frist of Tennessee, a medical doctor who is also an evangelical Christian, traveled to Khartoum with Franklin Graham and visited the hospital. He blogged about his visit for Fox News in an article entitled "Religious, Medical Progress in Khartoum Sudan."[20]

II

"MISSIONARY MAYONNAISE"

On the Monday morning of December 8, 2003, Graham set out for the palace to meet President Bashir. Graham's motorcade crawled through the clogged streets of downtown Khartoum, where Land Rovers jostled with donkey carts. Khartoum is no dusty backwater. The air, soaked with diesel, thrums with money from the Arab world, and from China, thanks to Sudan's oil. It feels in many ways like Dubai; its wealth as a city stands in radical contrast to the abject poverty of its people. I rode in the press shuttle behind the line of black Mercedes sedans in which Graham and close members of his entourage were traveling. The gray gates of the presidential palace swung open, and our caravan glided through. Inside the gates, it was quiet enough to hear the soles of Graham's ostrich-skin boots kick along the marble steps. On the palace grounds, in 1885, Graham's hero, an evangelical Christian named Charles "Chinese" Gordon, was murdered by the jihadis of Muhammad Ahmad ibn-Sayyid Abdullah, a man who called himself the Mahdi, or "the divinely guided one." He called himself an Islamic savior who would save his people from the infidel West. Now, more than a century later, the coattails of Graham's blazer fluttered as he went to meet the man who claimed to be the modern-day Mahdi. It was like watching history chase its own hundred-year tail; little had changed except for the names.

At the top of the stairs, a glittering hallway led to a meeting room, and at the room's far end, President Omar Hassan al-Bashir—bald, freckled, and dressed in a sparkling white turban and jellabiya—grinned at Graham from an ornate, mustard-colored sofa. Bashir was born poor in 1944 in Hosh Bannaga, a tiny village sixty miles northeast of Khartoum, but after almost two decades of military rule, he looked comfortable with the trappings of power. When the famous preacher's entourage entered the room, Bashir chuckled indulgently like a knowing parent about to chide a petulant child.

"Many people will not believe you are actually here today," he said in Arabic, and an interpreter hovering over his shoulder translated. Peanuts and luscious dates covered in cellophane were laid out on porcelain plates around the room, but no one bothered to uncover the fruit. (Bashir's government has spent more than $1 million a day waging war against the south, and to the west, in Darfur.)[1]

"We know you're going to love Khartoum," Bashir added. His men led Graham to a chartreuse couch.

"I've flown above Khartoum, but I've never landed here," Graham responded cheerily in English. Then his own interpreter, a Lebanese pastor, translated Graham's not-so-veiled reference to his work in the enemy south.

"For many years, you've come to Sudan through the back door," Bashir retorted, not waiting for the translation. (It was clear that he understood English even though he chose not to speak it.) "Now we welcome you through the front. Many people didn't understand us as we really are, but now, thank God, we want peace."

"I want to be able to come back and go from one end of the country to the other, to preach, to evangelize," Graham said.

"I want freedom of religion because I would like to convert you. We will try to make you a Muslim," Bashir chuckled.

And so it went until Graham introduced his entourage, including Dr. Richard Furman, the head of World Medical Mission. Graham told Bashir that Furman was a surgeon who had operated many times at their southern hospital at Lui.

"Isn't that the hospital we bombed?" Bashir asked pointedly in English, turning to an aide.

"Twice. And you missed," Graham shot back.

Bashir's aides ushered most of Graham's entourage—including his personal photographer and me—into the palace's sweltering driveway, so the two men could speak privately. In the driveway, an aide removed the cellophane from a plate of nuts for us.

Graham told me afterward that while he was sitting on the president's couch, he was struck with the idea of offering Bashir a "W–2004" campaign pin he had gotten on a visit to Karl Rove's office earlier in the year. Graham knew the White House had scheduled a call with Bashir for later in the day.

So he reached into his jacket pocket, fished out the pin, and said, "Mr. President, I understand you'll be talking to my president later this afternoon. You might want to tell him you're wearing his campaign pin." Then, Graham told me, he offered the pin to Bashir, who reached forward and took it.

Five years later, the International Criminal Court indicted Bashir for crimes against humanity. Bashir scoffed at his arrest warrant. Dancing before a crowd of ten thousand supporters, he called Americans "the true criminals," claiming that Sudan would refuse to bend the knee as the United States tried to "colonize people anew and steal their resources." One day the world would try America on behalf of the Native Americans, the victims of the Hiroshima bombing and the Vietnam War. "One day we will take them to justice," he said.[2]

This is where my trek along the tenth parallel began: in a marble waiting room with Graham, an emissary of American faith-based foreign policy, and Bashir, the political face of militant Islam in Africa—on the very grounds where Graham's evangelical hero Charles "Chinese" Gordon had been beheaded by jihadis a century earlier. Graham and Bashir were perfectly aware that their meeting stood in for the broader encounter of Christianity and Islam along the tenth parallel.

This encounter, which had led to war over both religion and resources, was firmly grounded in a series of historical misadventures that began here in Sudan. Gordon's death was the culmination of an Islamic rebellion that would prove one of the bloodiest and most embarrassing massacres in the history of the British Empire, and it began as a fight not between Islam and the West but within Islam. In 1871, from Aba Island, on the White Nile near Khartoum, a charismatic Islamic preacher and a boat builder's son, Muhammad Ahmad ibn-Sayyid Abdullah, preached against the abuses of the Ottoman Empire—namely its horrendous taxes. Although the Turks and Egyptians were also Muslims, he called for their overthrow in the name of a purer Islam. In 1881, he declared himself the Muslim messiah—the divinely guided one, *al Mahdi al Muntazar*. Carving a space between his teeth to fulfill prophecy about the savior's appearance, he claimed to be heaven's hero sent to earth to liberate true Muslims from the corrupt rule of the Ottomans and, soon after—as the British colonial presence in Sudan grew stronger with industrial advances—from the poisoned presence of the infidel West.

Under the Mahdi, anti-imperialism and religious purification were fused into a single empowering message and delivered by a magnetic messenger. British observers noted the devotion of his jihadis, bowing like corn before a storm—an expression that used to describe Christian revivals. After the Islamic rebellion of Uthman dan Fodio, the Mahdi was the second Sufi reformer to strive to purify the African faith. Revival meant returning to the past, in the hope of reclaiming an idealized moment when the tenets of the faith were unsullied and true. It meant righting man's relationship with God so as to reform the society built upon this relationship. And, in time, it meant turning fury against the new infidel invader, the Christians of the West.

No jihadist was more ferocious than Sudan's Mahdi, who branded even fellow Muslims who opposed him as apostates, and executed them. He kidnapped at least fifteen Western missionaries in the name of eradicating every kafir, or infidel. Then he and his forces swept toward the last Ottoman stronghold, the city of Khartoum, where, by the 1880s, the British had established a bustling colonial outpost. The British, fearing the Mahdi's advance, sent Franklin Graham's icon, Major General Charles Gordon, to evacuate British occupants of the city. Gordon was an evangelical Christian and a hero of the Second Opium War, which forced China open to foreign commerce. Having been one of the first missionaries to arrive in Sudan, he had a decade of experience in the territory, and he relished the role of Khartoum's savior. Wearing a black turban and an unsheathed saber, he scowled for photographs, his muttonchops and walrus mustache clipped to perfection—every inch the romantic hero that Charlton Heston would portray in the 1966 film *Khartoum*.

And yet, like most evangelicals of his moment, Gordon was no unswerving imperialist. Instead, like David Livingstone, he was a staunch abolitionist. During the 1870s he had earned a reputation for battling slave raiders in the sultanate of Darfur. "I am quite averse to slavery, and even more so than most people," he declared. "I show it by sacrificing myself in these lands which are no paradise . . . I do what I think is pleasing to my God; as far as man goes, I need nothing from anyone."[3] He served as governor-general until he grew ill, and returned briefly to England in 1880. His abolitionist policies, while effective, were a highly unpopular challenge to the Arab elite whom the Mahdi represented. Although they opposed the heavy taxes of the Ottomans, many made their fortunes slave raiding among the black Africans south of the tenth parallel. Gordon's vocal stand against African slavery, and all who supported it, helped turn the fury of the Mahdi and his followers away from the Turks and onto the European Christian crusaders, whom Gordon embodied. When Gordon arrived in Khartoum to evacuate the city, he claimed the authority of a higher power, God, and spurned his superiors' directives to get the British out of Khartoum. He decided, instead, to take a stand against the Mahdi. His prerogative was not just to defend his countrymen—he saw himself as a liberator, seeking to free both Muslims and Christians from the yoke of Islam, and slavery.

This stubborn self-reliance proved to be his undoing, and that of those trapped alongside him in Khartoum. After allowing twenty-five hundred sick men, along with women and children, to escape to the Egyptian capital of Cairo, he hunkered down in the walled city with the remaining healthy male British citizens, refusing to let them leave. As the Mahdi neared Khartoum, he wrote to Gordon—as he had to Queen Victoria— asking him to convert to Islam. The ensuing back-and-forth between them sounds a lot like the one between Franklin Graham and President Bashir. Gordon refused to convert to Islam. So the Mahdi sent him a tattered jibba, or smock; Muslim prayer beads; a straw skullcap; and a turban: a believer's humble attire. Gordon bristled at the Mahdi's arrogance and challenged his theology, accusing him of being a false savior. The Quran, Gordon wrote angrily, expressly forbids the killing of fellow believers, which the Mahdi was clearly doing. "I am ready for you," he told the Mahdi. "I have men here with me who will cut off your breath."[4]

The Mahdi laid siege to Khartoum for 320 days, slowly starving its citizens, who waited in vain for British reinforcements to arrive. Finally, on January 25, 1885—a month before the colonial powers would meet at the Berlin Conference to divvy up Africa—the Mahdi's army overtook the city and its famished populace. Gordon was beheaded, it is said, on the marble steps of the British imperial palace. At the Mahdi's orders, his head was wedged in between two tree branches, and passersby were admonished to throw stones at it. Islam had defeated the British Empire in Africa.

The Mahdi died of typhus six months later, but his regime, the Mahdiyya, governed Sudan for thirteen years, from 1885 to 1898, when the British returned to avenge Gordon's death with the state-of-the-art muscle of the Maxim machine gun. They easily defeated the remnants of the Mahdi's army. One Sunday soon afterward, Sir Reginald Wingate, an intelligence officer who had helped Western clergy escape the Mahdi's clutches during the siege, held a Church of England memorial service in Khartoum to honor the new Christian martyr, Gordon. Wingate also destroyed the Mahdi's tomb, an act of revenge that met with approval at home. As *The Times* of London noted, "Any tenderness to such a memorial of savagery would be misplaced."[5]

As Wingate saw it, Sudan's future depended on obliterating even the memory of Islamic rebellion. So he ordered that the rest of the Mahdi's bones be thrown into the Nile. This was more than an act of humiliation and defilement; it was an attempt to make sure that the Mahdi could not be resurrected on Judgment Day.[6] He also gave the Mahdi's skull to his commander, Lord Kitchener, to be used as a drinking cup or an inkstand. Queen Victoria caught wind of the desecration, and declaring it "too much like the Middle Ages,"[7] she ordered the skull quietly buried in a Muslim cemetery. To this day, no one is quite sure where the Mahdi's skull lies. It is believed to be in an unmarked grave in Wadi Halfa, in northern Sudan.[8]

But Gordon's reputation as a martyr for Christ and empire could not be buried. Admiring poems and press accounts, and evangelical fervor in London, stirred poor and middle-class Christians to support mission hospitals and schools—the principal tools of evangelism—in the face of "fanatical" Islam.[9] Of Gordon, Alfred Lord Tennyson wrote,

> *Warrior of God, man's friend, not here below*
> *But somewhere dead, far in the waste Sudan*
> *Thou livest in all hearts, for all men know*
> *This earth hath borne no simpler, nobler man.*[10]

In the aftermath of Gordon's death, the British etched a line across the map of Sudan along the tenth parallel. The line, and the policies underlying it, would lead to nearly four decades of civil war in Sudan, and contribute to millions of deaths. As Carolyn Fleuhr-Lobban, coauthor of the *Historical Dictionary of Sudan*, said in regard to this historic division, "Trace a modern conflict to its source, and there lies the British Empire."

Following the Mahdi's defeat, to impress their imperial stamp upon the city, the British remapped the Muslim city of Khartoum in the pattern of their flag (as it still is today). Wingate and his superiors, many of them veterans of the battle against the Mahdi, and who had seen the impact of anti-imperial Islamic rebellion firsthand, were now serving in Her Majesty's Sudan Service. They did not want to rule Sudan, and now had to figure out a way to do so. Due to their plunder of the Land of the Blacks, the Ottomans had cobbled together the two very different worlds of the Arab, Islamic north and the black, "pagan" south. The British now governed Sudan alongside the Egyptians as part of the Anglo-Egyptian Condominium. At the same time, the north was still regularly subject to small-scale Islamic uprisings, which the British put down brutally and quietly.

Within a month of the reconquest of Sudan, missionaries from the Church of England, which had established a fund in the memory of their martyr Charles Gordon for the "Christianization of the Sudan," appealed for permission to evangelize among Muslims. Some hoped to restore Christianity to the Nubian kingdoms, where the royal eunuch of Acts had once made his home. The colonial authorities were lukewarm at best—some, downright hostile—to the missionaries' aims. One colonial agent sought to warn off a Pentecostal group from Canada by telling them that if they wanted to work in Sudan, they had better be ready to be served up as a "missionary mayonnaise."[11]

Given the fervor at home for the re-Christianization of Sudan, however, the British felt obliged to point the missionaries somewhere. "I have no objection to giving missionaries a fair field amongst the black pagan populations in the equatorial regions," wrote Lord Cromer, who, as the high commissioner of Egypt, oversaw the immense expanse of Sudan. "But to let them loose at present amongst the fanatical Muslims of Sudan would, in my opinion, be little short of insane."[12]

In order to avoid another large-scale confrontation with Islam, Sir Reginald Wingate, the British officer who flung the Mahdi's bones into the Nile, and his superiors decided to draw a line across the entire nation of Sudan. The boundary would reinforce the preexisting divide between the Muslim north and the southern Land of the Blacks, and it would begin in the impenetrable bog—the *sudd*—which marked the end of Sudan's sere north, and had (along with the vociferous tsetse) kept Islam from penetrating farther south for centuries. (The *sudd* belonged to the swampland that the ambitious German evangelist Karl Kumm and his unlucky expedition were forced to traverse.) As the British saw it, while traveling in steamships south along the White Nile, where the sandy riverbank grew dark with loam, Islam ended, and true Africa began.[13] This line was the tenth parallel.

No one knows exactly why the British chose this line. The tenth parallel was a strategic military divide along which they had defeated the French in a battle for Africa in 1898, just after destroying the Mahdi's army. It marked the geographic shift between the north's sandy soil, called *goz*, and the south's seasonal mush, called *gardud*, as well as the two different worlds that thrived atop each. It was also a good round number, and that was how colonial adminstrators sometimes made decisions.

In 1905, Reginald Wingate—now the forty-four-year-old governor-general of Sudan, who kept his mustache tips tightly waxed (and tucked a pith helmet under his arm)—declared it illegal for Christian missionaries to evangelize among Muslims to the north of the tenth parallel, and eventually Muslim traders could not travel to the south of it. He and his higher-ups could not allow for another Islamic rebellion, and nothing, they feared, would provoke violence more rapidly than missionaries trying to convert Muslims. The 1905 *Regulations and Conditions Under Which Missionary Work Is Permitted in the Sudan* reads, "1. No Mission station is allowed to be formed North of the 10th parallel of Latitude in any part or district of Sudan which is recognized by the Government as Moslem."

Among the multitude of missionaries who opposed this ban was the Reverend Llewellyn Henry Gwynne, a priest of the Church in Wales who became the Anglican bishop of Khartoum. Moved by Gordon's martyrdom, he had come to Khartoum in 1899 to work for the Church Missionary Society as a tough and athletic young priest[14] ready to lead Christianity's advance against Islam. But the 1905 ban essentially forbade him from doing his work. As he saw it, the ban threatened the future of Christianity in Africa. Gwynne, only in his forties, found himself a prisoner of his bishopric, located across the White Nile from the colonial government, reduced to playing football with British troops and attending teas with the officers' wives.

He warned Wingate that by allowing Islam a free hand north of the tenth parallel, Britain was advancing the interests of a rival religion, and an inferior one. In his opinion, the colonial authorities were making a grave mistake. "If they think that British justice and natural gifts for colonizing-civilization are of themselves going to lift up these Sudanese, they are very much mistaken." Without Christianity, Gwynne argued, Africa would become "a human zoo."[15]

Wingate responded, "You and I have discussed this subject ad nauseam

and I'm afraid our views remain somewhat divided." Despite such episto-
lary contretemps, Wingate actually liked Bishop Gywnne. He did not,
however, like the American evangelical firebrands who dominated the
Christian scene in Sudan. (The Americans were so energetic and omni-
present that *Americani* became the local word for "missionary.")[16, 17]

In spite of pressure from the missionaries, Wingate held his line, and
the northern Muslims remained mostly off-limits to Christian evangelization, up through Franklin Graham's visit with Bashir in 2003. Barred from
the north's Muslims, the missionaries were forced to focus their efforts on
the "pagans" of the south—who were not so controversial a group. (This
legacy explains why Graham's Samaritan's Purse and thousands of other
Christian groups work largely in southern Sudan today.)

In 1909, Karl Kumm arrived in Khartoum after his punishing trek from
Nigeria along the tenth parallel. When Kumm met with Wingate, he
warned the governor-general about Islam's southward advance. He hoped
to plant a mission in Sudan, and most likely asked Wingate for money to
fund it. Wingate refused. Kumm's self-promotional zeal—more American
than British in tone—and his hysteria about Islam disturbed Wingate,
who already feared that such sentiment would prompt more Muslim out-
rage and bloodshed. Wingate warned Bishop Gwynne to do everything he
could to "curb the excessive ardor" of Karl Kumm and his plans to build
fifty missionary forts and bush trading posts across Africa.

Gwynne felt otherwise: when Kumm came to see him at his shiny new
offices near the Gordon Memorial College on the southern bank of the
White Nile and warned him about "the rising tide of Moslem progress"
along the tenth parallel, the bishop told him, "Pour in and pour in quickly
as many missionaries as possible . . . A chain of Missions as close as possible to the frontier between the Arabs and the Pagans is the only hope of
stemming the tide. Ten years will decide whether all the territory with its
thousands yet unborn is to come under the sway of Christ or Mohammad . . . May God stir up the hearts of men to save from the deadening
grasp of Islam these Sudanese put under our care by the death of Gordon,
by God himself."[18] Gwynne took Kumm to see the statue of their common
hero and martyr. Nearly thirty years after his beheading, an enormous
bronze Gordon stood astride a camel—facing south toward the rest of the
African continent. Standing in the glaring heat, Kumm wondered aloud
why Gordon was "looking out across the vast dark realms of inner Africa,"

not facing north toward Britain. "He is waiting, sir, for morning to dawn across the Sudan," his local guide told him.

Two years after Sudan's independence in 1956, Gordon's statue, a visible symbol of empire and the Christian West, was shipped home to England, where it now sits outside a boys' school in the southeast county of Surrey. If Gordon's likeness were still facing south toward Bilad-as-Sudan today, he would be gazing at a population of African Christians forty times larger than the one he left behind—one that no longer looks to the West for guidance.

This is the south that Franklin Graham and thousands of other Christian groups inherited from the British. Shortly after forbidding missionaries from evangelizing among Muslims north of the tenth parallel, the British authorities divided the territory south of the tenth parallel into three main spheres of Christian influence—Catholic, Anglican, and American (Presbyterian)—and set the missionaries very specific boundaries within which to work. This land south of the tenth parallel was dangerous and disease-ridden,[19] and the British were only too happy to let the missionaries do the hard work of constructing an infrastructure, primarily schools and hospitals. (Graham's organization still runs the largest hospital in the south—the one at Lui, a village in Western Equatoria state—which the northern government has bombed.)

Mission work was little more than "subsidized soul snatching,"[20] in the words of one colonial official. Although they restricted the missionaries, by requiring approval over their curricula, for instance, the British also relied on them to extend the empire. The British were as interested as the missionaries were in stopping the spread of Islam, since they saw it as a fanatical threat to the order and existence of empire. To curb this expansion, they declared English, not Arabic, the south's official language; made Sunday, not Friday, the official day of rest; and banned Arabic names and clothing. By the 1920s, under the Closed Districts Ordinance, northern (that is, Muslim) traders were entirely forbidden to visit the south.

The missionaries' monopoly on health care and education in the south was such that anyone who resisted evangelization risked being left out of the modern world entirely. With Wingate's blessing, many missionaries focused on educating young men, or "Mission Boys," as they were called. This group of new Sudanese Christians was meant to form a barrier against the southern spread of Islam, and to create a new generation of military leaders, the Equatorial Corps, allied with the Christian West.[21] For these young Christians, the fact that Christianity was an intrinsically African religion was crucial to their identity. The biblical conversion story of the royal eunuch, and the legacy of the Sudanese Christian kingdoms to the north in what was once Nubia, empowered their fight for equality. The stories of early Christian suffering helped to make sense of what it meant to be marginal people.

But Christianity never caught on as a cohesive identity in the south, as Islam had in the north, for several reasons. First, the partitioning of the south divided Christian denominations and bred competition over converts. Whichever group offered more in goods and services attracted more potential Christians.[22] The British effectively set the Christians against one another. Second, the greatest impediment to Christianity's spread in the south was that the so-called border pagans were hostile to outsiders and their beliefs. As Karl Kumm had found when he evangelized at the base of Wase Rock, the border warriors who'd successfully defied Islam for centuries were not so eager to become Christians. The same power that had enabled them to resist Islam now created opposition to Christianity.[23] The indigenous traditions of the south were very strong, and remain so today.

Lack of infrastructure deepened the north-south divide. For decades, vast tracts of land in the south were left undeveloped while the British colonial forces continued to build bridges, roads, and other infrastructure in the north. These unequal patterns of development also led to Sudan's civil wars. On the eve of independence in 1956, the British—who saw the south as still a backwater, and the mission-educated southern elite as too unsophisticated to lead—handed power to the north. When the southern leaders (many of them former Christian Mission Boys) mutinied, the Americans and the British largely ignored them. As Jefferson Caffery, appointed the U.S. ambassador to Cairo in 1949 during the Truman administration, put it nakedly, "I do not understand why anybody should be bothered about the fate of ten million niggers."[24]

12

JUSTICE

When Islam entered the central parts of Africa, it clothed naked human beings,
civilized them, brought them out of the deep recesses of isolation, and taught
them the joy of work in exploring material resources. It brought them out of the
narrow circle of tribe and clan into the vast circle of Islamic community, and
out of the worship of pagan deities into the worship of the Creator of the worlds.
If this is not civilization, then what is?[1]

—SAYYID QUTB

One evening during my trip to Khartoum with Franklin Graham, I paid a
visit to Hassan al-Turabi, the architect of the most violent jihad of modern
times. At his invitation, Khartoum became a hub for many militant Islamist groups banned in their home countries during the nineties. One was
bin Laden's then little-known cadre of Arab veterans from the war against
the Soviets in Afghanistan. I arrived after 9:00 p.m., during visiting hours,
when Khartoum comes to life in the relative cool, but al-Turabi, now seventy-
two, sat alone in a formal salon in his home, gripping a cane with papery
hands. The salon's thirty red velvet chairs stood pushed against the walls.
This once-bright room—frequented by a broad array of terrorists, including bin Laden—was fusty and gloomy. The air seemed choked with savage,
disappointed ghosts, arguing with one another over which of their failed
versions of history would have saved Sudan.

Al-Turabi, too, had fallen out of power after a spat with President
Bashir in 2001. Hoping to placate America, Bashir had cast him out of the
government that year, but ever the political survivor, al-Turabi formed a
new alliance (tactical, at best) with the southern Sudanese, so Bashir had
the old man thrown into jail. Al-Turabi had been in prison many times
over the past two decades, and now, two months after his most recent
release, he seemed diminished; the spareness of his frame accentuated

his giant teardrop eyeglasses and prominent buckteeth. He was desperate for visitors, especially Americans, for whom he could audition his kinder, gentler approach to the West. Tracing his cane against the carpet, he groused about the government he had brought to power, the jihad, and his own infirmities. A vengeful Sudanese martial arts expert who spotted al-Turabi on the escalator in Ottawa's international airport in 1992 and attacked him, holding him responsible for so much death and destruction in Sudan, inflicted the worst of his sufferings.

Al-Turabi personifies the history of Islamic rebellion in Africa, and in the rest of the world. It began in Sudan and neighboring Egypt. Much of this history unfolds in direct response to the West, and its missionaries. Born in a northern village in 1932, he grew up as the son of a prominent Arab judge and expert on Islamic law. After earning a B.A. from Khartoum University, he furthered his education in the West—getting an M.A. in law from the London School of Economics, and then a Ph.D. in law at the Sorbonne. Like his spiritual brother, the disaffected Egyptian poet and supreme head of the Muslim Brotherhood, Sayyid Qutb (al-Turabi would later become the Brotherhood's head in Sudan), al-Turabi grew convinced while in the West that Islam should be the foundation for a new, postcolonial Sudan.

Al-Turabi's place in history was born of World Wars I and II. During World War I, the Ottoman Empire, already in decline, sided with Germany. After the Allied victory, Muslims watched in anger and humiliation as France and Britain divvied up huge swaths of Ottoman territory in the new "Middle East"—a term coined by Alfred Thayer Mahan, a U.S naval officer and a vocal evangelical Christian.[2] Suddenly the Muslims of this "Middle East" found themselves living under illegitimate rulers in arbitrarily established new nations, and powerless in the face of distasteful new policies, such as the 1917 Balfour Declaration, in which Britain called for the establishment of a new Jewish state right in the heart of the Arab world, Palestine.

American internationalism is a relatively new phenomenon. So is government-sponsored humanitarian aid. Until the middle of the twentieth century, missionaries, not foreign-service officials or aid workers, led the bulk of the world's relief and development efforts. As early as the 1920s, to many Muslims, Christianity appeared to be the principal instrument of their oppression. Apart from colonial authorities, most of the white faces in the new Middle East belonged to missionaries, who quickly became the straw men for imperialism. The most frequent flash point was education. Out of fear that Christian missionaries were trying to convert their children, Egyptian and Sudanese Muslims took to the streets in protest.[3] These protests became a part of a larger revivalist movement to call Muslims back to their faith. They were based on the Islamic equivalent of evangelization—the Arabic *da'wa*, translated as "the invitation" or "the call." Islamic leaders modeled their organizations on the Christian ones they were attempting to supplant. The Young Men's Muslim Association, the YMMA, founded in Egypt in 1927, created a summer program modeled in part on the YMCA's Bible camp. Like the YMCA, the YMMA hosted soccer games, held lectures on health and hygiene, promoted social welfare, and reached out to the poor with food and medicine.[4]

The YMMA's most influential member was an Egyptian schoolteacher named Hassan al-Banna. Al-Banna grew up during the first years of the twentieth century, when American missionary zeal and influence in Egypt were at their apex. Galvanized by this experience, he argued that Islam as a way of life was under threat of extinction at the hands of Western missionaries. He called for Muslims to guard themselves against missionaries and their imperial poison in order to combat the West's growing influence among them. An early and outspoken proponent of this new religious liberation, he went on to found Al-Ikhwan Al-Muslimeen, the Muslim Brotherhood, in 1928. (Four years later and a few hundred miles away, the Sudanese intellectual Hassan al-Turabi was born.)

For al-Banna, the 1948 defeat of Arab armies and the founding of the state of Israel provided more evidence that Muslim lands were under threat. Later that same year, members of the Muslim Brotherhood assassinated Egypt's prime minister Al-Nuqrashi, whom the movement considered too secular. And in retaliation, King Farouk's henchmen assassinated the Brotherhood's Supreme Guide, al-Banna, in 1949. The Brotherhood then went underground, but al-Banna's deputies carried on his religious revival. Al-Banna intended to reach every Muslim, not just a scholarly few, and restore Islam's rightful place in the world. He sowed fear of a shared threat—a common enemy—and argued that in order to be a good Muslim, a believer had to be willing to fight. He preached to young men that by dying in battle against unbelievers, they would bypass God's judgment at the end of the world. Those who fought were assured of salvation. Jihad was a shortcut to heaven. His concept of jihad was not only about admission to heaven; it involved bringing the kingdom of heaven to earth. The Quran, al-Banna stressed, provided a comprehensive life manual: a seventh-century how-to guide for what to wear, how to pray, what to eat.

On sports fields and in study groups, al-Banna laid the foundation for what would eventually become violent global jihad. Sayyid Qutb would follow in his footsteps—and al-Turabi would follow in Qutb's—building the Brotherhood into both an effective model for social welfare and an organization that would give birth to the likes of Al Qaeda.

The Brotherhood also vehemently opposed the secular Arab nationalist movement founded by the Egyptian president Gamal Abdel Nasser, who rose to power beginning in 1952 with a political coup d'état (they tried to assassinate him in 1954). Nasser did not like the Brotherhood much either, and outlawed religious organizations that threatened his authority. But in the fifties and sixties, Nasser's authority also alarmed America. As the cold war began in 1945 out of the aftermath of World War II, Washington watched anxiously as the Soviets attracted to communism those newly independent African nations that had thrown off the bonds of colonial rule, by offering aid and arms across the continent. By refusing to ally Egypt with either the United States or the Soviets, Nasser challenged the dominance of Western powers in the new "Middle East" and throughout Africa. Alarmed by his popularity, America looked for a means to challenge his power. At the time, America's enemies were communism and Arab nationalism—not Islam.

The presence of U.S. missionaries unwittingly fanned the flames of militant Islam in Africa. So, too, early U.S. efforts to employ Islam as a political weapon helped birth a movement that would grow to antagonize the West. In Europe, following World War II, the United States supported many Islamic defectors from the Soviet Union who laid the foundations of Islamism—the political and religious movement that opposes the West.[5] In the emerging "third world" of the time, the cold war contest was especially heated. There, too, the United States and its agents attempted to employ Islam against the Soviets. In the East African nation of Somalia, for instance, during the sixties, the former intelligence director Abdiqani Dahir Haashi received American books that supported the cause of Islam against the Soviet-backed military regime. (The Soviets sent him Mao Zedong.)

In Egypt, one curious footnote to history lies in the so-called search for the Muslim Billy Graham. As the flamboyant former CIA officer Miles Copeland, Jr., tells it in his memoir,[6] he was sent by the agency to West Africa's Ivory Coast during the 1960s to see an anthropologist named Dr. Hans Gruber. The doctor convinced him that "Africans were suckers for 'charismatic' leadership of the kind fundamentalist preachers used to entrance audiences in my own Deep South."[7] Copeland, who had been born in Demopolis, Alabama, left Ivory Coast convinced that he had seen the future for "winning" Africa. Once again, the West's approach to "winning" Africa would be built on religion; yet this time the religion was Islam. Copeland, who called himself a Unitarian but had little religious conviction of his own, figured that a Muslim preacher sympathetic to the evils of Communist expansion could mobilize his followers to support the United States against the forces of atheistic communism. After all, this was working at home in America, and not just in the Deep South; much of the country was enthralled with the charismatic revivalist preacher Billy Graham. As the most outspoken anti-Communist preacher in the world, Graham was rallying millions of American Christians to oppose the Soviets, thereby saving souls and advancing U.S. foreign policy at the same time.

So began what Copeland called "the Search for the Muslim Billy Graham," which took him to Cairo in the mid-fifties. Under the guise of an analyst evaluating Egypt's cotton industry, Copeland visited the haunts of various Islamic holy men—including a basement speakeasy called Milo's Den, where he watched Sufi dervishes bite the heads off live chickens. Later, with the help of a guide, he stumbled into a Muslim Brotherhood meeting, where saw Sayyid Qutb's successor, a spellbinding preacher named Sheikh Hassan al-Hudaybi. (The Egyptian government had executed Qutb in 1966.) Al-Hudaybi was "one hell of a speaker," and Copeland planned to recommend him to the CIA, but found out shortly thereafter that another officer had done so already. According to Copeland, his boss, Kermit Roosevelt, a director of the CIA's Near East Division, had already put the search for the Muslim Billy Graham into play.

Copeland died in 1991, and the definitive truth as to his role in the United States' early entreaties to militant Islamists died with him. However, Copeland's son Miles Axe Copeland III told me more of his father's story. (He is a music executive who started I.R.S. Records, and has managed bands, including his brother Stewart's band, The Police.) As a teenager, Miles Copeland III traveled to Egypt in the fifties with his father, tagging along at meetings with Nasser and other leaders. His father believed that religion could be a strategic asset in controlling other nations. America could further its interests by playing to the irrational devotion of foreign powers. "My father was always interested in manipulating religious conviction. It was part of what he liked to call his bag of dirty tricks," his son said. He recalled his father as an amoral man who saw morality as a perversion—an obscuring of the cold, hard facts of human behavior— and religion as an ideal cold war weapon, which enabled spies to exploit believers' weakness and naïveté.

The author Robert Baer, who served with Copeland while working at the CIA, never heard Copeland speak of a search for a Muslim Billy Graham. "It's absolutely possible that he could have this idea; it is right up Copeland's alley," he told me, "but spooks are always talking about things they never do, and war is ninety percent myth."

Much has been written about the CIA's next move: after the Soviets invaded Afghanistan in 1979, the agency, along with the Saudis, decided to back a group of Islamic holy warriors, the Mujahideen, against the Soviets, channeling money to them through Pakistan's intelligence service. One of those holy warriors, Osama bin Laden, would prove that Copeland's dream of tugging the strings behind a Muslim Billy Graham could backfire incalculably.

In 1965, when Sayyid Qutb was on trial in Egypt for attempting to overthrow Nasser's government, the acerbic and quick-witted Hassan al-Turabi took the Brotherhood's helm in neighboring Sudan, with no Nasser to outlaw the organization, the Muslim Brotherhood thrived. He then married Wisal al-Mahdi—the Mahdi's great-granddaughter—thus securing his connection to one of Sudan's most powerful families, and one with impeccable religious credentials. His ideas about Islam served as the basis for the nascent Sudanese state and its vision of "civilizing Africa." For the next four decades, he would connive to head the militant Islamist movement in Africa, becoming, in the nineties, the "pope of terrorism."[8]

Like any other political ideology, Islam's role in the Sudanese state was not foreordained. After independence in 1956, the Muslim Brotherhood was one of a number of players—Communist, nationalist, Islamist—all bidding to determine what political shape the new state would take. With the platform that Islam should build the new nation, Hassan al-Turabi rose above them all, gaining influence both politically and theologically, until, in 1983, the military dictator Jaafar Mohammad Nimeiri—a former socialist conveniently turned Islamist—began to fear al-Turabi's political reach. Although the two were ostensibly allies, Nimeiri had to show his religious authority to secure his grip on power. So in order to outdevout al-Turabi, he declared his brand of Islamic law the law of the land. His chosen form of Sharia proved brutal for Muslims and Christians. For arbitrary crimes—and to perpetuate a state of fear—"Courts of Prompt Justice" ordered cross-amputations, such as cutting off a hand and an opposite foot, and other extreme punishments sanctioned by the Mahdi a century earlier. Apostasy, or leaving Islam, was punishable by death.

In Sudan's most infamous case of apostasy and sedition, Mahmoud Muhammad Taha, a Sufi mystic and powerful Muslim reformer, went on trial for the last time in 1985. Taha was the leader of a small but influential movement called the Republican Brothers, whose progressive theology threatened the rigid dogma that was shaping Sudan's political future. Nimeiri, acting on al-Turabi's instructions (or so he later claimed), ordered Taha hanged in prison. A helicopter spirited his body away immediately. "Up to this day no one knows his burial place," Abdullahi An-Na'im, Taha's most influential student and one of Sudan's leading religious reformers, told me.

Taha's crime was distributing a Christmas Day pamphlet entitled "Either This or the Flood." In it, he made the case that Islamic law could never be applied justly in Sudan's plural society, because Christians were *dhimmi*—non-Muslims living under Islamic law—and so were second-class citizens by definition. This was in line with his broader contention (set out in his revolutionary book *A Second Coming of Islam*) that Islamic law was in dire need of reinterpretation. Taha highlighted the tension between two sets of verses in the Quran. First, there were those supposedly revealed to Mohammed in his forties and early fifties in his hometown of Mecca, in which he calls himself simply a "warner," and preaches to a beleaguered minority of believers. Second, there were those revealed later in the so-called Prophet's city, Medina, where Mohammed acted as a warrior statesman. The Meccan verses contain a universal prophetic message about humanity and Judgment Day. The Medinan verses are more legalistic and address the codes and conflicts of a new Muslim state.

Taha believed that the time had come for modern Muslims to move away from the strictures of the Medinan verses and return to the earlier, more inclusive Meccan verses. In his interpretation, the Meccan verses represented an egalitarian message to all of humankind, regardless of sex, race, or religion.

Many scholars, including Hassan al-Turabi, saw this argument as heretical, a challenge to the infallibility of God's message as given to Mohammed. Some analysts hold that al-Turabi—Sudan's most senior religious scholar at the time—signed Taha's death warrant. Others, including Abdullahi An-Na'im, think this is unlikely, given the tensions at the time between President Nimeiri and al-Turabi, and conclude that the latter had little to do with the actual execution. Either way, al-Turabi and the hard-line machine of the state benefited from the silencing of one of their most potent critics.

Sudan's recent history is littered with such missed opportunities—moments at which a Khartoum-based cabal destroyed efforts at reform from the periphery, striking down those who had risen to challenge centralized power in the name of Islam, Christianity, or any other means of self-determination. In 1989, backed by Hassan al-Turabi, Hassan Omar al-Bashir, then a general stationed along the north-south border, seized executive power through a military coup. Shortly after, in the name of purifying Sudan and advancing Islam, Bashir declared a jihad against the Christian and non-Muslim south. By unifying the north under the banner of religion, and in a war against the south, Bashir, under al-Turabi's direction, set the north at common purpose and made a bid for the country's oil in the name of Islam—murdering thousands with al-Turabi standing by.

Al-Turabi is known as a tyrannical talker, and that night in December 2003 he wanted to hold forth on his new enemy, Bashir, and how foolish America would be to believe a word the president said. "This current government cannot be trusted," he snapped. He was bitter and eager to deflect blame for decades of organized campaigns of rape, murder, and scorched villages away from his former militant platform and onto the government. "I am indebted to Human Rights Watch for getting me out of prison," he said, but his professed fondness for America and its human rights groups eroded as he spoke about the civil war. He had only contempt for the backward, non-Muslim south, and for the American evangelicals who, in calling for an end to the civil war, envisioned a fictitious peace that would never arrive.

"The people are tired of war—they want anything called peace, even if it's a dream," he said. But in assessing the popular mood, al-Turabi would be proven wrong once again—as he had been wrong about building a successful militant Islamic state in Africa, wrong in offering Osama bin Laden safe haven as a way to strengthen Sudan, wrong in publicly backing Saddam Hussein during the first Gulf War in the hope of garnering support in the Arab world. And in point of fact, a peace—if a wobbly one— did arrive in the form of a 2005 deal between north and south.

For al-Turabi, the steady stream of American evangelical leaders visiting Khartoum at Bashir's behest was evidence of a historical cycle repeating itself. One hundred years ago, the colonialists took Africa in the name of Christianity. Nowadays, with neocolonial America at war with the world's Muslims, as he saw it, men like Graham and Bush were using religion to mask their desire for conquest.

"The American Right seems to have inherited the worst of 'The White Man's Burden,'" al-Turabi declared, pausing to be sure I had caught the allusion to Kipling, who coined the phrase in 1899 at the apogee of the British Empire's power, and a year after the United States had bought the Philippines from the Spanish for $20 million. By this he was calling attention to what he saw as the Christian right's moral imperialism in American foreign policy, its role in a war against Muslims, and a new crusade for oil. Kipling's poem begins:

> Take up the White Man's burden—
> Send forth the best ye breed—
> Go bind your sons to exile
> To serve your captives' need;
> To wait in heavy harness,
> On fluttered folk and wild—
> Your new-caught, sullen peoples,
> Half-devil and half-child.[9]

13

CHOOSE

Although no one told Franklin Graham, many of Sudan's Muslims objected to his visit following his "wicked and evil" comments. While the comments had ricocheted around the Arab-language press, criticism of Graham's visit did not. There is virtually no press freedom in Sudan, and the Bashir government had threatened the handful of independent papers, saying that if they reported negatively about Graham's visit, they would be shut down. Apparently not knowing this, Graham held a press conference at his guesthouse in Khartoum, and Ni'ma al-Baghir, a northern Sudanese Reuters reporter in her late twenties, raised her hand.

"You say that you are here to promote religious tolerance and coexistence between the faiths," she began, "but bearing in mind your documented views on Islam and your vehement criticism of it, do you not think that your visit to Sudan at such a sensitive time is miscalculated and is liable to inflame matters?" The room was silent. "I just want to be really clear about this," Graham said, fixing al-Baghir with his inscrutable smile, "I was *asked* to come to Sudan. Dr. Mustafa Ismail [the minister of foreign affairs] called *me* up and asked *me* to come and I was worried that if I refused to come it would be seen as me not supporting the peace process. So I prayed to Jesus and decided that I should come."

After the conference, as the rest of the reporters filed out of the guesthouse, al-Baghir scribbled her phone number on a piece of paper for me, and several days later I called her. With her elder brother at the wheel of a Land Rover, she picked me up and we drove around the colonial city listening to Stevie Wonder. "You have this person blundering in, believing that he can use the might of Jesus and the might of the American administration to protect something he doesn't even understand," she said. Her question had been a deliberately pointed one: her father was the editor of one of Sudan's independent newspapers, *Al Khartoum*; before Graham's arrival, he had written an editorial about the infamous evangelist, entitled "We Do Not Believe What You Believe," and the government had threatened to shut down the paper, as it had many times in the past.

Khartoum lies within the 10/40 Window, but proselytizing to Muslims here is strictly illegal, and Christians caught doing so can be arrested—an issue Graham had raised with President Bashir. Sometimes entering closed countries requires an undercover mission, or "creative access." Teaching, nursing, running fabric mills—some missionaries adopt these or other legal businesses in order to share the Gospel. I asked al-Baghir if she knew of any such business; she thought for a minute. "The aerobics studio," she said.

The next day she took me to a wealthy old colonial district of Khartoum. The homes were set back from the streets and hidden by the neem trees' feathery leaves. Inside a one-story bungalow, a Sudanese woman stood behind a wood-paneled reception desk on which a Christmas tree twinkled with tiny colored lights. A schedule for aerobics (4:30–5:30 p.m.) and a kickboxing class, Tae-bo (6:00–7:30 p.m.), sat on the desk. When I asked her if I could speak to the Americans who owned the place, she looked at me nervously and picked up the phone.

I poked around their computer room while we waited. Al-Baghir, who had recently returned from studying finance at the London School of Economics, sat outside on a café's brick terrace hidden from the street by eight-foot-high walls. The café, in the same building as the aerobics studio, did not allow men, which meant that the women could order pizza and smoke cigarettes there without being bothered or scolded by the brothers or male cousins normally obliged to escort them in public at night. Al-Baghir and her friends chatted about their courses and blew smoke rings into the air.

The dust was constant here, especially in the summer, when its heavy gusts stung like fiberglass splinters. Sudan lies within the catastrophe belt, where the dry air dropping from the northern hemisphere and the wet air rising from the equatorial south collide. Khartoum, a desert city, lies in Africa's arid north, where the desert is advancing. On the terrace, a late fall breeze blew in from the barren north and drew the smoke rings skyward through red dust.

At last a woman approached me—a large-boned and harried woman, an American, her high auburn ponytail swinging in synch with her no-

nonsense gait.[1] She had two rambunctious redheaded boys, of four and five, in tow. When I told her I was an American writer, she blanched and said that she could not speak to me without her husband there.

She picked me up at my hotel the next day and took me to their home, a dark, high-ceilinged place built by the British. As the redheaded boys wrestled in a corner of the living room, she offered me tea and chocolates. Her pale, tall husband explained that they were missionaries who belonged to the Assemblies of God, the largest Pentecostal church in the world. He had grown up as a Pentecostal MK, or "missionary kid," in East Africa, and had attended a Christian college in Missouri, where he'd met his wife.

"We love the Sudanese so much, it's our driving passion to have as many as we can in heaven," she said, and he agreed. "I felt this call to Sudan. I love the Muslim people. In the Arab world there are so many millions who haven't heard the word." Here in Sudan, Christianity dated back to the first few years following Jesus's death and resurrection, he explained, recounting the story of the royal eunuch's baptism and his return to evangelize North Africa.

"It didn't take," he said ruefully. In 1964, less than a decade after independence, the northern-led Muslim government expelled the remaining missionaries from the country. That didn't really stop evangelization, however. "Since 1964, through creative ways, missionaries have been coming to Sudan." To this couple, these creative ways have included teaching English and offering basic computer classes to Khartoum's working-class Muslims.

"Our desire is to have a place ladies can feel comfortable and that can be a blessing to them," the husband said. In a male-dominated Arab culture, where many young women had to be escorted almost everywhere by one male relative or another, an all-female café was a radical idea. Although some might argue that the couple were creating conditions conducive to reaching the women for their own purpose of evangelizing, they saw their café as a form of cultural empowerment—and, quite simply, as a pleasant place to be. "We're also looking for treadmills and a real cappuccino machine," his wife added. I found it difficult to fathom how it could be worth evangelizing a woman who could be killed by her family for converting to Christianity. For nonbelievers, this was hard to understand, her husband said, but not for those who had the confidence of faith. For them, the effort of conversion was an act of love and service designed to help others reach heaven, or at least to have a chance at heaven. In their eyes, they were simply providing a doorway; whether to walk through or turn away was an individual's choice.

"We love Jesus very much and we want others to know that love as well. We don't ram that down anyone's throats," he said, with the gentle matter-of-factness of one used to explaining his beliefs.

"How many people have you saved?" I asked.

"None," he answered.

Franklin Graham held a final prayer meeting with Sudanese Christian leaders before piloting his plane from Khartoum back to Boone, North Carolina. These leaders represented an array of denominations—from Roman Catholics, to Anglicans, to charismatic Protestant revivalists. Many were black southern Sudanese who had lost everything but their lives while leading their people on an exodus from the battlefields of the south to the relative safety of the Khartoum slums. This was the paradox: the two million southerners living in the north were safer in exile than they were at home. In the guesthouse parlor, these Sudanese Christians beamed as they prayed with Graham. After all, they had survived. And although few bought into Khartoum's invitation to Graham as anything more than an act of political self-preservation, they were still pleased to meet this famous American pastor. After so much persecution, they saw his visit as a sign that America and President Bush had not forgotten them. Yet politics fell quickly by the wayside. This was a religious experience: reliving the suffering of the first Christians, who died as minority believers at risk in a hostile land. Many of the pastors saw Graham as a hero for trying to protect fellow Christians from an Islamic onslaught. He seemed to see himself in terms of his heroes Livingstone and Gordon, furthering the work of the Great Commission.

In the hallway a few minutes later, Ken Isaacs, Graham's second-in-command—a tall, hard-jawed North Carolinian who would go on to head the Office of U.S. Foreign Disaster Assistance under President Bush—approached me and asked, "What's your background?" Originally, I came from Philadelphia, I told him. "That's not what I meant," he said. Was I a believer or not? Salvation was absolute. Saved or damned. There was no in-between. Which was I?

To me, the question required a more complex answer. I was raised as the daughter of an Episcopal priest, and I grew up in a rectory in suburban Philadelphia during the seventies and eighties—a particularly progressive moment for the church. Worship included Passover Seders, *Jesus Christ Superstar*, and doing the Crop Hunger Walk, as well as gathering around an altar and eating homemade organic wheat bread at the Eucharist. This was the bustling, clamorous world of public religion. Talking and listening to God involved a quiet conversation, and words, I was sure, were the way to reach his ear. For me as a six-year-old girl, going out to play often meant sneaking next door to the dark, cool church. I learned to read by standing at the pulpit and practicing the Bible's cadences out over the empty pews. I saw the Bible—sitting open on the brass lectern, a red satin ribbon marking the page—as a book of spells, one whose extravagant metaphors, whose terrible and powerful parables were ways to call God down to earth. In college fifteen years later, I read the work of the twentieth-century Romanian historian and theologian Mircea Eliade. When I came across his concept of hierophany—the spaces where the sacred and secular worlds meet and people's attempt to create them through ceremony—I understood what I had been up to as a child.

At Sunday school, a boy my age once asked me if my father was God. "No, he's God's best friend," I replied. I saw my loving, distant, distractible father caught between two worlds. One was a place of worldly decisions and unexpected telephone calls; once I watched him rip the rectory's black rotary phone right off the wall. The other was a sacred realm in which he was a servant, not a leader. When I was twelve, he was elected the Episcopal bishop of Chicago, and so we moved from a Philadelphia suburb to the urban shore of Lake Michigan. At his consecration—the rite in which a person formally offers himself to God as a bishop—my father, following long tradition, lay facedown on the cathedral floor with his legs extended and arms outstretched, his body forming the shape of a cross. There was something about this act of utter surrender that terrified and angered me. What right had God, and the several thousand midwestern strangers in the pews, to demand my father's life?

"When are they going to let Dad up?" I asked my mother. Although I feared for my father, I also feared for myself. What did God want from us, anyway? As a teenager, I grew petrified of God's will: What if He were to swoop down and ask me to submit also? What could faith cost me? It could cost me myself, I concluded. Frankly, I was afraid God would ask me to be a nun. My father's uncompromising commitment to the articles of his faith proved difficult for me to reconcile with his progressive values and his critical intelligence. I spent those years wondering how it was that smart people could believe in God.

When I traveled with Franklin Graham to Sudan sixteen years later, my father was serving as the presiding bishop. The consecration of Gene V. Robinson had just taken place, upsetting not only African bishops such as Akinola but also conservative American evangelicals such as Graham, with the blessing it obviously conferred on homosexuality. This was evidence to them of the lethal moral lassitude of the West, where whole churches were bent on denying God's will as revealed by scripture.

For Graham, the contemporary confrontation with Islam was sharpening the Christian faith, giving it moral fortitude. Western sinfulness and moral slackness were weakening the faith worldwide, and Christianity needed the West to shape up if it was going to win the fight. But for Graham, as for others, the consecration of Gene Robinson as the bishop of New Hampshire was not just a sign of weakness, a falling away from the old true faith. It was a full-on repudiation of the sexual morality that some Christian evangelicals believed set them apart from others. As such, it marked a divide among Protestants worldwide over what it meant to be a Christian—over whether progressives or conservatives had the right to speak in the name of God. The Reverend Franklin Graham and Presiding Bishop Frank Griswold stood on opposite sides of this divide, and the gap between them was widening.

And I was the presiding bishop's daughter. "You have thirty seconds to tell Franklin," Isaacs said. Graham was in the dining room eating a lunch of oxtail soup with twelve members of his entourage. In the doorway, I hesitated.

"Thirteen seconds," Isaacs said, standing behind me. I sat down at the table and told Graham who my father was. Graham listened, then looked at me and flashed a smile: not the familiar high-watt public beam, but a private and mischievous grin. He and I were kin. For although we were raised with very different understandings of what it meant to be a Christian, we were also fellow PKs, or "preacher's kids"—mottled sheep who had grown up caught between religious parents and private rebellion.

But that's where our similarity ended. As far as he was concerned, the fact that I had not accepted Jesus Christ as my personal Lord and Savior meant I was going to hell.

"There is no middle ground: salvation is black and white," Graham told me. He had made this choice for Christ himself. Why hadn't I?

I asked him to clarify. What did he mean by praying to Jesus? How was that different from praying to God? The clatter of soup spoons ceased. Graham looked at me and said, "Jesus is the only one who died for our sins. Mohammed didn't do that. Buddha died still searching for truth." He quoted what I later learned was the Gospel According to John 14:6—"I am the way, the truth, and the life. No one comes to the Father except through me." There was only one way to be saved and to be assured a place in heaven: through faith in Jesus Christ. "If your plane crashes tomorrow," he asked, "are you absolutely sure you'll go to heaven?"

I thought for a moment. "No."

"Would you be willing to pray with me now?"

I had wondered, before coming to Sudan with Graham, if the question of prayer would arise. I had prayed with believers of all kinds—Sufis, a Sunni friend in Pakistan—so why not with Graham?

"Yes," I told him. We proceeded upstairs and knelt together, prayed a version of the Lord's Prayer together, and asked for the forgiveness of our sins together.

"I know you think you came to Sudan to interview me," Graham said, as we rose. "But I believe the Lord brought you here to pray with me."

That afternoon, vertiginous and queasy, I stood on the tarmac and watched Graham's Gulfstream rise from Khartoum, glinting like a lure against the cloudless sky. What had I done? Had I handed over my soul to his version of God? Had I prayed to please him, or had I broken a professional code by sharing such an intimate act with a person I was writing about? Right or wrong? Open-minded or a sucker? My mind spun; I was searching for a place to come down on one side or the other. But I could not. Meeting believers along the tenth parallel, I tried to parse their distinct identities as Muslims or Christians, northerners or southerners; but like them, I suddenly understood, I was a compound of multiple identities, observer and questioner and believer all in one.

What about him? Was he playing me in the hope of favorable coverage? No, I decided, he was just doing what he does. For Graham, there was little difference between Nada and Shirain, the mother and child in the pediatric hospital, and me: lacking Christ the Lord, we were all lost souls. Offering us a chance at salvation was the most loving thing he could do for us.

Yet his work was not really about us, not us as people; it was about fulfilling his own duty to God. In this, he resembled my father spread-eagled on the cathedral floor, a man who sought to give himself over to a greater power.

It was one thing to offer your own life to God, though, and quite another to offer someone else's. My family would not kill me for kneeling on that rug. Graham did not risk my life in the hope of saving my soul, as he did for many thousands of would-be Christians in Sudan.

Later that December, a few days before Christmas, I went to see Graham at his home and headquarters in Boone, North Carolina. On the wall of his personal office in the sprawling compound hung a framed letter from a woman named Ada, who had sent Graham a penny and a nickel, along with a note: "Dear Franklin, I have prayed that you will receive all the money you need for your mission for God. This is all the money I have and I will pray that God will make it possible for me to mail this letter."

I asked Graham about the human cost of evangelizing in the restricted Muslim countries of the 10/40 Window. Didn't he worry that trying to save people could actually kill them? In reply, he framed a dilemma. "So I keep my mouth shut," he said, "don't tell them about what God has done for them, keep them in spiritual darkness, they'll live out their life, and they'll die and go to hell. Or I tell them about God's son, and if they receive Christ, then I know that their soul is in his hands. Now could their life come to an end? Yes. All of our lives are going to come to an end. Some of us just a little sooner than others."

A package from Graham awaited me when I returned to New York. Inside was the black leather-bound New King James Bible, with Jesus's words printed in red ink. In the Gospel According to John, Graham had bracketed with a pen: "And I give them eternal life, and they shall never perish; neither shall anyone snatch them out of My hand. My Father, who has given them to Me, is greater than all; no one can snatch them out of My Father's hand. I and My Father are one" (John 10:28–30). For much of the next seven years, I used the red-letter version Graham had sent me to look up the biblical verses Christians cited to me during my travels between the equator and the tenth parallel—some of them, words by which they had watched their families die; others, words in which they found a license to kill—until one day, absentminded on a train from Boston to New York, I left it behind.

14

SPOILING THE WORLD

Is the black color of skin such a thing
That the government should draw its guns?
—DINKA SONG[1]

If Sudan splits along the tenth parallel, it will become two countries, one black and Christian, the other more Arab and northern. When I traveled to the north-south border, and to the frontline village of Todaj, in 2008, I was startled by how aware people were of the tenth parallel's significance as both a geographic and ethnic divide. Partly this was a result of the failed 2005 peace deal, which was supposed to give both sides rights to the land along the tenth parallel: leaders from both sides knew the lines on the map, since they determined whether or not the whole town would survive. But it wasn't the town that mattered this time; it was the oil beneath, and I wanted to see it. I'd flown above the fields—thousand-mile grids sliced into the *sudd*—from above. Swamp water shone through the slots. I'd thought of the determined Karl Kumm nearly swimming across what he'd called "one vast lake that culminates between the seventh and the tenth parallel." From the ground, oil was a more mysterious affair, and that was no accident. Occasionally, I would get a whiff of its acrid tang, but the signs of oil extraction are not so easy to see. Sometimes a red knob in a sandy clearing led to a few yards of exposed white pipe, or a telltale hummock that looked like a woodchuck's tunnel. These, I was told, were signs of the 2003 oil pipeline buried under six inches of barren soil. I decided to try to visit the largest oil fields around.

For thousands of square miles, the Greater Nile Petroleum Operating Company was extracting the light, sweet crude oil that makes petroleum prospecting in Africa so lucrative. GNPOC had its headquarters at Heglig, which lies within fifty miles of the tenth parallel in the state of South

Kordofan. It was a four-hour drive from Todaj (which lay in Zone Four) to headquarters, beneath an incandescent sun. Along the way I saw no sign of life except a few fishermen, who stood ankle-deep in puddles scooping Nile perch and mudfish into nets. The fish, at first glance, looked like snakes. So late in the dry season, the puddles were too shallow to cover the fishes' whole bodies, leaving their muddy fins to writhe above the water. These would-be fishermen depended on a battery of international aid agencies, although their fishing hole was at the edge of a vast oil field. Aid dollars were pumped in to feed them while their country's wealth was pumped out from beneath their feet.

GNPOC did not welcome visitors, but thanks to a favor from a well-placed friend, I was granted an appointment with the chief of security at headquarters. My reporting was supposed to be restricted to the company's community development programs, but what I saw were communities being destroyed.

The territory within GNPOC's barbed-wire perimeter, which lay about an hour north of the town of Bentiu, seemed like another country, or several countries. In the trailer that served as a lobby, oil workers in red, green, and beige jumpsuits—from China, Malaysia, India, and Sudan—scurried through a waiting room, where a sign in Arabic read, "Use the Waiting Time to Ask for Forgiveness."

I was taken to a GNPOC-built hospital on a company road not far away. Since the headquarters sat on the de facto border between northern and southern Sudan, the hospital saw patients from both sides—northern Arab nomads, and Dinka from the south. Medical treatment was free, as long as those seeking it could pay the three-dollar bus fee from the nearby town. And most people could not. "The culture is our biggest problem," said the hospital's doctor, who had come south from Khartoum. "There's no civilization here. Africans and Arabs both, all they do is fight."

That spring, the Arabs and the Ngok Dinka were doing all they could *not* to fight. Most nights in the nearby oil town of Abyei, well-armed teenage bullies played a lethal game of chicken, as soldiers from both sides cruised the oil company roads in land-borne gunboats—open Jeeps mounted with antiaircraft guns called technicals.

But no one who actually lived there wanted more war. The nomads were in a terrible position. As in Nigeria and across much of Africa, the desert and seasonal droughts were squeezing them off their land. In Sudan, the Khartoum regime intensified this crisis by leasing land along the nomads' migration routes to commercial farmers. (For years, Osama bin Laden was one of the largest.) No longer able to go north, the nomads had no choice but to push farther south, into Dinka land. Both nomads and Dinka recognized these patterns, and neither wanted trouble. The elders also understood that their people were not simply competing for grazing land, or even oil; they were pawns in a larger conflict.

Most evenings the elders gathered at the sprawling whitewashed mud compound of the Ngok Dinka's paramount chief, Kwol Deng Kwol. Lesser chiefs such as Nyol Paduot looked to the paramount chief for guidance. But so did the Arab Misseriya, thanks to ties between the two groups.

Kwol Deng Kwol is a gentle giant in his forties. Seven feet tall and wearing a pink tattersall shirt and khaki trousers, he made his way around the banquet hall greeting his guests, a mobile phone in each hand. He inherited this role by blood; his father was the legendary Ngok Dinka chieftain Deng Majok, who married nearly two hundred wives and fathered a thousand children. Deng Majok also forged a peace with the Misseriya chieftain Babo Nimr. When Deng Majok died after a long illness in 1969, Khartoum had his most powerful son and rightful heir assassinated. Both men were buried outside the hall in what looked like a small parking lot, the sarcophagi slathered over with cement so that no one could defile the bodies.

Fear lent the evening a festive air. The chief was laying out hot platters of roasted goat, cups of wild honey, and china bowls of sour cheese called *kisra*. Sometimes the signs of imminent conflict—crowded roads, a sudden excess of food—are easy to mistake for prosperity. Yet at the chief's banquet, everyone knew they were waiting for war.

At the edge of the hall, one black man towered over the tall crowd. He was wearing the white cap and robes of a northerner—a Muslim—but his height and skin color clearly marked him as belonging to the Ngok Dinka. His name, it turned out, was Maulana Alor Deng and he was one of the paramount chief's hundreds of brothers. He was also an imam in the local mosque—had been, at any rate, until the northern government kicked him out several years earlier because, as he said, they did not want a black man leading prayers.

Maulana Deng converted to Islam in order to get an education, and upon doing so, he was compelled to forswear his parents' spiritual beliefs and take on a Muslim name. Over time Deng's practical assimilation had become a genuine experience of religious conversion.

With a bowl of amber honey in his lap, he laid out the conflict between north and south in terms an outsider like me could understand. "In the north people think that they are better," he said, because they are Muslims and ethnic Arabs. "The south is more blessed with resources. That's why the north wants to control it." That meant oil for the government, water and viable pastureland for the nomads. As a Muslim, Maulana Deng was ordered by the northern government to fight against his non-Muslim Ngok Dinka brothers during the most recent jihad. He prayed for God's guidance, and, he says, God told him not to go. So he refused to fight. "I didn't give in because I know what jihad means, and this was not real," he said. As a result, he was tortured. "If my faith wasn't strong, I would have left Islam," he said.

A blind woman, eyes blued with cataracts, one earlobe ripped in two and a safety pin pushed through the other, entered the mud hall, which was redolent with the aromas of honey and hay. Dragging a gnarled wooden staff and wearing a white shawl so frayed her clavicles showed through its weft, she looked like an oracle, and was singing low in her throat about Abyei, this town, which was named for an acacia tree. She was a praise singer, Maulana Deng explained, a cultural relic of another time. The song she sang—of war, attrition, and stubborn return—was a song of the past, but she could have been singing about the future.

Three weeks later the northern army laid siege to Abyei and destroyed the town. By satellite phone, the paramount chief told me that the whitewashed mud house where we had eaten supper had been looted and burned to the ground. He had taken shelter with twenty other men in a single hut too small for them all to lie down in at once. Aid workers did not have enough tents or tarps to go around. At night, the men took turns standing out in the rain. "My people are living under trees," Kwol Deng Kwol said. Here at least there were trees.[2]

SOMALIA

*Now brother will deliver up brother to death, and a father
his child; and children will rise up against parents and cause
them to be put to death. And you will be hated by all for My
name's sake. But he who endures to the end will be saved.*

—THE GOSPEL ACCORDING TO MATTHEW 10:21–22

*We sent to you [Muhammad] the Scripture with the truth,
confirming the Scriptures that came before it, and with final
authority over them: so judge between them according to
what God has sent down.*

—THE QURAN, THE FEAST 5:48

15

"THE REAL SUPERPOWER"

"Take off your veil!" a soldier shouted, grabbing
a woman's black face veil with his left hand and

steadying the butt of an AK-47 against his shoulder with his right. "Why are you coming so close to us? You have explosives?" The soldier, working for a government of warlords, stepped forward until his gun's muzzle grazed her nose. She was a suicide bomber, he was certain; he fixed her with a glassy, pink-eyed glare. Fearing he would shoot her, or that she would explode, I closed my eyes. The afternoon's bedlam didn't recede; it flooded my eyelids with green.

Here at this crossroads in the Somali capital of Mogadishu in June 2007—deserted except for this woman, a passel of soldiers, and a man selling fresh mango juice from a wooden table (his stall had been blown up several days earlier)—everyone and everything held its breath. A piece of trash, a pile of rubble, a woman waiting for a cup of mango juice—any of these could be a bomb rigged by the Islamic insurgents called al-Shabab, "the Youth." The insurgents ruled this neighborhood, Tawfiq. Their bunkers—hidey-holes littered with cracker wrappers and old tissues—rutted the sandy streets.

"I just want a juice," the woman pleaded, trying to back away. Suddenly exposed and embarrassed, she broke into a jester's forced grin. The juice man watched from behind his table, trying to wipe the distress off his face, keep his features neutral, *careful, careful.* He probably knew her, since she lived nearby, and he had sold juice on this corner for the past twenty years. For all I knew, she could be his daughter. Maybe her family was watching from the curtained window of a house down the street. Maybe tomorrow, to avenge their daughter's shame, they would send their son to join the insurgents.

Nearby, grazing cows and a group of children sniffing glue competed for something to eat in the same pile of garbage. A sign on a daub wall read, "New Fallujah Café," linking Somalia to Iraq and the legendary city there where Muslim resistance defied American might. This arid strip of badland clinging to the continent's northeastern edge was fast becoming the most violent nation of Africa's fifty-three. Six months before I arrived, on December 26, 2006, neighboring Ethiopia, which has been governed by Orthodox Christians since the fourth century, officially invaded Somalia, whose nine million people are Muslims. In the name of defending their Somali nation and their Islamic religion against Ethiopian "crusaders," al-Shabab, an Islamist militia, had launched a rebellion against the Ethiopians. This local battle had global repercussions: it was bleeding into a proxy war between Al Qaeda and America, who saw in this fight between Somalia and neighboring Ethiopia a struggle for an ideological and logistical foothold in Africa.

The battle-by-proxy for Somalia was not new; during the cold war, the United States and the Soviets vied for control of the tiny country to gain access to the oil routes on its long coastline. Since the fall of Somalia's Soviet-backed military dictator, Siad Barre, in 1991, the country has endured seventeen failed attempts at government. Somalia is the longest-running failed state on the planet; for much of its history, it has been ruled by warlords. In 2004, a nascent Islamist government, the Islamic Courts Union, rose to challenge the warlords' power. The Islamic Courts Union began as a network of neighborhood courts that meted out justice according to Islamic law. It consisted of a coalition of businessmen, religious leaders, and militants, including, according to U.S. intelligence, at least three members of Al Qaeda. From the start, the coalition was riddled with divisions: Sheikh Sharif Sheikh Ahmed, a forty-six-year-old soft-spoken former Somali schoolteacher, headed the more moderate political wing, and was frequently at odds with the sixty-two-year-old hard-line military commander Sheikh Hassan Dahir Aweys, who was on both the U.S. and UN terrorist watch lists. Sheikh Aweys led the Islamists' military wing and their militia, al-Shabab, and by 2005, under Aweys's leadership, the Islamic Courts Union was showing the usual signs of a conservative Islamist regime staking a claim on its people and their habits.

Almost all Somalis, like most North Africans, are Sufis, and for most, religion is a personal, not a political affair. But the Islamic Courts Union was burning and banning the mild leafy stimulant *qat*, outlawing movies, and demanding that men wear beards and keep their hair short. In January 2005, al-Shabab raided the graves in an Italian colonial cemetery, dug up the bones of the "infidels," and dumped the human remains by the airport.

Ethiopia's 2006 invasion, tacitly backed by the United States, aimed to overthrow the Islamic Courts Union. Ethiopia fears, above all, having a hostile Muslim government next door because the Christian-led government is afraid of its own restive and growing Muslim population. (Of Ethiopia's eighty-five million people, 50 percent are Coptic [called Orthodox] Christians, 10 percent are Protestants, and more than 30 percent are Muslims.) Ethiopia's leaders have long viewed their country as "a Christian island in

a Muslim sea." President Meles Zenawi told the U.S. senator Arlen Specter in August 2002 that the American-led "war on terrorism" was "something of a godsend."[1] The Ethiopian invasion of Somalia was supposed to
send thousands of Somali fighters and a handful of suspected terrorists
down the Somali coast, where U.S. and allied forces would kill or capture
them. But the invasion backfired, and so did the Bush administration's
policies in Somalia, such as backing loathed warlords and launching Tom-
ahawk missile strikes against civilians.[2] By the end of 2009, the fighting
had left at least 8,500 people dead. According to the UN, 1.5 million had
lost their homes and 3.8 million were at risk of famine. America and its
allies had created the very enemy they had sought to destroy.

Al Qaeda, like America, hoped to plant a friendly flag on this strategic
battlefield—an effort waged as much by Al Qaeda's aptly named media
wing, As-Sahab ("Clouds"), as by actual militant boots on the ground.
This ideological tug-of-war filled the vacuum the cold war had left behind;
as Al Qaeda cast it, the battle between communism and capitalism had
given way to "the eternal struggle" between the godless and the faithful.
As bin Laden has claimed in the past, "God is the real superpower."[3] Now
his lieutenant, the Egyptian Ayman al-Zawahiri, called for Somalis "to be
steadfast in this new Crusader battlefield [sic], which America, its allies,
and the United Nations are waging against Islam and Muslims." He called
for ambushes, the laying of mines, and "martyrdom-seeking campaigns"—
endorsing suicide bombings and exhorting the "lions" of Yemen, Egypt,
Sudan, and the rest of Muslim North Africa to send their brothers money
to fight against America and "its slaves."[4] (To insult the Ethiopians, he
used *abd*—the word for "slave" and a Torrid Zone slur against blacks.
Months later, he would call President Barack Obama *abd-al-beit*, which
translates to "house nigger.")

And al-Shabab responded to this call: on September 20, 2009 (six days
after the United States killed a thirty-year-old Kenyan Al Qaeda member,
Saleh Ali Saleh al-Nabhan, in a helicopter air strike), the group issued a
forty-eight-minute video entitled *Here I Am at Your Service, Oh Osama*.
Amid local scenes of Somali battle, the video replays George Bush's
September 16, 2001, comment that the war on terrorism is "a crusade";
then it cuts in Bush's successor, President Barack Obama, seated in front
of a large, brightly lit crucifix. The video's highly sophisticated visuals
and screen grabs call for little translation.

For Al Qaeda, Somalia, "the gateway to the Arabian peninsula," is a strategic fault line; it is a doorway marking the end of Dar-ul-Harb, the profane land of war, and the beginning of Dar-ul-Islam, the holy land of Islam. This worldview is partly a matter of geography, of the divide between Christians and Muslims in East Africa, created, once again, by century-old patterns of trade driven by weather.

The Horn of Africa is a dry, knobby jut on the continent's easternmost edge. It includes Eritrea, Djibouti, Somalia, and Ethiopia. The Horn stretches west into Sudan and south into Kenya. Here, the demographics of Christianity and Islam shift from the north-south divide that defines most of inland Africa, to a west-east split between highland Christians and lowland Muslims. More than two thousand years ago, Judaism arrived by way of a diaspora from Israel.[5] Christianity, then Islam, followed. Today, Africa's Jews have largely disappeared. Much of Africa's east coast is predominantly Muslim, with Christians living inland. Arab traders began traveling to the East African coast before Islam even existed, beginning around the year 500, when they dubbed the coast the land of *Zinj*, another Torrid Zone term for "black." As Christianity spread inland with European colonialism in the nineteenth and twentieth centuries, a divide opened up between the Muslim coast and the Christian heartland here and in countries such as Kenya and Tanzania. In the years since Al Qaeda's 1998 bombings of U.S. embassies in those countries, that divide has sharpened, and thousands of East African Muslims have been rounded up, interrogated, and detained in the name of counterterrorism. Many Muslims living along the coast say that they feel like suspects—not citizens—in their own countries. This is part of a hardening of religious identity that has occurred along the coast over the past decade; it has led, once again, to the importance of religion surpassing that of nation.

By June 2007, nine million Somalis caught in the middle of this proxy battle were paying the price of Ethiopia's occupation. Those injured during the occupation and insurgency filled the sixty beds of the Medina hospital. Dried blood glued sand to the concrete floor—the ground gritty and sticky—and the wounded overflowed into the hospital's hallway. On one gurney, a former teacher clutched the drainage tube protruding from his own stomach. Ethiopians had shot him, stolen his $1,000 in savings, and left him in the street to die. An eighteen-year-old rape victim in another bed had been admitted several days earlier bleeding from his rectum, violated by members of a rival clan so as to humiliate his own. In intensive care—a dank and fetid room with stained curtains half drawn over dusty windows—a woman waited for her sister to wake from a coma after being shot during a carjacking. "Under the Islamic Courts Union," she said, "it wasn't possible for anyone to do this." Meanwhile, in a crowded room next door, a woman named Rogia poked at the cast on her right knee, where an Ethiopian sniper had shot her. When I asked if she was sure the sniper had seen her, she snorted. "Of course he saw me. I saw him. The Ethiopians hate our religion." Embarrassed, the hospital's one doctor translated for her: "Muslims wouldn't do anything like this."

Ashen and haggard, slumped behind the desk of his bullet-riddled office in a Mogadishu suburb, Ahmed Abdi Salem, forty-seven, a prominent businessman and a co-owner of HornAfrik FM radio, had had it with proxy wars. "For most people, this war has nothing to do with Somalia," he said. "This is all about international issues: Islam versus Christianity, the war on terrorism, Ethiopia versus Somalia."

Abdi Salem had returned home to Somalia from Canada several years earlier. In the hallway, there were hopeful cartoon murals of reporters holding microphones: "We Are Responsible to the Public. We Must Treat Them Fairly" and "The Media Are Free" and "Be Aware the Harm That Media Can Inflict on Conflict." The signs, which looked like children had painted them, seemed tragic and forlorn; recent relics of one more failed attempt at building a functioning society. It seemed that conflict could inflict harm on the media, too, by the looks of Abdi Salem's office. Shrapnel had made a moonscape of the plaster walls and shattered windows, the result of an insurgent firebombing months earlier. More recently, the Ethiopians had lobbed mortars at the station and decimated the BBC satellite dish mounted on the roof. HornAfrik was under fire from both sides. No one wanted a free press. Ignorance served all parties better, Abdi Salem explained. So far that year, seven local journalists had been murdered. In 2007, 2008, and 2009, according to the Committee to Protect Journalists, Mogadishu proved more perilous for local reporters than Baghdad. Salem was losing colleagues every month. "There has been so much fighting in this city, people do not care anymore," he said. "The level of hopelessness is worrisome."

Fueled by this sense of hopelessness, Islam's role grew larger in Somali life, Salem said. "This is a secular community, but the more they see themselves as marginalized, the more they turn to religion." Plus, there were no other organizations to turn to anymore, he added. "When I was growing up, you had other institutions, communities, youth clubs, schools. There are children of children here who haven't gone to school. What will a father who never went to school teach his children? Religion comes in because it's education for free and we all have it."

This pattern began decades earlier, during the eighties, when Siad Barre, the cold war dictator, used the machinery of a police state to spy on, interrogate, and oppress his people. Islam came to provide a toehold of truth and authenticity in lands ruled by dictatorial regimes such as Somalia's—regimes based on silence, lies, and a false view of the world. When the Soviets fell, the West stepped in to back these same corrupt dictators. Muslims naturally turned against the West. By sheer dint of its size, it seemed there was little way for America to win public opinion; the United States was either a foreign invader or a callous Judas.

In the mid-nineties, the United States and the United Nations left Somalia following the 1993 "Black Hawk Down" debacle, when the warlord Mohammed Farah Aideed's militia shot down two American military helicopters and killed eighteen U.S. Army Rangers. Although the UN and other Western aid groups had pulled out, Islamic aid groups had not. For many Somalis, this was proof that only Muslims helped Muslims. I'd heard this familiar story while on the border between Afghanistan and Pakistan. When the cold war ended and the Soviets left Afghanistan, America pulled out too, ending its alliance with the Mujahideen who had opposed the Soviet occupation. There, as here, Islam seemed the only solution, and the West's departure was seen as abandonment.

"Because of Black Hawk Down, because eighteen boys were killed here, America thinks that we are their enemies," Abdi Salem said, considering his brutalized office walls. He was one of the few who could still leave Somalia if he chose. But he did not, and that decision seemed to hang around his neck, a yoke stooping him slightly. He took me up to the roof to see the remnants of the BBC's satellite dish, its bowl crushed and tipped over, its legs in the air, and its shell hollow like a dead bug's carapace.

Abdi Salem looked out over the city: cheerful sun-bleached pastel houses dozing against a tropical sea. Not a soul was visible. It could have been siesta on the coast of Spain, but it was siesta in Somalia. There was nothing to suggest that by night skeletal young fighters would emerge from hiding to assassinate civil leaders or target media outlets such as Abdi Salem's. "A young generation with no hope; religion gives them a sense of purpose," he said. So did having an enemy. "America's against us, they're infidels," he mimicked the young militants. His voice died away. They were responsible for their actions, but the system meant to raise them into responsibility was also broken. "You had every reason to see this was happening," he said.

"The only way out is to come up with a system that gives people a sense of hope—schools, a government essentially." Weeks later, Abdi Salem's business partner and his star reporter were assassinated. By the time I returned to the city a year later, in 2008, Abdi Salem had become, for a moment, Somalia's deputy prime minister—the one job more hazardous than that of a reporter or an insurgent.

Later that afternoon, I met an insurgent commander at a deserted compound in the once-wealthy neighborhood called K4, four kilometers from the sea. Until Somalia descended into the chaos of civil war in 1991, the vast, once-verdant compounds of K4 housed an international community of Russians, Americans, Chinese, and wealthy Somalis. Now refugees had crept into the blasted homes, hospitals, and university buildings; two widows were squatting in what was left of the villa that had been the American embassy.

I was waiting among the wild honeysuckle vines on one abandoned villa's veranda when the compound's iron gate swung open and two men slunk in, their faces mummified in rags. As they passed the cracked, netless tennis court, one pulled the cloth from his face, revealing skin that clung to his skull like a wet washcloth. This was Ahmed Mohammed Hashim, a twenty-five-year-old insurgent commander; his companion was his bodyguard. We settled beneath the courtyard's bower, with Dini, the interpreter and assistant manager of the Peace Hotel, where I was staying. I asked Hashim who he took his enemies to be. "Ethiopia is our first enemy," he began. "Right now they go into our mosques and shit and pee there." Second was the Somali government, which Ethiopia backed, "because it is illegitimate." And third: "America. America is the father of our enemy. America is using the Ethiopians to take over our country and we are against them."

Hashim was the product of an older war. He was nine when Siad Barre fell from power in 1991, and the country descended into the chaos of civil war among warlords. One day during the war, while Hashim was at school, a mortar ripped through his family's clay house. His mother and brother were killed instantly. (His father, a soldier, was already dead.) In hindsight, he had come to believe that the war was punishment for their being bad Muslims; as he put it, "We had forgotten our religion." After that, Hashim spent much of his time in mosques, which became safe havens for those trying to escape the violence in the streets—a matter of protection, as well as devotion. Religious rituals, too, grew more popular: people performed ablutions before leaving the house each day so as to die, if they died, in a state of grace. For Hashim, this war was both global and local. Somalia's shared religion was the practical, local solution to transcend the rivalries among powerful families that were ruining his country.

"Everything is based on clans," he said. "Only God is strong enough to defeat both the warlords and America."

Down the road from the rich man's house, one hundred refugee families were living within the stucco walls of another ruined household, in igloo-like wooden framed domes covered in a patchwork of cloth scraps and feed sacks. The camp's inhabitants shared whatever food they had. A six-foot-high bramble wall guarded the entrance to the community school, and inside it a dozen children under the age of ten sat in an oval. A twelve-year-old boy patrolled the circle with a switch. Each of the children had a wooden paddle on which boys and girls were inking a verse from the Quran. Every morning, from seven until eleven, the children rocked back and forth in the dirt chanting verses in Arabic, a foreign language they neither spoke nor understood. Only ten out of one hundred Somali children attended any school at all, Abdi Salem had told me, and only one out of one hundred of those schools was secular.

Beyond the bramble wall, someone was singing. Ducking out of the makeshift school to see who it was, I found camp residents gathered around a bearded man dressed in white and carrying a staff. He was a Sufi fakir—an Islamic monk and miracle worker rolled into one.

"God created all people from Adam and Eve," he sang. "We are all the same," he continued, smiling fatly at me. "The Prophet Mohammed wanted to unite people and so we, the Sufiyah, are trying to unite people."

When he finished, the listeners gave him a little money and wandered away. He lingered to talk to me. "I come here to praise the Prophet Mohammed so these people will help me," he said. A fakir is at the mercy of those he blesses, who decide what they will pay for his blessings, or *barakat* (the Arabic root of the name Barack). This one lived as a squatter in a bombed-out Russian hospital, along with eleven other Sufi singers. Sufi prayer flags—green squares trimmed in fuchsia—fluttered over Mogadishu and marked camps all over the city. The skyline looked like a medieval encampment, with pennants from different battalions tugging against the Red Sea's balmy spindrift. Months later, with the mounting influence of al-Shabab—which promoted a hard-line Sunni rather than local Sufi theology—the Sufi religious leaders would be forced to flee the city as Sunnis and Sufis fractured and battled each other. Before the exodus, the Islamist government had cracked down on the fakirs. "The Islamic Courts didn't let us come and sing like this," the fakir told me. "They said we were telling lies about the Prophet." When the religious police tried to stop him from singing, the fakir argued with them. "I said I had a right to praise Prophet Mohammed how I wanted." For this, he received eighty lashes with a cane. He stopped singing and began to beg instead. Begging was safer.

16

"THEY'LL KILL YOU"

When I returned to Mogadishu on April 8, 2008, many of the people I had hoped to see there had either left the country or been killed. As our shuddering Daallo Airlines flight turned in the sky above Mogadishu's airport, now frequently under fire by militants, I noticed the grids of oil excavation off to the left, through the airplane's filthy window. Somalia, it turns out, has virtually no oil; the grids date back to the fifties, when the country seemed laden with economic promise. In 2008, it had no promise. A few hours after the plane touched down, there were two suicide bombings, which resumed that day after a several-month hiatus. The threat of mobile-phone-detonated homemade bombs rendered movement in the city virtually impossible. The technical know-how to make such weapons hadn't existed in Somalia the year before. But now, as militants migrated from one field of battle to another, or linked up on the Internet, the global networks of lethal technology, like ideology, had grown stronger. Here, as in Sudan, war globalized: it linked disparate battlefields through common ideology and killer gadgets.

The world ignored the mounting dead. In Iraq and Afghanistan, Americans were dying, but in Somalia, Somalis were dying. It seemed to them that America had made a brutal calculation: to catch only three suspected members of Al Qaeda, it was worth placing four million people at risk of famine—more than a million lives upended for every suspect. In Somalia itself, this was fast becoming a war between moderate Muslims such as Sheikh Sharif Sheikh Ahmed, the former political head of the Islamic Courts Union whom I'd met in Kenya while he was negotiating with the UN, and hard-liners such as Sheikh Hassan Dahir Aweys, the ICU's former military head, in exile in the nearby country of Eritrea. The culprit, the scapegoat, for every mounting ill was America, America, and America.

Rational or not, part of this Somali ire stemmed from the fact that in 2008, the United States and the UN were backing yet another failing attempt at a transitional federal government led by some of the country's most rapacious warlords. To see how these warlords actually controlled the lives of average Somali citizens, in April 2008, I went to meet one of the most notorious, Mohammed Dheere, who was the mayor of Mogadishu. With a head of thick, well-oiled curls and a double-wide girth, he rarely left the seaside rubble of the whitewashed colonial city, the territory where the transitional federal government held on to its last scrap of power against the Islamists. Dheere was an obese Captain Bly, a land-bound scourge who out-awfuled any penny-ante pirate at sea. He used to tax mothers giving birth in the hospitals he controlled—more money for having a boy than a girl.

As mayor, he told me, his two top priorities were "security and taxes." Security, I knew, meant his private militia, which robbed people at checkpoints. Taxes meant that he would make the few people left in Mogadishu—those too old or poor to flee—pay for the right to live in a war zone.

Because Somalia lies within a few hundred miles of the equator, it is particularly prone to weather-borne catastrophe. Thanks to environmental change, fickle weather patterns are making it impossible to predict the right seasons for crops and migration. In 2008, the seasonal *gu* rain was late. Since most Somalis are herders, their pastoral way of life was at risk as the land dried up. Half the population was facing extreme food shortages due to drought and war profiteering. Herders were especially at the mercy of the worsening weather, and in Mogadishu, the price of a barrel of water—a day's worth—was then an inconceivable ten dollars. Residents bought their water right off a donkey's back; boys led the donkeys, strapped with yellow barrels, through the streets, delivering each day's precious supply.

In economic terms, the Somali shilling was falling so fast in value that shopkeepers no longer accepted it. Corrupt political leaders and businessmen were minting shillings as fast as possible and flooding the market for personal gain, as insurgent attacks shut down the city and hundreds of thousands of residents fled their homes for squalid camps as near as a few miles outside of town, and as far as Dadaab refugee camp, five hundred miles away in northern Kenya.

One afternoon, Dheere took me along to a city council meeting at a large private home called the Richmond Residence. The lady of the house, a mammoth gray-haired Somali American woman, lounging on a beach chaise in Coney Island sunglasses, cackled gleefully to see a fellow U.S. citizen. "I named this place for my home in Virginia!" The city council's sleek members dined on roast chicken and relaxed afterward in a cool lounge drinking peach soda and chewing *qat*, legal again and back in full force since the ouster of the Islamists a year and a half earlier. Dheere, seated as if enthroned before a leopard pelt nailed to one wall, laid out his tax plan. It was simple. Everyone had to pay.

"But my area is too small to collect tax. We don't even have a market," one local official protested.

"No place is too small to pay tax!" the mayor shouted. Laughter rang off the walls.

Dheere defended his policies in the name of battling Al Qaeda. He was a member of a group of Somali warlords, the Alliance for Restoration of Peace and Counter-Terrorism, which the CIA backed in return for the group's help in capturing and killing suspected terrorists—until the plan was publicly exposed in 2006 and discontinued. "The Americans approached us," Dheere explained. "They had their own intelligence about the number of international terrorist suspects using Somalia as a safe haven."

According to Dheere and another warlord named Mohamed Qanyare Afrah (who preferred to be called "a very, very, very successful businessman"), after a 2002 terrorist attack on the Israeli-owned Paradise Hotel in the coastal Kenyan city of Mombasa, Americans and Israelis came to the warlords for help. They gave the warlords a list of people to kill, capture, or kidnap, and paid for these services with suitcases of American dollars. The U.S. officers then flew the suspects in secret from Qanyare's heavily guarded private airport to places unknown. The Somalis involved claimed they turned over about twenty people in this manner, and to this day, they believe they deserve both gratitude and support from the United States for protecting its security interests. (In 2009, a CIA spokesperson, Marie Harf, told me she could not comment on the warlord's accusations. A Special Forces commander told me that some of his soldiers had traveled along with CIA operatives to Somalia, and had been disturbed by their naïveté in dealing with the warlords.)

"Americans should not treat their friends like this," Qanyare chided me gently when I met him in a Kenyan hotel in 2008.

His former colleague Mayor Dheere was especially loquacious about the capture of Suleiman Abdalla Salim Hemed, aka Isa Tanzania. Tanzania, whose moniker *Isa* is Arabic for "Jesus," is a Yemeni linked to the 2002 attack on Mombasa's Paradise Hotel. Dheere brags about his henchmen capturing Hemed in Somalia in 2003 and handing him over to the Americans. According to Hemed's lawyer, Tina Monshipour Foster, executive director of International Justice Network, an NGO that provides international legal assistance, Hemed was flown to Afghanistan and held at Bagram Airbase until eventually he was returned to Tanzania. According to Foster, Hemed claims that he was tortured while in U.S. custody.

Since the CIA program that funded the warlords came to light and was terminated in 2007, Dheere had been forced to make his money elsewhere. Here, his title as mayor came in handy: his greatest source of revenue was the main checkpoint, about eight miles out of Mogadishu, on the only viable escape route from town. Here, in trucks strapped with mattresses, on foot, and by donkey cart, almost all of the nine hundred thousand residents who fled Mogadishu were forced to pass a posse of Dheere's sometime soldiers. Many refugees left their few possessions at home in the shelled city, preferring to risk losing their family photographs or clothes rather than carry them through these checkpoints and have them stolen.

The blanched two-lane byway called the Afgooye Corridor was a road of horrors. Trucks carrying food and other forms of aid from the far more secure town of Afgooye, fifteen miles away, to Mogadishu were often kept waiting for weeks because they could not pay whatever "tax" the militia demanded. Sometimes the soldiers took potshots at passing vehicles only because they were bored. One afternoon in April 2008, these soldiers strafed my convoy—the Toyota Corolla I was riding in and the 4Runner of armed guards traveling behind me—with automatic fire. My driver stopped the car, which I thought seemed suicidal after these men had just shot at us. He yelled at the shooters, who, to my baffled relief, looked sheepish and apologized. They had fired at us simply because we were moving, the driver told me when he returned to the car. No other reason.

About six months earlier, in October 2007, not far from this checkpoint, workers distributing UN food supplies at a refugee camp clashed with Dheere's militia. Shots were fired into the crowd, and although several people were killed, the refugees (miraculously, it seemed) forced the militia to retreat.

This camp, walled with a labyrinth of scavenged wood shanties, sat atop a hill along the main artery out of Mogadishu, on the way to Afgooye. Dr. Hawa Abdi, a Soviet-trained gynecologist in her fifties (her education a relic of cold war alliances), had founded the camp. Each time I visited in 2007 and 2008, the camp's main hill swarmed like a domed beehive with new arrivals. Women, in pairs, bent bare boughs and wove them into oversize baskets, then planted the baskets, like giant upside-down birds' nests, into the high, sandy hummock. Once Dr. Abdi handed out tarps, these frames became houses. But there were never enough tarps to go around, and the doctor had to negotiate in high-speed Somali to stop fights from breaking out among the waiting women.

For generations this scrubland had served as Abdi's family farm, but two decades ago she opened a one-room women's hospital here. Then, during the famine of the early 1990s, women who knew and trusted Dr. Abdi, a divorced mother of two, flooded her farm by the thousands with their families, believing she would help them. (She had even set up a jail—an empty storeroom with a barred window—where she sequestered husbands accused of beating their wives.) First, she sold her family gold to feed them. Then, as the famine worsened, she had to pay gravediggers in food to bury the more than ten thousand who died. For a moment, her humanitarian work had made her a national hero. When President George H. W. Bush visited Mogadishu in 1992, she shook his hand.

The hill on which we were standing was a mass grave.

"We buried ten thousand and seventy-eight bodies underneath here," Dr. Abdi told me as we cut through the press of new arrivals and picked our way down the steep slope to the place she euphemistically called the neonatal ward: a cracked veranda where half a dozen babies lay dying of chronic diarrhea, which is treatable. Abdi stuffed her worn hands into the frayed pockets of her white lab coat. When I first visited in June 2007, twenty thousand people had fled to her farm for safety; when I returned in April 2008, that number had quadrupled to eighty thousand. Yet this new wave hadn't brought interest from the international community with them. Many of the aid dollars—and the shiny, white SUVs of the United Nations and nongovernmental organizations—earmarked for Somalia ended up in neighboring Kenya, where it was safer to work.[1] Dr. Abdi received some help from the UN World Food Programme, and Doctors Without Borders had set up a sand-colored field hospital tent on her land, which they were finding difficult to staff. No foreigners could stay for more than an hour, or they were likely to be found out by the insurgents and killed. So, for the most part, she was left to do her work—and to defend her camp from attacks, such as the one by the mayor's militia—alone.

"I'm ready to kick the militia's asses," Dr. Deqo Waqaf said to me. She was Abdi's daughter, a Somali American in her thirties. She had come from Atlanta to help run the camp's hospital for women. From the life in her eyes, framed by red Prada eyeglasses, I could tell that she had not been here for more than a few months; she still seemed indignant, unwilling to believe she was stuck. She was desperate to talk about America, her home, as if she feared she had only imagined it. Dr. Abdi came to sit with us. She peeled back her head scarf to reveal a scar on her skull just above her forehead. In the past year, she had battled brain cancer, she told me, laughing at the unlikely list of misfortunes she had survived. That laugh, too, was a celebration that she was still alive. Returning from treatment in the Netherlands, she summoned her daughter to help, and though Dr. Waqaf wanted desperately to go back to Georgia, her mother needed her too badly, and so she had stayed.

"I am stuck," Dr. Waqaf said. She was scared. During her years in America, she told me, Somalia had changed profoundly. Recently, al-Shabab had stopped her sister while she was running an errand in town because her face was not covered with a veil. The mother and her daughters waited in dread for the Islamists to decide that women could not run a refugee camp, or a hospital, because they considered such powerful female roles "un-Islamic."

"Mogadishu is way more religious," Dr. Waqaf said. She saw this especially in the growing presence of religious NGOs. Over the past decade, as the UN and other aid agencies moved to the Kenyan capital of Nairobi, and the conflict in Somalia dropped out of the Western headlines, Somalis had been left to fend for themselves. Religious NGOs—some from Saudi Arabia—stepped in. They now did most of the aid work, and used their funds to spread a more conservative, "Arabized" Islam. Some Saudi

NGOs, for example, gave women fifty dollars to wear traditional Islamic clothing. This was not unique to Somalia; in many conflict zones with significant numbers of Muslims—Chechnya, Afghanistan, the Balkans, Central Asia—aid workers brought religious revival along with bandages and high-protein biscuits, attempting to plant a more conservative strain of Islam while offering humanitarian aid. In Somalia, most doctors would not even tell patients that they had HIV, Dr. Waqaf said, because the diagnosis carried such a stigma. This shocked her, and she told the doctors so.

"Don't use your Western mentality here," they responded. "They'll kill you." This was not paranoia. Insurgents killed thirty-five aid workers in 2008. All of the international relief workers had fled. By 2010, the insurgents controlled the Afgooye Road and Dr. Hawa's camp was cut off from the outside world.

As in most wars, women bore the brunt of this conflict, mother and daughter explained. Partly as a result of rapes by militias, but also due to the new religious conservatism, women could not move as freely as they had in the past. As in Afghanistan under the Taliban, women could no longer travel alone. This new step backward for women scared Dr. Waqaf, and she was seeing an unusually high number of miscarriages; the reason, she said, was that some pregnant women were loath to seek medical care. Many women told her they'd stayed away from the doctor because the militias did not want women in the streets—or anywhere outside the home. This was not the Islam that Dr. Waqaf had grown up with. "The Prophet's wives were educated," she said. Until there was a state, things would get worse, her mother said. She retied her scarf over her surgical scar and got ready to go back to the operating room. "How many millions are being wasted on Somalia in other countries?" she asked. "Aid is a business."

The next afternoon I came across the aftermath of a food riot. A crowd had thrown stones at a man driving a sugar truck, striking him in the head and causing him to crash the truck. With cups and sacks and buckets, the looters took what they could before the "police" showed up. Many people were no longer eating every day, but the mayor continued with his plan to beautify the shattered city. He didn't begin with schools or feeding centers or hospitals, but with the central bank, which he painted robin's egg blue.

17

PROXY

Most of the spoilers, has-beens, and hangers-on who were controlling Somalia's proxy war were not in Somalia; they were holed up nearby, in the mile-and-a-half-high, modernist city Asmara, the capital of Eritrea. Asmara's boulevards are lined with airy Bauhaus villas, which Benito Mussolini built in the 1920s and '30s when he attempted to establish an African empire here. Now all but forgotten, Asmara has become a sar-cophagal city, a legacy of empire's febrile dreams. In one of those blunt and boxy Fascist-era villas, Sheikh Hassan Dahir Aweys, the militant com-mander whom the United States named as a wanted man on November 7, 2001, for his connections to Al Qaeda, was living in open hiding. I paid him an unexpected visit in April 2008.

That summer it was practically impossible for an American citizen to procure a visa to Eritrea. The State Department was threatening to name Eritrea as a state sponsor of terrorism for hosting Sheikh Aweys, and when I went to the consulate in neighboring Kenya, the Eritrean consul general looked at my U.S. passport and then at me. "*You* cannot apply," he said, apologizing, and then offering me an espresso.

So I turned to a fellow American citizen living in Asmara: Hussein Farah Aideed, the son of the notorious warlord Mohammed Farah Aideed, whose militia had shot down the two American Black Hawk helicopters in 1993. The younger Aideed, forty-two, belonged to a group called the Alli-ance for the Restoration of Somalia, which opposed the ongoing Ethio-pian occupation. He was living in Asmara on the Eritrean government's dime, plotting to kick Ethiopia out of Somalia. But the alliance was com-ing apart at the very moment I arrived in Asmara. One faction, led by Sheikh Sharif Sheikh Ahmed, was becoming more moderate and willing to negotiate with the United States over Somalia's future. Soon he would become president, and so was distancing himself from hard-liners by moving to Djibouti. The other faction, led by Aideed's cousin, Sheikh Hassan Dahir Aweys, refused to negotiate with America, and it was stuck in Asmara. By accident, not conviction, Aideed had ended up as a part of the less-powerful group in Asmara. He hoped that an American reporter like me might bring him much-needed recognition, so he procured me a visa with a few phone calls to high places.

Eritrea and Ethiopia, governed by cousins, loathe each other. They are the Hatfields and McCoys of East Africa. Eritrea won its independence from Ethiopia only in 1993; the two are still fighting over their borders. Here, national borders *do* matter, and matter greatly. To undermine Ethiopia, Eritrea was willing to pay for hotel rooms and a breakfast buffet for the Somali opposition indefinitely. This included Aideed, a complicated figure whose mixed-up identity as a Somali, a political refugee, an American citizen, a U.S. Marine, a warlord, and, briefly, in name, Somalia's president, made him a toothy, shambling objective correlative for the maddening chaos of Somalia.

More as a court jester than as a king, Hussein Aideed was being dragged through history. He was sixteen when his father was caught scheming to topple Siad Barre's government and thrown into a Somali prison. Shortly after, Hussein Aideed and his family fled to Washington, D.C., as political refugees. They were granted U.S. citizenship and moved from D.C. to West Covina, California, east of Los Angeles, where Hussein Aideed attended both high school and Glendora Community College, learned to cha-cha, and became proficient in martial arts. During high school, he joined the Marine Reserves and hosted weekend barbecues for his fellow soldiers. He was working as a civil engineer at West Covina's City Hall in 1990 when he was shipped out to Kuwait during Operation Desert Storm. He spent 257 days there, and after the U.S.-led coalition's victory in Kuwait, Hussein went back to his desk job at City Hall. In August 1992 he said he was tapped to become a Marine interpreter in Mogadishu. The once-picturesque tourist town, with glittering piazzas and al fresco bars, lay in ruins as a result of the civil war his father was then fighting for control of the city against an archrival, another clan-leader-cum-businessman-cum-warlord named Ali Mahdi Mohamed. When relations soured between the United States and Mohammed Farah Aideed, the Marines sent Hussein back to West Covina. He returned to his engineering job at City Hall, while his father masterminded a battle against America in Mogadishu's streets. It was not easy to have the last name Aideed, and in his bulky frame, two rival identities—embattled Somali and U.S. Marine—squeezed in next to each other, like hostile strangers on the same subway train. "It was like *Apocalypse Now*," Aideed told me of that dark time when I finally met him in Asmara. In 1995, he returned to Somalia to marry a Somali. "I came back just to say hello and get a blessing from my father," he said. But seven months later his father was assassinated, and Hussein took over the leadership of part of the clan, and even, briefly, the title of president—for what it was worth.

The nature of power had changed in Somalia. Blood still mattered, but the cold war era of African big men was over. Without the funding from the Soviet Union and the United States, would-be leaders were searching for new claims to power. Now for the first time in history, religious authority was the most important credential for leadership. Even Aideed, the Marine and cha-cha aficionado, was looking to shore up his religious credentials. In the ongoing scramble for power, Islamic authority was de rigueur.

When we met on a bracing spring day in Asmara, Aideed wanted to take me on a walking tour of the seemingly deserted city of glass. At nearly eight thousand feet above sea level, the city's thin, dry air lifted the hem of his flowing white robe. He lumbered down the staircase of the enormous Italianate Great Mosque, another of Mussolini's projects, built in the hope of winning Muslim approval for his African empire.

Aideed, like most devout Sufis, prayed five times a day. He'd come late to Islam, and was taking online classes with a Sufi study group called the Straight Path. The downloaded lessons were part of a larger, progressive mystical Islamic awakening, one more entry in the global religious marketplace. Aideed believed that promoting Sufism, with its tolerance and mysticism, would help to safeguard the continent against Sunni Arab extremism, which seemed to be gaining ground in war-torn Somalia. These radicalized newcomers disdained Sufi practices. And blood meant nothing to them. "They say you Muslims are not Muslims," Aideed said. Who were *they* to claim what true Islam was?

From the mosque, Aideed and I forged steeply uphill along Haile Mariam Mammo Street. Out of the corner of my eye, I watched elegant old men in hand-tailored suits sip espresso at open-air cafés. (At a glance, the scene seemed idyllic, yet the espresso was probably all the men would consume that day.)

And President Isaias Afwerki, a rebel hero turned tyrant, kept his shipping-container prisons far away from the boulevards. In those prisons, Afwerki routinely imprisoned evangelicals, Pentecostals, Jehovah's Witnesses, and some Muslims, calling all of their practices a threat to religious stability in a country nearly evenly balanced between Christianity and Islam. (Really, he feared any religion's ability to mobilize against him.) In Eritrea, reliable religious statistics are impossible to obtain, since the state officially recognizes only four faiths: Islam, Coptic (Orthodox) Christianity, Roman Catholicism, and traditional (not evangelical) Protestant sects. All other forms of worship are illegal. Religious repression is so virulent in Eritrea that in September 2005, the Bush administration took the first-ever action under the International Religious Freedom Act and imposed new sanctions against military aid to Eritrea.

At the top of the hill, on Harnet Avenue, we could see the dark brick spire of the Orthodox Cathedral (another gift of Mussolini's). Heading toward the cathedral, we passed a white-tiled façade inlaid with a large Star of David, its padlocked gates painted UN blue. It was a synagogue, constructed in 1905 and still maintained by sixty-two-year-old Samuel Cohen, an Asmara native and the youngest of Eritrea's few surviving Jews. This community had swelled to five hundred during the 1950s, with Jews coming from as far as Sudan and Yemen. Although the Greek-style façade had been recently scrubbed, Cohen was nowhere to be found. The tended-to tiles were still a reminder that despite the current government's oppression, the three Abrahamic faiths—Judaism, Christianity, and Islam, in that order—had existed peaceably for more than a thousand years in the Horn of Africa. In the Bible's first Book of Kings, this relationship begins with Solomon, the ancient king of Israel, and the queen of Sheba, Ethiopia, as the Greeks called the Land of the Blacks. (The Quran also tells a similar story, in 27:22.) In the biblical version, from her African kingdom that stretched into Yemen, Sheba hears of Solomon's devotion to God. Skeptical and curious about his faith, she loads her camels with spices, "and very much gold, and precious stones," and heads north for Jerusalem to meet King Solomon and "to prove him with hard questions."

And when the queen of Sheba had seen all the wisdom of Solomon, the house that he had built, the food on his table, the seating of his servants,

the service of his waiters and their apparel, his cupbearers, and his entryway by which he went up to the house of the LORD, there was no more
spirit in her. Then she said to the king: "It was a true report which I heard
in mine own land about your words and your wisdom" [1 Kings 10:4–6].

The queen of Sheba converted to Judaism on the spot, which meant
that her subjects did, too. Although the Bible does not mention any romantic relationship between them, Ethiopian tradition holds that Solomon fell in love with the virgin queen on sight, and tricked her into
sleeping with him. She gave birth to a son, Menelik, and sent him to Solomon for his education. Menelik I became the king of Axum in today's
Ethiopia. For hundreds of years, his Jewish descendants worshipped the
God of Israel—until, in the fourth century, a slave named Frumentius
of Tyre (Lebanon) converted the king, and much of his kingdom, to
Christianity.

In the ancient capital of Axum, farmers uncovered a seven-foot-high
roadside stone in 1981. It chronicles one King Ezana, who ruled the kingdom from 330 to 356. The stone is inscribed with Ezana's declaration of
his Christian faith, and his demand for tribute from all who pass along the
stretch of the now-forgotten road that once linked Africa to the faraway
kingdoms of Arabia and Jerusalem.

While King Ezana's conversion is a matter of historical record, the
union between King Solomon and the queen of Sheba, and the birth of
their son, remains the stuff of legend. Still, Ethiopia's modern emperor,
Haile Selassie, and today's Orthodox Christian leaders have relied on this
legend to legitimize their authority. Its most powerful symbol still rests in
Axum. Unseen by human eyes save those of its keeper, a guardian monk,
lies an ancient relic that Ethiopians believe to be the Ark of the Covenant,
carried by their Jewish forebears from Jerusalem thousands of years ago.

From Judaism to Christianity to Islam—the most important bond
forged between Christians and Muslims in East Africa dates as far back
as the Prophet Mohammed's lifetime. In 615, when Mohammed had
to flee his hometown of Mecca, he sent his family to the Christian king
of the Ethiopian empire, then called Abyssinia (yet another name for
Land of the Blacks), for safekeeping. In thanks, he warned his followers
not to attack the East African Christians, according to the following
Hadith: "Leave the Abyssinians alone, so long as they do not take the
offensive!"[1]

And for more than a thousand years, as Muslim traders from Egypt, Yemen, and Oman, among other places, arrived along the east coast of Africa, they coexisted peacefully with Christians out of respect for the fact that an African Christian king had once saved the Prophet's family from death at the hands of fellow Arabs.

Somali Muslims have waged jihad against their Christian neighbors only twice. First in the sixteenth century, then from 1899 to 1920, under the banner of a Sufi reformer and persuasive poet, Mohammed Abdullah Hassan, known as "the Mad Mullah." Alarmed by the Christian influence in Somalia under the British, Hassan founded an army of dervishes who aimed to drive the infidels into the sea. Hassan was the third and last of Africa's Sufi teachers—like Uthman dan Fodio in Nigeria, and Sudan's Mahdi Muhammad Ahmad Abdullah before him—to wage a major African jihad, until today.

A familiar Somali hero, or antihero, depending on whom you asked, was emerging in 2008. His name is Sheikh Hassan Dahir Aweys, and when Ethiopia invaded Somalia in 2006, he fled to the coast with his fighters, dodged American air strikes, and disappeared, only to resurface in Asmara a year later. After months in hiding, he was the guest of the Eritrean government—much to the dismay of the United States. Aweys led a homegrown Islamist movement that had begun in the seventies, when a group of influential sheikhs opposed Siad Barre as un-Islamic because his "Family Law" gave equal rights to women. When Barre executed the sheikhs for being "religiously backward," many young Somalis came to believe that their religion was the only solution to Barre's godless "scientific socialism." University students traveled to Cairo, Karachi, and Riyadh on secret Islamic scholarships; others went to Afghanistan to fight in the anti-Soviet jihad. Aweys became their icon, in part because of his historic relationship with Al Qaeda.

Al Qaeda's first-ever attempted attack on Americans occurred in 1992, when bin Laden blew up a hotel in Yemen where U.S. soldiers were billeted on the way to Somalia. (Fortune had it that the Americans had already left.) The group's direct relationship with Somalia—and with Aweys—began when a dozen or so of Osama bin Laden's operatives, called the Africa Corps, arrived in Somalia from Sudan in late January 1993. Al Qaeda agreed to fund Aweys's now-defunct organization al-Ittihad al-

Islami (AIAI), which promoted Islamic law in Somalia. In return, Aweys's group helped the Africa Corps start terrorist training camps in southern Somalia, where Al Qaeda struggled from the start. The salaries it offered didn't compare with what Somalis could earn as freelance gunmen working for warlords. And the "spiritual benefits package"—the millennial brand of faith that guaranteed heaven to those willing to fight and die for the faith—meant nothing to Somalis who did not buy into the movement's violent Islamist ideology. In letters seized by U.S. intelligence and analyzed by the Combating Terrorism Center at West Point, the Africa Corps's operatives, who traveled from neighboring Sudan to Somalia, couldn't get cells up and running, and complained about the cheap and lazy Somalis who were willing to let their wives starve to death rather than kill their cattle. Al Qaeda and the Africa Corps never found a foothold in Somalia. Costs outweighed benefits. A handful of Al Qaeda members still used Somalia as a base, including the Comorian Fazul Abdullah Mohammed, the alleged mastermind of the 1998 U.S. embassy bombings in neighboring Kenya and Tanzania, as well as the 2002 attack on the Paradise Hotel. Most such fighters, however, decamped for Kenya. Weak states, not failed ones, serve terrorists best.

Aideed and I climbed into a tiny taxi to meet Sheikh Aweys in the once-swank diplomatic section of Asmara called Tripolo. We were early. From behind the gate of the compound came a boy's voice; then a man in wire-rimmed glasses and a blue tracksuit opened the door. Aweys grinned hello. It was the same rictus that stared out from his wanted photo on the U.S. terrorist watch list, his hair and beard the same Halloween hue of pumpkin henna.

He welcomed us inside the empty government villa, and then excused himself. I heard voices and wandered down the hall. Behind a half-opened door, four women sat on beds, minding small children. The youngest of these mothers was one of the sheikh's wives. She hated Asmara and missed Mogadishu, she explained, while rocking a newborn baby. The conversation—a little English spattered with Arabic punctuated by gestures—was a bit like bilingual charades. She worked to communicate to me that there was something about the altitude that was making her sick; the baby had been born too early. A boy of four or five chased a smaller girl around the room, pretending he was a lion. "Halas, Osama," his mother said half-heartedly. *Osama, enough!*

Aweys appeared at the bedroom door—he had changed from the blue tracksuit into a white robe—and led me back to the parlor, where he served popcorn and tea. He also set up his laptop computer and a microphone to record our conversation, showing me how my voice leaped across the screen. It was a gesture of accountability, and an attempt at intimidation. I nodded earnestly and crunched popcorn into the microphone to make the electronic needle spike. Inevitably, talk turned to Al Qaeda.

"Let's assume I met with Al Qaeda. Is there a sin in it?" he asked. I held my tongue as Aideed translated for his cousin. "Al Qaeda was a small baby. My commitment was much bigger," he said.

The sheikh's infamy was local, not global, he strained to tell me, as he recounted the heroic story of his own life, including a near execution in 1986, when Siad Barre sentenced Aweys to death by firing squad. (He was saved when other international Muslim leaders intervened.) The question of Christianity in a Muslim land was a tricky one, he said, recounting an incident during the early nineties when he was working at the Mogadishu port and found a shipping container full of Bibles delivered as relief supplies. He took the Bibles—Bibles!—to Hussein Aideed's father to prove what the Westerners were secretly up to. Hussein grinned and nodded in agreement. I tried to catch his eye, but he gazed back at me unseeing, as if he had slipped into a role of devotion, or maybe favorite son, for the ease of it. He told me later that Aweys was one of his father's closest allies, and a respectable sheikh, who, like his father, had been misunderstood by history.

Aweys protested that he did not belong on the U.S. terrorist watch list just because he had met with Al Qaeda and was in charge of a few militant groups. Okay, so perhaps his followers launched several attacks on Ethiopian soil over the years, but he had never taken action against America. Still, he refused to denounce Al Qaeda—a demand he says the West uses to divide Muslims. "The hammer and big stick coming from the West affects all Muslims," he said. The more the West attacked Somalia, the more Muslims around the world would unify against America.

He led me to the door of the villa. His son Osama was playing on the stairs outside. "Osama?" I asked, pointing to his son. His eyes widened in alarm: oh no, he explained, his son was not named for Osama bin Laden, but for Osama bin Zayd, one of the Prophet Mohammed's adopted sons, who, by the age of twenty-seven, became a famous general.

Returning to Somalia's battlefield in April 2009, a year after our meeting, Sheikh Aweys took command of a new militant group called Hizbul Islam, "the Islamic Party." He turned his self-proclaimed jihad against the five thousand African Union peacekeeping troops from Uganda and Burundi stationed in Somalia. Calling the peacekeepers "bacteria," Aweys fought alongside al-Shabab to destroy the African Union troops and defeat his former friend and the Islamic Courts Union political chief, Sheikh Sharif Sheikh Ahmed. With UN and U.S. support, Sheikh Ahmed had become Somalia's latest transitional president in January 2009. (On August 6, 2009, as a gesture of U.S. support, Sheikh Ahmed met with Secretary of State Hillary Clinton.) Disgruntled, Sheikh Hassan Dahir Aweys claimed that his former ally had become an American patsy, and in late February 2009, he joined forces with al-Shabab in a vicious battle against the African Union troops, killing nearly fifty peacekeepers and wounding three hundred more. Inevitably, as the new fissures between Sufis and Sunnis continued to branch, the militant groups splintered and began to fight one another, too.

18

"GATHER YE MEN OF TOMORROW"

The Peace Hotel, where I stayed in Mogadishu in 2007 and 2008, flew eight white flags as a symbol of its neutrality. Its manager, Bashir Yusef Osman, thirty-three and unmarried, had fended for himself in the midst of a civil war for the past seventeen years. His family, like many of Somalia's wealthy families, had gone to America and Canada during the fighting, but he had stayed on to oversee their interests. Wearing Timberland boots and a caterpillar mustache, Osman could have been a Brooklyn hipster—a savvy everyman in any culture.

"Most of the ones who have left, they think they are going to make it big in the States," he said. "But they end up cleaning toilets." In an inversion of Mogadishu's wartime remittance economy, Osman sent money abroad to keep the family afloat. His cousin Jamma, who was about the same age, had recently returned from Canada to help Osman run the hotel for a few months. Although he was terrified, Jamma could not refuse to lend Osman a hand. Jamma owed him.

Jamma was slight and as big-eared as a field mouse. He anxiously twirled his cufflinks, which were custom-made in Canada and embossed with the Somali flag: a white five-pointed star against a pale blue background. The color was United Nations blue. The familiar hue was a reminder of its lack of national identity inherent in the patchwork of colonial borders. Now that the borders no longer applied, religion was filling the space they'd left behind. The points on the star reminded Somalis of their cousins living beyond the nation's five borders—especially those in the Ogaden region of Ethiopia, where that country was starving its own Muslim population.

Convinced that he was going to be shot at any moment, Jamma kept repeating, "It's all good, it's all good." An obvious outsider, he was hoping that his cufflinks would keep him safe if he were caught in a tight spot;

they were both a mark of his allegiance to Somalia and easy lucre for a bribe.

Jamma hated guns and the culture of guns. "These insurgents would just as soon shoot me. I am much more like you," he said one May afternoon in 2008, as we sat in the back of Osman's Corolla waiting for our armed security guards to lead the way into the colonial patch of town by the sea.

That afternoon, like most, Osman drove. We were headed to meet the prime minister, and to visit a Catholic cathedral I had seen on a postcard near his office. Osman was the only one cool enough to handle the ever-changing checkpoints, all of which seemed to be manned by armed teenagers, surly boys too small to fill whatever piece of camouflage "uniform" they had managed to cadge. The gunmen belonged to the clan of Prime Minister Gedi, a former veterinarian who has since been ousted from power. Gedi was, to put it bluntly, an Ethiopian stooge, and his transitional government had retriggered old tribal animosities. We were stopped every block until we reached the ex–Italian colony, which a Somali friend of mine dubbed the Lime Zone (to Baghdad's Green Zone). The failing government had hunkered down here in a last-ditch effort to protect itself. Curious boys peered into the car as we drove past. Seeing a foreigner—and a woman—they puffed out their child-size chests. I fixed my gaze beyond them to the sullen sea, and the fishmongers in a Romanesque piazza.

We passed the post office where the U.S. Army Rangers had barricaded themselves and were killed in 1993. We passed the U.S. embassy where the two childless widows were squatting. We passed the old sea wall along which Osman and Jamma's family had once kept a bar. And we passed mounds and mounds of rubble of every kind: stone, garbage, and indistinguishable waste. Trash hung in the trees like bleached prayer flags, or a doll's laundry.

"Friday night, this place was packed," Jamma said, recalling the boozy fun of more than twenty years ago. We had stopped briefly to look through a hole blasted in an old stone wall. Through it we could see a square of dance floor, and beyond that, a beach, where music used to spill into the surf at night. (I had seen a postcard of this same beach with Italians in shorts and bare chests strolling across the white sand.) "Look at what God gave to us and people are missing," he said.

A little farther down the road, the cathedral we had come to see had been blasted into stone toothpicks; its spires looked like bleached bone shards splashed with cerulean paint, it seemed, to indicate heaven.

Prime Minister Gedi was waiting for us in a second-floor office in the three blocks of the old city his government was able to hold. "There are terrorist elements hiding in this city," he said as we sat in leatherette chairs. His favorite argument, like that of his Ethiopian ally President Meles Zenawi, was that Al Qaeda was "a clear and present danger." His second-favorite argument was that the Islamists were "human rights violators," which he seemed to believe, and which was sure to catch the attention of an American journalist. "The United States is *very* cooperative," he said. "Somalia is a very important country from a geopolitical point of view in the war on terror."

A few hours after we left, a suicide bomber crashed a truck through his office gates, killing six people in the parking lot and injuring ten more. The bomber's hand was left hanging from a tree. The prime minister was rushed to an undisclosed location. It was the fourth attempt on his life. Soon after, my phone rang. It was Prime Minister Gedi looking for me. An assassination attempt was an unparalleled opportunity for spin. "This bombing will make the international community pay attention," he said hopefully, connecting the ideological dots lest I miss them. "It is the mark of Al Qaeda." I listened, not saying that it would take much more than a suicide bombing against Ethiopia's man in Mogadishu to get America's attention.

That night, a salty wind lifted the hotel's eight white flags from their posts. After a supper of scored halves of mango and *zuppa di verdura*—Gigi, the cook, was Italian-trained—I sat at the sole table in the empty parking lot. Dini, the hotel's assistant manager, strolled outside to show me old newsreels he had bought in the market. They were from the time of Black Hawk Down, when his cousin, Mohammed Farah Aideed, had ruled the city. During the day, Dini served as the hotel's Internet guru, always futzing with a landline to find a miraculous connection. At night, he wore a yellow mesh tank top and a wraparound sarong. He wanted to be an entrepreneur like his boss, Osman. And like Osman, he was proud of his toys. His blinking phone, his streetwise getup, and his laptop all came from Dubai. He wanted to see how my laptop worked. A MacBook with iTunes might be worth another shopping trip, once things calmed down, *if* they calmed down, in Mogadishu. Those early days of occupation were like the first few of flu: Somalia was coming down with something and no one knew how bad it would be.

Despite having no government, Somalia had better telecommunications than most African countries, until the 2006 Ethiopian invasion. And Somalia had one of the most sophisticated informal banking sectors on the continent until after September 11, when the United States shut down the leading hawala company in Somalia, Al-Barakat. Hawala is a money transfer system—the Somali equivalent of Western Union—that made it possible for Somalis in America and elsewhere to send about $790 million annually home to their country. A man could walk into an office in Michigan and give the agent $1,000, and within a matter of hours, his mother in rural Somalia could pick up the cash from her local office. This money kept Somalia afloat until Hussein Farah Aideed claimed Al-Barakat was linked to Al Qaeda. The United States shut down the company, destroying Somalia's economy in the process. Alex de Waal, program director of the Social Science Research Council, refers to this act as "the equivalent of a financial carpet-bombing." The September 11 Commission never found a link between Al-Barakat and Al Qaeda. (Aideed, however, owed Al-Barakat $40,000.) The attackers, it turns out, hadn't used Somalia's hawala system to pay for 9/11; they'd used interbank wire transfers at the SunTrust Bank in Florida.

In the darkness, Dini scrolled through icons on his laptop, looking for the Somalia news footage. As he searched, my eye caught the name of another file: "Toora Boora [sic]," the name of America's largest battlefield in Afghanistan. "What are you doing with that?" I asked. Dini said nothing and pushed Play. On the screen, a Libyan named Sheikh Abu al-Lai'th al-Libi sat in the darkness before a campfire. The light glinted off his square pharmacist's glasses. He named the other men sitting around the fire, then lectured on the absolute oneness of God—*tawheed*—and talked about an upcoming operation in Shkai, a Pakistani village of South Waziristan on the Afghan border, where Al Qaeda had a training camp. (Mention of this border village gave me a start: I had been in Shkai during the spring of 2004, days after Pakistani troops bombed it. To punish a militant leader named Nek Muhammad for sheltering Al Qaeda, the Pakistanis had reduced the village to muddy craters. It looked like an archeological dig.) The video cut to a daytime scene of pairs of sweating men running some kind of wheelbarrow race up a rocky hill. Another cut in the video, and another activity. This time, chicken fights: one man mounted on the shoulders of another, grappling with his opponent on the grizzled slope. It was laughable, really, but lethal, too: these men were training to kill American soldiers. It was a rudimentary promotional video likely dated around 2004, nothing like the slick high-tech work of al-Shabab in 2009. A song played as a soundtrack in the background: "Gather ye men of tomorrow. Join hand in hand for an important and dangerous struggle . . ."

Dini then found the Black Hawk Down footage: Hussein's dad, Mohammed Farah Aideed, strutted along a hallway wearing a straw fedora. I recognized a pair of plaster swan planters from the Peace Hotel foyer. Rounds of failed peace talks had taken place where we were now sitting. Then Black Hawks whirred against the blue of a Mogadishu sky. Soon, some of these same Black Hawks would spin and fall.

Rapt, Dini leaned forward. His awe seemed to be less about Islam than about power and the human fascination with violence. These grainy images were the first public shaming of America in the Al Qaeda era. In essence, these were the first jihadi videos—the first moment the world order was shown to be shakable, when boys like Dini, shut out of the West's system, saw that the status quo could be punctured and America could be wounded. America could lose, even. After the eighteen U.S. Army Rangers died, Al Qaeda's correspondence begins to refer to the American squeamishness at losing soldiers as a "Vietnam complex," with bin Laden's recruits claiming responsibility for a victory they had little, if any, part in. "The youth were surprised at the low morale of the American soldiers and realized more than before that the American soldier was a paper tiger," bin Laden said later.[1] God, indeed, was the real superpower.

PART TWO

ASIA

INDONESIA

And whoever lives and believes in me shall never die.
—THE GOSPEL ACCORDING TO JOHN 11:26

Anyone, male or female, who does good deeds and is a
believer, will enter Paradise and will not be wronged by as
much as the dip in a date stone.
—THE QURAN, WOMEN 4:124

19

BEYOND JIHAD

A Muzak rendition of Beethoven's "Ode to Joy" echoed through the Jakarta airport's domestic terminal shortly after dawn on May 9, 2006. A forty-year-old man wearing knock-off Ray-Ban Wayfarers and an Al Jazeera baseball cap shuffled along with a large cardboard box poked with holes tucked under his arm. A minor celebrity within the world of international jihad, Farihin Ibnu Ahmad, aka "Yasir," was barely known outside of it. He was renowned for his violent pedigree, although few people other than militants would have recognized his broad, hangdog face. He sidled up to a plainclothes security officer and thrust the box toward him.

"Will the X-ray machine kill them?" he asked. The officer pulled back one of the box's dog-eared corners to reveal a pair of rabbits, mottled black and white, noses twitching wildly at the unfamiliar smells of stale coffee and perfume. Ibnu Ahmad (*ibnu* in Indonesian, like *bin* in Arabic, means "son of") wanted to know if he should check the rabbits or if he could carry them on the plane. The officer glanced up from the rabbits to Ibnu Ahmad's face, half hidden beneath the baseball cap. Though I was there to meet Ibnu Ahmad, I scooted furtively to the other side of the corridor, certain he was about to be arrested.

The rabbits should have been the least of the security officer's concerns: Ibnu Ahmad was a killer, and member of Jemaah Islamiyah, a lethal group of Southeast Asian militants most notorious for the 2002 Bali bombings, which left 202 people dead. The militants' ties to Al Qaeda were precisely through men like Ibnu Ahmad.

For generations, Ibnu Ahmad's family has been part of an Islamist movement—first opposing Western colonialism and later fighting for Indonesia to become an Islamic state. When he was sixteen, Ahmad's family offered him a choice: Did he want to be an Islamic teacher or a fighter? He chose to be a fighter, and in 1987 he shipped out to Al Qaeda's Al-Sadda camp in the saw-toothed, snowy mountains on the border between Afghanistan and Pakistan, to fight in the jihad against the Soviets. He learned to build explosives and heard a couple of sermons given by Abdullah Azzam, the Palestinian preacher who served as Osama bin Laden's spiritual mentor. Azzam believed that every Muslim was duty bound to fight in—or pay for—global jihad until the holy lands of Islam were restored to their former glory. He preached that Islam's future lay in reviving its ideal, seventh-century past by whatever means necessary.

When Ibnu Ahmad returned to Indonesia in the nineties, he brought with him a bloody, millenarian worldview intended to overthrow the secular government, and a network of contacts. In Jakarta, the nation's buzzing capital, he became one of Jemaah Islamiyah's most ardent deputies. In 1996, when Khalid Shaikh Mohammed, one of the architects of the 9/11 attacks, visited Jakarta, Ibnu Ahmad served as his tour guide. He did the personal bidding of Hambali (aka Riduan bin Isomuddin, known as Al Qaeda's kingpin in Southeast Asia), and he helped plan an attack on the American embassy in Jakarta.

"The instruction was to drive a suicide truck into the U.S. embassy, or get a helicopter to bomb them from above," Ibnu Ahmad said. The plan, apparently, did not work out. His surveillance photographs of the embassy building proved too blurry to show to Al Qaeda higher-ups in Afghanistan. In August 2000, the group ended up bombing the Philippine ambassador's residence instead, killing two Indonesians and injuring the ambassador. Most recently, Ibnu Ahmad was imprisoned twice for waging jihad against Christians on the island of Sulawesi, one of the largest of the seventeen thousand islands that make up Indonesia's vast archipelago.

With 240 million people, 8 of 10 of whom are Muslims, Indonesia is the most populous Muslim country in the world. (Protestants make up about 6 percent of the rest of population; Catholics, 3 percent; Hindus, less than 5 percent.) Indonesia is also a vibrant young democracy, which held its first presidential elections only in 2004. In 1998, after thirty-two years in power, the strong centralized government of President Suharto collapsed and political power spread to the outlying islands. On Sulawesi, power became something worth fighting for, and Christians and Muslims began to battle over local elections. As in Nigeria (where military dictatorship ended in 1999), in Indonesia's wobbly new democracy, political and religious affiliations soon reinforced one another.

Once the religious violence began, Ibnu Ahmad traveled by boat to Sulawesi to train his Muslim brothers in how to fight a guerrilla war against infidels. His training in Afghanistan hadn't been about killing Christians, however, but about overthrowing the secular government. Back at home in Indonesia, there were arguments among the militants as to whether these skirmishes were the right ones to fight. Ibnu Ahmad went to Sulawesi anyway, where he was caught carrying thirty-one thousand rounds of ammunition, tried, convicted, and imprisoned. He wasn't interested in talking about the electroshock or waterboarding he was subjected to in prison. "My brain doesn't work right—it's like a broken computer," was all he would say. But evidence of his treatment seemed all too visible in his absent stares and broken teeth.

Apparently the security officer at the Jakarta airport didn't recognize Ibnu Ahmad: after allowing the rabbits to be checked, he let him go without incident. Ibnu Ahmad strolled back across the gleaming terminal to where I stood with Zamira Loebis, a journalism professor and *Time* reporter in her forties, who was traveling along with us to interpret. From beneath her blunt bob, Loebis's eyes found mine in disbelief that Ibnu Ahmad had been allowed to check the rabbits as luggage. An animal lover, she had a household full of cats and dogs; she'd even rescued two parrots from different religious battlegrounds. (One could say, "Allahu Akbar!"; the other, "Alleluia!")

These rabbits were a gift for Ibnu Ahmad's newborn son and his second wife, Farhia, twenty-eight, whom he had met while still in prison on Sulawesi, where the three of us were headed this morning. "Fathers used to come to the prison to marry their daughters off to us," he said wistfully.

Otherwise, Ibnu Ahmad was broke. This is where I came in. For the price of his plane ticket home, and the chance to see his wife and child, he was going to show me how he had grafted a war of worlds onto this local conflict. He missed the days when he was a folk hero, when the difference between good and evil was glaringly clear, when identity and ideology were as simple as fear, a face mask, and the scrawl of a cross or a crescent on a wall. For the past two years, lack of funding and divisions over the meaning of jihad had been tearing Jemaah Islamiyah militants apart, and their beliefs and tactics seemed to have lost favor among local people and prospective recruits. Several months before our trip, three Christian teenage girls had been beheaded on Sulawesi while walking to school; one's head, wrapped in a black plastic bag, was dropped on the front step of a local church. A fourth teenager, Noviana Malewa, had also been attacked, but survived. No one had been arrested yet for these crimes, but most thought the attackers must have come from among the hard-core fighters such as Ibnu Ahmad. Now the former heroes were pariahs.

On the flight to Sulawesi, Ibnu Ahmad listened to John Lennon's "Imagine" over and over through a pair of flimsy earphones. "Al Jazeera," he would joke from time to time, pointing to his cap. He liked to tease me about the differences between our two worlds, which he viewed as being in opposition: America and I and all Christians on one side, he and Al Jazeera and the world's Muslims on the other. The conflict in Indonesia, however, was much more complicated. Every government arm that received counterterrorism funding from the international community—namely the United States and Australia—had a stake in the ongoing conflict. It was clear that the conflict had little to do with religion per se and everything to do with competition over who controlled the local government and, by extension, the economy. These realities hadn't occurred to Ibnu Ahmad, who clung to his worldview and the peace of mind it seemed to provide him, oblivious to the fact that the rest of his country, had moved beyond the jihad he thought he was fighting.

Ibnu Ahmad's rabbits were shivering but alive when they came out of baggage claim, their brown fur spiked like hedgehog quills. We were in Palu, Central Sulawesi's main city; the dingy airport was full of scowling men in sunglasses and short-sleeve button-down shirts, the universal uniform of intelligence. Along with jungle rot and sea brine, menace hung in the moist air. Palu felt like a place of exile and disappearances.

Palu lies about sixty miles south of the equator, at almost the same latitude as Mogadishu, which is five thousand miles to the west, over the Indian Ocean. These are the fattest, lowest latitudes; the heart of Aristotle's Torrid Zone. The soil was the color of saffron, as if egg yolk had been beaten into the ground. Here, as in Nigeria, tropical rainstorms had leached the gumbo of all minerals but iron, and the ground was so vibrant it almost pulsed with what it could grow, which was why it was soaked in blood. By the paved road, farmers dried cloves on a blanket—the same cloves that had brought the Spanish and Portuguese to these islands five hundred years earlier. But cacao, which the Spanish brought from the Americas to Southeast Asia, was the real gold now.

Ibnu Ahmad had managed to secure himself a small cacao field out behind the shack where his second wife, Farhia, had lived a few years earlier in the midst of the fighting. The night we arrived, Zamira Loebis and I went to meet her. Farhia's broad face opened when she saw us. Then she returned to chasing the baby around the shack floor; he had begun to crawl since Ibnu Ahmad last saw him. Spying the rabbits, the baby shrieked gleefully, grabbed a dinner plate, and dragged it along in one small hand. *"Clinchi, clinchi,"* Ibnu Ahmad repeated the Indonesian word for "rabbit." Reaching one rabbit, the baby took the edge of the plate and drove it into the fur between the animal's skull and shoulders. He was trying to lop off its head with this makeshift ceramic guillotine. Ibnu Ahmad beamed. He planned to send this son to a Jemaah Islamiyah school, where he would learn to fight as his father had

Early the next morning, we hired a young driver in an old Land Cruiser to take us to Poso, Ibnu Ahmad's former battleground. The road snaked southward along the coast; as we approached Poso, where most of the fighting had occurred, the conflict's lines were disturbingly easy to see. The Muslims, mostly fishermen and traders, lived by the sooty ocean; the Christians lived inland, where the island rose, like the spine of a sleeping creature, up a steep green ridge. The fighting had sharply segregated the two communities, reestablishing the colonial-era patterns of coastal Muslims ringing inland Christians.

With a stranger from Palu driving, we stopped to pick up a local guide, who would ride with us and serve as negotiator in case anything went awry. An odd man, shrunken like a dried date and unable to stop talking, he crowed with a sycophant's delight when he spied Ibnu Ahmad in the rear of the Land Cruiser. Ibnu Ahmad, it turned out, had commanded him on Sulawesi battlefields. "We all fought," he shrugged. "Even the mayor was involved. You'd be lying if you said you didn't."

The man's nom de guerre was Hunter (others included Marlboro, Jet Li, and Osama). He was shrouded in a robe that looked like a maroon tablecloth, with a matching napkin on his head—a polyester costume that made him resemble an extra from a Bollywood remake of *Lawrence of Arabia*. "I prepared my outfit for men," he said in defensive apology, his eyes falling on Loebis and me. The robe was meant to show his Yemeni roots, though it was like no outfit I had ever seen in Yemen, or anywhere else. In the early days of Islam, many Muslim sailors, missionaries, and traders had come to Southeast Asia from the Hadhramaut in southern Yemen. Some present-day Hadhramis claimed descent from the Prophet; others, from Muslim traders from along the east coast of Africa. Osama bin Laden's ancestors migrated to Arabia from this bleak and rough region—a fact of which Hunter was especially proud, for it, like his robes, suggested a distinguished Arab lineage, and his corresponding fantasy of authority.

We approached the charred remains of Sepe, a Christian village that Ibnu Ahmad had attacked in December 2000. The Christians were gone now, Hunter explained: they had fled, first selling their land to their enemies at rock-bottom prices. (The Muslims who'd lived in predominantly Christian villages inland were forced to do the same.) Ibnu Ahmad remained silent in the back, earbuds plugged into his ears. The music was loud enough that John Lennon's plaintive keen whined like a gnat in the car.

Mangroves had reclaimed most of the five hundred abandoned wooden houses. Relics of a massacre moldered among the tree roots. A whitewashed wall painted with a blue cross read, *"Dani Jesus,"* or "Jesus Lives." Next to it, someone had drawn a competing peace sign in green paint, and written "Islam" beneath it. The meaning was clear: Islam means peace. But there was no peace here. On one side of the road a steep hillside marked the beginning of what was now Christian territory; on the other, the Muslims' wooden shacks clustered along the edge of the pigeon gray sea. The two worlds met along the sandy road, where Muslims were beginning to rebuild. Up the ridge, in predominantly Christian communities, the pattern was happening in reverse. No one wanted to risk living among people who would turn against him the instant trouble started. Safety lay only in being a part of a larger whole, in numbers.

As we drove the beachside road slowly in Sepe, the newly arrived Muslims looked up from their piles of lumber and stared into the car to see who was driving by. Hunter grinned and waved; he was proud to be seen with foreigners. Ibnu Ahmad slid down on his jump seat, seemingly ashamed of the havoc he had wreaked; so much for the conquering hero.

The engine idled, but no one got out of the car.

Ibnu Ahmad reluctantly pulled the earbuds from his ears and pointed a stubby finger toward the overgrown hillside. This was part of our deal: he would map the battlefield for me. Now that we were here, he did not want to detail what he had done. In a monotone, he began, "On December 23, 2000, I came down that hill with twenty-five fighters I'd trained." Our driver, who didn't know him or his story, fell quiet. "We went at nighttime and infiltrated. Sometimes it went wrong and we burned the wrong houses. It was easy to make mistakes and kill the wrong people."

Fighting in this steaming, sleepy village was much more difficult than in Afghanistan, he reasoned. In Afghanistan, the Mujahideen stood at a distance from their Soviet enemies, who were dark blots against a snowy mountainside. Not here. In this kind of jihad, the holy warrior saw the face of every man he killed. The victim would sweat and weep and plead his innocence, with his wife and children around the kitchen table, watching Ibnu Ahmad's face for a flicker of mercy that never came.

"Muslims were being oppressed," he argued against the air-conditioned silence. It was the Christians' fault, he added vaguely. Plus, he and his cadres had burned only a few houses. Within two years of that first attack, his colleague Omar Al-Faruq, an Al Qaeda operative, returned to burn the rest of the five hundred houses in Sepe. The goal of this bloodshed, Ibnu Ahmad tried to explain, had been to drive the Christians out of Sulawesi entirely, so as to establish a safe base—a *qoidah aminah*—from which his colleagues could rebuild the perfect-seeming past of the seventh century.

"The first step of jihad" is what Ibnu Ahmad called this *qoidah aminah*. "It's what the Prophet established in Medina." He had learned this during the eighties, in Afghanistan, from the Palestinian preacher Abdullah Azzam. *Qoidah* is the Indonesian word for "base"; in Arabic, it's *qaeda*.

As a safe base, Sulawesi offered a perfect staging ground for a holy guerrilla war, Ibnu Ahmad said. (Later, his former commander Nasir Abbas—a Jemaah Islamiyah leader who trained fighters in the nearby jungles of the Philippines, and who defected from the group after his arrest in April 2003—confirmed this account to me.) JI's plan was to forge the nations of Indonesia, Malaysia, Singapore, and Brunei, and the southern Philippines, into one Islamic megastate, using extraordinary acts of violence, such as the Christmas Eve church bombing in 2000 and then the Bali bombings. Sulawesi's long, gentle coastline provided ideal ground for landing boats in secret; its high verdant ridges, like their bleaker equivalent along the Afghan border, formed a perfect natural defense; and revenue from the booming chocolate market would soon fill their coffers, as Abbas, the reformed commander who planned this strategy, told me. Chocolate would be a source of terrorist funding, like opium in Afghanistan or diamonds in West Africa. But the plan didn't come off. The beheading of the three schoolgirls turned locals, Christian and Muslim alike, against the radical outsiders from JI, a shift in his status that Ibnu Ahmad was still struggling to comprehend.

During the long, sticky hours in the car, Ibnu Ahmad fell into a reverie for the good old days in Afghanistan. He seemed to find it easier to imagine himself as a hero there, wounded by Soviet shrapnel, than to recognize himself as a killer in Sepe. Mostly we compared notes about the craggy border between Afghanistan and Pakistan, and discussed the war he had "won" against the Soviets. "I miss it sometimes. It's a way to heaven." (Fittingly, he also liked the Led Zeppelin song "Stairway to Heaven.") There he had learned the radical Islamic teaching that a martyr bypasses the judgment of God, and that jihad is the shortcut—or escalator—to heaven.

Yet Ibnu Ahmad was disappointed in the direction the holy war had taken in Indonesia. JI had run short of cash: "When Hambali was here, there was plenty of money; now there's none," Ibnu Ahmad said. Hundreds of militants had been arrested, including Ibnu Ahmad. Ideological divisions were also ripping the group apart, especially the question of whether holy war allowed the killing of civilians. Although no one in JI liked to admit it, their bombings generally killed innocent bystanders: fellow Muslims, not enemies of Islam.

Ibnu Ahmad opposed the killing of fellow Muslims as a way of spreading radical Islam. In theory, he was intent on returning to the seventh-century way of life, dress, and devotion practiced by the Salafs, the first three generations of the Prophet's followers. Many Salafis, like Ibnu Ahmad, abhorred what was happening to contemporary jihad, because they believed these current struggles were political—not religious. For instance, fighting against the Indonesian government—fellow Muslims— was not religious, it was political, he argued. "Salafis don't get involved in politics," Ibnu Ahmad said. Jihad did not condone killing fellow Muslims. True Salafis, he believed, did not even use prayer mats when they knelt and faced Mecca, since these were a post-seventh-century innovation. The concept of what it meant to be a Salafi was splintering fast, between Salafi jihadis who employed unconditional violence and those who opposed such violence on the grounds that there was no supreme leader— no caliph—to sanction it.

Within his family, these rifts were emerging. Ibnu Ahmad's little brother Salahuddin, thirty, had been arrested on terrorism charges about a week before we left for Sulawesi, and Ibnu Ahmad was in anguish. Salahuddin's view was that anyone who did not espouse all-out war in the name of Islam was a kafir, an unbeliever, and every unbeliever must be killed. To Salahuddin, Ibnu Ahmad was such a kafir. Salahuddin now swore allegiance to a new leader, Noordin Top, the Malaysian-born head of a JI splinter group who espoused this ideology; Ibnu Ahmad called Top "a psychopath."

"Kill, kill, kill—he's destroying Indonesia," he said.

That afternoon we drove to Hunter's house for tea to be beyond prying eyes. Ibnu Ahmad could go almost nowhere on the island. Locals feared him; his fellow fighters knew that he had informed on them during his arrest and torture.

Hunter lived a hundred yards from the lapping waves of a small harbor. He had recently completed a second story on his wooden house—a large, empty veranda where he liked to nap in the afternoon with the sea stretching before him to the equator's hazy band. On the way, Ibnu Ahmad confessed one thing he hated about Afghanistan: the arrogance of the Arab fighters, who believed, by virtue of their Arab ethnicity, they were better Muslims than locals and Southeast Asian foreigners, including the Indonesians. "The Arabs were *zolim*," he said, which means "cruel" in Arabic. "They smoked, chased women, and ate unclean food," he said. "Arabs are the wickedest people on earth."

Hunter howled his approval. He, too, hated the attitude of those in Europe and the Middle East, be they Caucasian or Arab: it was the classic arrogance of those in the temperate zone couched in religious superiority. To me, this insulting of fellow believers sounded sacrilegious.

"It's not sacrilegious," Ibnu Ahmad answered. "It's in the Holy Quran. That's why the Prophet was sent down among the Arabs: to save the wickedest people on earth." Although it was unclear how he had arrived at this argument, Ibnu Ahmad said that the Quran's ninth chapter, "Repentance," supported his claim. In it, God instructs the Muslims on what to do with the Arab tribes that have broken their treaties and returned to the worship of many gods: "They have sold God's message for a trifling gain, and barred others from his path. How evil their actions are!" (9:9). According to Ibnu Ahmad, God was calling Arabs evil. Look at the Saudis, he said; they were the worst hypocrites. They tried to export Islamic law and practices to other places while letting their princes do whatever nasty things they wanted behind the closed doors of their desert palaces. He seemed to have extrapolated these ideas about who was a good Muslim and who was not from Al Qaeda's condemnation of the Saudi royal family. For bin Laden and the Arab fighters along the Pakistani border, the Saudi princes were Islam's worst enemies. Here in Indonesia, however, the battle lines were different: it was Christians, not fellow Muslims, who were cruel.

"Muslims don't have justice yet. If we don't get it yet, we'll rise up again," he warned no one in particular. He had stopped making sense. Ibnu Ahmad's febrile brain—that "broken computer," as he called it—was loaded with glitches. Hunter shifted his gaze out to sea; he was either bored or discreetly trying not to notice his leader's mounting confusion. Hunter had changed out of his ceremonial outfit and into a T-shirt and shorts.

Both men knew that of the two of them, Hunter was lower on the pecking order. After the war, many of the most brutal fighters, like Ibnu Ahmad, stayed on, started schools, and got married. Some were still trying to impose their "purer" seventh-century observance on the townspeople, and to cleanse the people of the syncretic taint of their mysticism and folk belief. When Ibnu Ahmad went downstairs to take a nap, Hunter confessed that no one admired Salafis like Ibnu Ahmad.

"They came and they stayed and they began to have an effect on our community," he said, and locals resented the puritanical way of life being foisted upon them, as well as the haughty lectures about being good Muslims. The worst part was that these conservatives were dividing Sulawesi's Muslim community by whipping up fervent youth in their schools against their more tolerant parents, and this was beginning to affect local culture.

Burying the dead, for instance, had become a controversial practice. The locals bathed and buried their dead as quickly as possible, as Islam mandates, yet they held a service afterward, with prayers and singing. This the Salafis abhorred, calling it *bidah*, or "innovation," and as such, it was expressly forbidden. Hunter did not agree. "The Salafis treat their bodies like animals," he said. The struggle over custom betrayed a deepening struggle over authenticity.

One day, the Salafi missionaries chided Hunter for wearing shorts to the mosque. "My house is less than one hundred feet from the mosque. I had time to get in and out of my shorts. I wore them deliberately to annoy them," he said. That day, he told them to mind their own business: true scholars should concern themselves with the Quran, not with clothing. "How many pages is the Quran? How many chapters? How many verses?" he asked them. These, he believed, were the basic truths any real Islamic scholar should know. When the missionaries could not answer him, he told them, "I'm already a Muslim. Go preach to nonbelievers."

Now on the terrace, he added, "Honestly, I don't know where they think they'll find nonbelievers in Indonesia, because we all have religions."

Hunter led me to the railing of the new veranda, which smelled of sawdust and salt. Before us, swells scudded across the cove. Turning his back to the sea, he pointed inland to where the dun-colored sand ended and a series of red switchbacks running up the drowsy green ridge began. The sandy edge marked the end of the Muslim fisherman's domain and the beginning of the inland Christian farmer's carnelian highland. "It's like the Berlin wall," Hunter said; the border between two ideologies. The shift from sand to loam reminded me of Africa's fault line. In Africa, however, the pale sand marked the beginning of the desert, where two kinds of land underlie divisions between peoples and religions. Here it marked the edge of the sea. Both sea and desert signified Islam, a religion spread by travel and trade over the Sahara, and over the Indian Ocean. Geography was religious destiny; like gangland turf, the changes in terrain told stories, spoke of divisions that outsiders could not see. To us, they were barely worth noticing, since we could cross and recross them at will. Yet for the locals, these boundaries were indelible, marking out matters of life and death. In Poso, Christians and Muslims used to intermarry. "I used to be married to a Christian," Hunter confessed. During the fighting, she had had a heart attack and died. Now he was on his own.

20

NOVIANA AND THE FIRING SQUAD

Late one spring afternoon in 2006 we took the road behind Hunter's veranda. It twitched back and forth up the green ridge for forty-three long
and lurching miles until, after dusk, we reached Tentena, a Christian
town in the highlands. Main Street looked deserted: an ominous, un-
friendly place trying to bar its doors against any more suffering. At three
thousand feet above the Molucca Sea, the jungle grew eerily cold and
dank; brackish clouds of rain and sea mist swung low through town like a
crowd of salty, ill-tempered ghosts. The Land Cruiser's high beams caught
a dog sleeping on the concrete doorstep of a shuttered mosque. Awakened
by the glare, he flashed his amber eyes in the dark and disappeared. If
there was ever a sign that there were no Muslims left in a once-integrated
town, it was this dog sleeping on the mosque doorstep. (Dogs are considered unclean in Islam.) From other small details, it was clear even at
night that the Muslims were gone. By day, the market's butchers slaugh-
tered pigs (also considered unclean). (When Dutch Protestant missionaries from the Netherlands Missionary Society arrived in Celebes—today's
Sulawesi—in 1892, they found that Islam had already "won" the coastal
kingdoms. They bushwhacked inland to convert the indigenous people,
and to halt Islam's spread. Discovering that the landlocked highlanders
already ate wild boar as their staple protein, the missionaries were able to
graft their theology onto local conditions.) Weird, disembodied choral
music rang through the empty market stalls. I thought there must be a
celebration going on nearby, maybe a wedding. Listening closer, however,
I heard William Blake. It was the hymn "Jerusalem": "Bring me my bow of
burning gold, / Bring me my arrows of desire, / Bring me my spear—O
clouds, unfold!" The hymn was blasting from a pair of tinny loudspeakers
attached to Tentena's mobile-phone office, and this happened on most
ordinary nights. The speakers were so loud, I wondered if perhaps they

had once competed with the muezzin's call to prayer from the nearby mosque. The muezzin had moved down the mountain to the safety of his people along the Muslim coast.

Somewhere nearby, in Tentena, Noviana Malewa—the teenage girl who had survived the beheading of three of her friends months earlier—lived under police protection at her sister's home. Zamira Loebis and I had come to find her. Ibnu Ahmad stayed down the hill; as a Muslim militant, he was not welcome here in the Christian highlands. To ask about Noviana, we went from the market to the home of the local minister, the Reverend Rinaldy Damanik, who was also the president of the Christian Church of Central Sulawesi, a mainline, Dutch Reformed Protestant church that claims 188,000 members today.[1] The minister's two guitars were sitting on the couch, but he was not at home, and his wife directed us down a hill to a house with a pig tethered outside. After the attack, Noviana had moved from Poso's minority Christian community up to the segregated safety of the highlands to stay with her sister. The clouds broke on our way to the house, a rough-hewn shack. Rain blew in through the splintered walls, and there seemed to be no door, just a cloth snippet tacked to the lintel, billowing against the storm. Shivering, we waited for Noviana to return to her sister's house for the night.

Both Loebis and I were chilled, and I felt as if my soul had caught cold and was lying like a lifeless slab of liver under my ribs. It had been a long several days of listening to litany upon litany of bloodshed. On this island, there was no denying the dead. A few days earlier, the exhumation of two mass graves had begun on the road between the two towns. The police had cordoned off a section of the jungle. Inside the muddy clay pits lay what was left of the Muslim men massacred on May 28, 2000, at an Islamic school called Walisongo. Already, the police had unearthed seventeen bodies in one pit and eleven in the other, including the corpse of an eight-year-old boy. Before leaving Poso to drive up to Tentena, we had visited a hotel abandoned by its Christian owner, where Muslim widows who'd survived the Walisongo massacre were now squatting. In May 2006, each family was allowed to send a member with the police to search the mass graves. The police had waited so long for the exhumation because they were cautious that digging up the past would breed new violence. Most family members were still waiting to hear if their fathers, brothers, and sons could be identified by anything: a scrap of shirt cuff, a rubber shoe sole. One Muslim widow, Suwarni Hariani, thirty-five, had lost nine male members of her family during the massacre. The women had been captured, stripped of their clothes, frightened, and humiliated. "I believe they held us hostage until they had killed all the men," she told me. Hariani had recognized one of her attackers, a local Catholic man named Dominggus da Silva, who had greeted her by name that day as she stood before him in her bra and underpants.

Three Catholic men, da Silva, Fabianus Tibo, and Marinus Riwu, had been convicted of orchestrating the Walisongo massacre, killing the men, then herding the women into the school, ordering them to take off their head scarves, and checking their vaginas for magic amulets. Many were raped. Now the three convicts were awaiting execution by firing squad in a prison in the Central Sulawesi capital city of Palu, where, several days earlier, I had gone to visit them. Tibo, the ringleader, had dyed his gray hair shoe-polish black. His two sidekicks were brawny, wore crocodile smiles, and denied everything. "The Protestants got more lenient sentences than we did, because we Catholics have become barter between the Muslims and the Protestants," Tibo said. He argued that all Christians should stick together. Because I was a Westerner, the men assumed that I, too, was a fellow Christian who had come to see them in solidarity, out of our shared belief in fighting for Christ. They hoped I could carry their message to fellow believers in the United States.

"The pope wrote to us," Tibo said. He claimed they had received a papal pardon. While it was true that Pope Benedict XVI had recently sent a letter to the three men in prison, a local Catholic priest explained that it was certainly not a pardon, simply "a message of union." Still, the convicts believed they were protected by outside powers, and this belief gave them a shared identity larger than the prison. Also, they were quick to explain, they had changed their ways. Tibo, who had admitted previously to killing 40 people, was now a prayer healer, laying his hands on those who came to be saved by a condemned man. He claimed to have healed 537 people.

"It's not me. It's God," he said, simpering. "I want the world to know that this case shows injustice. As a Christian, I gave my left cheek and my right." This was the same revisionist call I had heard in Nigeria, the one that the one-armed pastor, James Wuye, used to make before he renounced religious violence: that Christians had a right to defend themselves. He had left that call behind, but Tibo hadn't.

Four months and eleven days later, the three men were executed by firing squad. Federico Lombardi, S.J., a spokesman for Pope Benedict XVI, called their death "a defeat for humanity." He was careful, however, to make clear that this was not a statement about the men's innocence. It was a defeat for humanity in the sense that all capital punishment is a defeat for humanity.[2]

At last, Noviana Malewa, her dark hair tucked behind her small ears, appeared in the shack's doorway. A deep, shiny scar cut across her right cheek. Although she was a teenager, she could have been ten years old, and her tiny, well-muscled form looked like a gymnast's. Noviana was dripping with rain. She was wearing a pink rubber bracelet that read, "HE IS RISEN!" A policeman carrying an AK-47 trailed behind her, sending text messages.

Once I saw Noviana, still gasping from the steep climb up the wet, oily hill, I did not want to ask any questions, and I could see by Zamira Loebis's face that she did not want to translate them. This was all too raw; this girl had suffered too much, and her frailty was palpable. "He cut through to my teeth," she began, speaking below a whisper—just a breath, really. Her small jet eyes squeezed shut involuntarily when she talked, as if she had a tic. While walking to school, as they did every morning, she and three friends had taken their usual shortcut from home down a narrow path through plantations and jungle. They were laughing, talking about their boyfriends, when a group of men attacked them. Noviana had no idea how many, and she had survived only because she was the last of the four filing down the narrow path. "I only found out my three friends had died three days later. They were my best friends at school, at home, and at church." The other three had been beheaded, but she—Loebis and I realized as Noviana spoke—did not know this. Either she had seen nothing, or her conscious mind had refused to entertain the images.

We talked about God, instead of what had happened that day. "I pray more now," she said. "I pray for my friends whom I've lost. I pray so the perpetrators get arrested. It was all because of God I survived, not because of me."

On some Christian blogs and on YouTube, Noviana Malewa had become a heroine: an earnest Christian girl with a round, scarred face and a clear, child's voice talking about her faith made stronger by suffering, and about persecution by Muslims. The story came to support the notion that Muslims were persecuting Christians. After the attack, Noviana received letters from evangelical Christians worldwide that reflected this. "Hello Noviana I am 20 years old. Jesus loves you so much. I love you too! I will pray for you!" They sent her Bible verses, including one from the apostle Paul's letter to the Philippians, written from prison: "I know both how to be abased, and I know how to abound." All of the letters drew parallels between the suffering of the early Christians and what Noviana had endured. One person had sent her the pink rubber bracelet she was now wearing. The gift reminded me of the shoe boxes from the Reverend Franklin Graham's Operation Christmas Child in Sudan—gifts intended to reach people with the Gospel at vulnerable moments. They made me uncomfortable; to me, they seemed less about supporting Noviana than about promoting the sender's worldview. But they had worked. In the midst of her suffering, Noviana had surrendered her life to Christ and been born again. She now believed that we were living in End Times, and that the attack against her signaled the coming of the end of the world. She cast back in her memory for warnings or threats she had missed. Once, before the attack, she said, she had passed a woman's house on the way to school and had heard the woman joking with her grandson outside their house, teasing the girls about murdering them. This casual threat, she now believed, was a hint, a forewarning.

"The conflict has a huge effect on children," Rinaldy Damanik, the Protestant pastor, said when I found him at home the next morning. Damanik was elected president of the Christian Church of Central Sulawesi while in prison for two years, charged with arms possession during the religious violence. During the crisis, Damanik had become a reluctant leader, he explained. In fact, he never wanted to be a pastor; he wanted to be a doctor, but had twice failed his medical exams. He came from northern Sumatra and belonged to one of the country's largest ethnic groups, the Batak. As a pastor, he was also essentially a missionary among these people.

Since the fighting, the Christians had tried art therapy, offering kids pen and paper and having them draw whatever they wanted. "They drew war, people with crosses attacking mosques," he said. In clashes, the children witnessed Muslims yelling, *"Allahu Akhbar!"* while the Christians yelled, *"Alleluia!"* Now, the community was self-segregating. "Even now, if you ask a child why he moved up here to Tentena, he'll say he was attacked. Ask by whom, he'll say Muslims," he said. To an outsider, Christians and Muslims looked exactly the same. Their ethnicities were different in that the Christians came from inland indigenous peoples and the Muslims had lived along the coasts often visited by traders. But it was really deliberate choices in their appearance—clothing sometimes, and sparse beards on Muslim men—that told them apart to an outside observer like me. The pronounced differences in dress were relatively new, one more aspect of the revivals in both faiths that had made believers increasingly conscious of who they appeared to be.

"People seem to get used to the conflict, and that's dangerous," Damanik said. Here in Tentena, the Christians were competing day to day with Muslims over fertile forestland for ebony and cacao. Yet simultaneously, the two struggled over which worldview and way of life would dominate in Poso. This was both a spiritual and a material conflict, and one storyline really couldn't be separated from the other. During the fighting, a little anonymous book circulated among the Christians of Tentena that retold the Bible story of David and Goliath to argue that the Christians were duty-bound to fight against the oppressive Muslim population. These days, there was no way to separate the practical tensions from the ideological ones. As one group grew more violent, the other responded in kind. They were creating each other.

Local people had accused Damanik of a curious charge: of "internationalizing" the conflict—self-consciously employing globalization as a means of defense. He had contacted Western churches and tried to gain their attention and support with stories of Christian persecution. He didn't deny it. This was a battle fought locally and exploited globally, he explained. When Damanik saw that the Muslims were bringing in fighters such as Ibnu Ahmad—and funds—from outside, through a worldwide Christian network he alerted churches about the threat against Sulawesi's Christians by their Muslim neighbors. If the Muslims could sound the warning and get outside help, then the Christians could, too.

Soon this complex, small-scale conflict became part of the larger narrative of a global clash between Christianity and Islam, and Damanik knew he was partly responsible for this escalation. When the Western churches responded to his call, they retold his story in terms of a jihad against Christians, which he admitted was only part of the story.

"I'd say, wait a minute, hold, but since they have their own international network, they immediately spread the word to the world," he explained. This was a marked difference between mainline Protestant churches like his, and the more conservative evangelical and fundamentalist ones, he said. "The difference between me and the evangelicals is that I don't hate Muslims, and they see nothing good in them." In some ways, he seemed to be the mirror image of Hunter down on the coast—welcoming outside help, only to learn that help came with an agenda.

Damanik's concern about Christian militancy could have been convenient hindsight, but others told me that jail had sincerely changed the minister. He had been imprisoned with Ibnu Ahmad's bosses, the founders of Jemaah Islamiyah, and in the close cells, the leaders on both sides of this violent revival passed the time discussing religion. But JI's kind of Islam—the violent kind—came from outside, not from this island, he said. These outsiders with their funny seventh-century short pajama pants and strict ideas were creating problems for local Muslims who did not like being forced to change their ways. From the hills, Damanik explained, he was watching cracks appear in the Islamic community below.

Before we left, Loebis told Damanik that she belonged to the same ethnic group as he—Batak. It has a checkered history with Christian missionaries. In 1834, the Dutch colonialists assigned American Baptist missionaries to the Batak to block Islam's spread among them. The Baptists refused to learn the local language, and were generally disliked for their haughty ways. The Batak turned against the missionaries and, according to locals, ate them.[3]

21

BEGINNING ON THE WIND

Until the eighteenth century, the term *trade winds* had little to do with commerce; the phrase simply meant "to blow trade," which meant to move steadily in the same direction. The trade winds consistently blew toward the equator from both the northern and southern hemispheres, making it possible for early explorers and merchants to travel vast distances on predictable winds. These winds carried first Muslim, then Christian explorers southeast over the Indian Ocean to Torrid Zone islands more than five hundred years ago. In a sense, the trade winds blew Christianity and Islam together. For more than five centuries in Southeast Asia, Christians and Muslims have gone through periods of peaceful coexistence and moments of intense competition and conflict, which have usually begun as a scramble for economic power in a political vacuum. This pattern began with the sixteenth-century competition over the nutmeg and cloves of the spice trade.

Islam and Christianity, like Hinduism and Buddhism before them, arrived in Southeast Asia over water. All these religions traveled under the battered sails of traders and missionaries from Yemen, China, India, Portugal, Spain, and the Netherlands. Even before Islam arrived, the archipelago was part of a trade network that linked the Mediterranean to China, East Africa, and other parts of Southeast Asia. Yemeni traders were traveling through these islands on their way to China by 900. By then, Indonesia's main island, Java, was under Hindu rule. Indonesia did not adopt Islam until the thirteenth century, and contrary to popular history, it was Muslims from India—not from the Arabian Peninsula—who led most of the trade that drove the religion into new territories. According to the Quran, being a trader is a holy profession, in part because trade was seen by the Prophet as one of the most effective and egalitarian ways to spread the new faith: "You who believe, do not wrongfully consume each other's wealth but trade by mutual consent" (Quran, Women 4:29).

In Indonesia, as across North Africa, intermarriage, not armed conflict, advanced the geographic borders of the Muslim world. Polygamy played a role. Muslim sailors, who traveled without their wives, married local women when they reached the islands of Southeast Asia. Although these wives took Islamic names, they were typically only nominal converts; their children, however, were Muslims from birth. By the end of the thirteenth century—as Marco Polo noted in his Southeast Asia journals while returning to Venice from China in 1292—much of today's Indonesia had adopted Islam. Linked to a wide world of culture and trade through Arabic, the language of Islam, Southeast Asia flourished intellectually and economically. At the same time, local people blended their existing practices of Buddhism and Hinduism with Islam, so that Islam in Indonesia took on a colorful array of expressions, while following the core tenets of the faith.

The bustling ports of Southeast Asia welcomed a host of international traders. Indian dhows jostled for moorings among Chinese junks and, eventually, the galleons of the Portuguese, which carried Christianity to the islands in the sixteenth century. Although the crusades had ended two hundred years earlier, Spanish and Portuguese explorers still stitched crosses to their sails to display their vociferous opposition to Islam. As in East Africa, they cast their mission in terms of their search for the fabled Christian king Prester John. Somewhere among the savages of the Torrid Zone, the legend went, there was a lone and isolated Christian kingdom, and it became a Portuguese mission to find it. In the meantime, the Portuguese wrested control of Muslim shipping lanes. At last, in 1511, after a month-long siege, they defeated the Islamic kingdom of Malacca (part of contemporary Malaysia), exiled Muslim traders from the city, and razed the great mosque. To drive home the message of their newfound power, they built their Catholic fort, A Famosa, atop the mosque's ruins.

To defend themselves from such attacks, Southeast Asian Muslims turned to Islam as a unifying force and source of rebellion. Muslim scholars, religious teachers, and traders fled west to the Sumatran province of Aceh, nicknamed the Porch of Mecca, as millions of Muslims set out from its shores for the hajj.

————————

Soon after the Dutch landed in 1596, their Protestant influence replaced much of the Catholicism left behind by the Spanish and Portuguese. Like their predecessors, they were vehemently opposed to Islam as a rival religion and found, much to their dismay, that Muslim kingdoms flourished along the coasts. Intent on stopping "Mohammedanism" from spreading any further among their new subjects, the Dutch encouraged Protestant missionaries to sail eastward toward the peninsula's far-flung islands, which Islam had not yet claimed.[1] Many Dutch colonial officers and missionaries, as with their counterparts in Africa, sought to establish a human bulwark against Islam by evangelizing among non-Muslims and baptizing them as Christians. Since Muslims already lived along the coasts as a result of trade and intermarriage, the Protestant missionaries forded rivers and pushed inland up steep ridges to reach indigenous non-Muslims. If the race to stop Islam looked like a line of converts across Africa, then here in Southeast Asia, conversion began with a series of bull's-eyes: islands on which a Muslim coast ringed around a staunch Christian core, as on the island of Sulawesi.

Also, as in Africa, conversion to Christianity offered indigenous people a link to a powerful new world, one in which they would no longer be isolated and marginalized as they had been under an Islamic system. The Dutch were more aggressive than the British in their attempts to undermine Islam. One Dutch provincial authority openly paid people (two crowns and forty pennies) to be baptized. This was to "stimulate others to adopt the reform faith as well, and to show how we appreciate that our pagan and Moorish [Islamic] community attempt to seek their salvation through our only savior, Jesus Christ."[2] The government banned any religious practices other than Christian ones, and publically referred to Islam as "evil" and from "the Devil."[3] Christian instruction was mandatory in all government schools, and the colonial authorities tried to weaken Islam's grip on society by subverting Islamic law and promoting the use of *adat*, "customary law," instead.[4]

The Dutch were especially keen to keep a tight grip on their territories after the discovery of oil in 1883. Indonesia is home to some of the world's first functioning oil fields, and for more than a century, oil has been one of the country's main sources of wealth. A twenty-year-old Dutch tobacco farmer discovered oil on Sumatra in 1880, and in 1907 the Dutch and British together formed Royal Dutch Shell.[5] (The name comes from one of the founder's family businesses, importing seashells to London.)[6] Indonesia currently has reserves of 3.8 billion barrels of oil, and currently exports 977,000 barrels of oil daily, making it the world's twenty-third-largest exporter.

At the same moment, partly as a result of the Dutch efforts to supplant their religion, Indonesian Islam was undergoing a revival, and during the late 1800s, Muslims began to violently oppose the Dutch, reinforcing the centuries-old story that Christianity was the oppressor's religion, and Islam the means of liberation.

The Japanese occupied Indonesia throughout World War II. Two days after Japan's global surrender to Allied forces, Indonesia declared its independence from the Netherlands. That was August 17, 1945. But Indonesia's people struggled for four years against their colonial masters before gaining their freedom. During the struggle, Islamic fighters fought alongside nationalists to liberate the country. When the Dutch recognized a free Indonesia at last, the country's first president, Sukarno, faced the daunting prospect of forging a single nation out of the populace of more than seventeen thousand islands.

Much to the dismay of many devout Muslims, Sukarno decided against the formation of an Islamic state. Instead, he adopted Pancasila, a political program based on five principles: "belief in one supreme God, humanitarianism, nationalism, consultative democracy, and social justice." Indonesia's motto became "Unity in Diversity," and Christianity, Islam, Buddhism, Hinduism, and initially Confucianism were all state-approved religions.

The Islamic militants who had fought alongside the nationalist Sukarno to help him win the war against the Dutch were enraged at this turn of events. Under the leadership of one of Sukarno's former allies, Sekarmadji Maridjan Kartosuwiryo (an erstwhile follower of Gandhi), some militants formed a group called Dar-ul-Islam, the Land of Islam, which went underground after independence and kept fighting against the nascent state—and against the Christians who now enjoyed state-sanctioned religious freedom. Ibnu Ahmad's grandfather, father, and uncle all eventually joined Dar-ul-Islam. From generation to generation, this early anti-colonial struggle would develop into the battle against the neo-imperial, neocolonial West, and the new fight would fall to sons such as Ibnu Ahmad.

Sukarno ruled the country for nearly twenty years, until, in 1966, after a failed coup attempt, he fell from power and his former subordinate, Major General Suharto, rose in his stead. Staunchly pro-Western and anti-Communist, President Suharto became a cold war darling of Nixon and Kissinger; his mid-1960s pogrom against alleged Communists left at least five hundred thousand dead.[7] (And militant Islamists manned Suharto's death squads—a dirty open secret of Indonesian history.)[8] Since converting to a state-approved religion prevented people from being charged as godless Communists, many Indonesians did, and religion consequently became more important in their lives than it had been for their forebears. Ostensibly to combat communism, the state outlawed the Chinese practice of Confucianism; most Chinese turned to Christianity instead. During the 1960s, thousands of Chinese chose to be baptized as Catholics and Protestants. These numbers laid the foundation for a broader religious awakening, and the shift toward charismatic and muscular Christianity that would contribute to religion's outpacing ethnicity as the primary mark of identity.

While the Christian reawakening took place mostly among the middle-aged, its Islamic counterpart was really a youth movement. Particularly on college campuses, during the 1970s, religion became a way to organize socially under the oppressive grip of Suharto. During the 1980s, following the Iranian Revolution, a groundswell of Islamic devotion swept Indonesia, as elsewhere. Only a generation earlier, many Muslims had looked down upon praying five times a day as antimodern; by the late 1980s, praying, and other forms of public devotion such as head scarves, had grown fashionable. By the 1990s, President Suharto, the staunch anti-Communist, needed religion to bolster his waning authority and his strained relations with the military. He built mosques and prayer halls in villages and schools, went on the hajj, promoted Islamic education and scholars, and placed Muslims, instead of Christians, in high military positions. Yet his signs of outward devotion did little to undo the corruption of his government. In 1997, an economic crisis tore through Southeast Asia as Thailand unpegged its currency, the baht, from the U.S. dollar; the tumbling economy set off a financial domino effect throughout the region. The crisis, also called the Asian economic flu, triggered the collapse of

Indonesia's currency, the rupiah, as well, and in 1998, after widespread rioting, Suharto was forced to resign. His decades-long grip on a strong central government suddenly collapsed. In the ensuing political vacuum, there arose the question of who would hold power and by what authority. All sorts of groups long silenced by the absolute rule of Sukarno and Suharto seized the chance to speak out. This new populism led to religious strife—a pattern similar to what would happen one year later in Nigeria, when military rule ended and Christians and Muslims began to compete for political advantage. So, too, in Indonesia, religious identity became the arena in which rival groups began to compete for newfound political power.

From Jakarta to the outlying islands in the east of the archipelago, where, due to the legacy of Dutch Protestant missionaries, Christians and Muslims were more evenly divided than elsewhere, rival gangs and militias sprang up on both sides. In the name of defending Christianity or Islam, they vied for dominion over markets, neighborhoods, and local governments. Yet this competition was fueled not only by local conditions; the worldwide revivals in both religions compounded the problem. On the eastern island of Sulawesi, for instance, Christians had begun to use loudspeakers outside of churches[9] (and mobile-phone offices) to reach their flock, as the Muslims did outside mosques. The two were vying for the airwaves in the thousand-year-old question of whose prayer had the right to be louder. Both were building larger, fancier places of worship as emblems of their power—emblems that became the first targets once the bloodletting began.

This competition over religion fit easily on top of centuries-old animosities. On Sulawesi, for example, Christians were poorer than their Muslim neighbors and had been for a hundred years. While their Muslim neighbors fished along the coast, and gained access to global trade routes, the isolated Christians farmed crops such as rice, crookneck winter squash, cucumber, Chinese eggplant, and peppers.[10] In short, Christians saw their coastal neighbors as greedy; Muslims saw the Christians as lazy.

The world's demand for chocolate made things worse. Much of the world's cacao crop comes from Indonesia, and in the 1990s, its price exploded. To grow cacao on Sulawesi, Muslims began to buy up traditionally Christian land. The envious Christians could not afford *not* to sell; even if they kept their land and harvested the cacao themselves, they did not have the means of competing in the global marketplace. Resentment grew over the green seedpods, and soon, along with newfound democracy, the price of chocolate would help to fuel a local power struggle between Muslims and Christians, and men such as Ibnu Ahmad would rush in to fight under the banner of global jihad.

22

"NO MORE HAPPY SUNDAYS"

More than four hundred churches in Indonesia have been bombed, burned, or forced to close by Islamic militants in recent years. It is virtually impossible for Christians to build new churches in Muslim areas. Under a law instituted in 2006, Christians may not open a new church unless certain conditions are met: there must be at least ninety church members living in the neighborhood, sixty Muslims in the neighborhood must sign a petition in favor of the new church, and the government must issue a permit. Needless to say, the government rarely does so. The law has widespread support from most of Indonesia's Islamic leaders, both conservative and moderate. Even moderates argue that in a Muslim country, freedom of religion cannot mean the right to preach to whomever you want. "Christianity and Islam are both expansionist religions," said Din Syamsuddin, the chairman of Muhammadiya, a mainstream political and religious party with thirty million members. "Their aim is to grow." Proselytizing creates competition, and in Indonesia, that competition leads to violence.

In lieu of church buildings, many Christians gather to worship in houses, malls, and high-end Chinese restaurants such as Yen Yen in Jakarta, where the Reverend Ruyandi Hutasoit, a fifty-six-year-old urologist turned evangelist, walked among a floor full of well-heeled ethnic Chinese, many of them clutching Louis Vuitton purses, to preach one Sunday evening in May 2006. Hutasoit, who is not aligned with a particular denomination, preaches a version of the prosperity gospel based on Success Motivation International, a program developed by Paul J. Meyer, a motivational speaker from Waco, Texas.

"This is the wheel of life," he said, drawing a large circle on a white board and lancing it with spokes labeled "Wealth," "Health," and "Hygiene." Hutasoit follows the plan himself. Upon entering the restaurant, he had swept past me to go brush his teeth; an aide told me, "He is very tidy and clean." The plan, the reverend said, made it possible for him to play golf twice a week, to continue to perform urological surgery, to start a Christian political party called the Prosperous Peace Party 2001, and to run for president in 2004, on a platform of increasing the number of Christians in Indonesia from roughly 9 percent to half of the population. He lost. Five years later, in the 2009 presidential and legislative elections, his party won less than 2 percent of the vote. "If we don't struggle with our faith, we are lost," Hutasoit said. "We will conquer Goliath."

For many of Indonesia's conservative Muslims, Hutasoit is Public Enemy Number One. Having survived attempts on his life, he is frequently accused of *Kristianisasi*, or "Christianization," a controversial concept with a history dating back to the arrival of the Portuguese ex-crusaders. Christianization refers to the (real and imagined) effort to make Indonesian society Christian—and hence Western—by converting its citizens to the Gospel. Indonesian Muslims grew fearful of such an effort half a century ago, with the arrival of American groups such as Campus Crusade for Christ International, an evangelical mission founded by Bill and Vonette Bright at UCLA in 1951. At the time, CCC—which professes a mission to reach the entire world with the Gospel—proselytized aggressively among Muslims. Today, Christianization provides a ready source of fear for conservatives looking to whip up the need to defend Islam, and Hutasoit is their bogeyman.

In the eighties, the pastor started an evangelical seminary, a health clinic, and an insane asylum founded on the message of the Great Commission. Young preachers, as well as sick and mentally ill people, came to the compound to attend the seminary and to be healed. After the economy collapsed in 1997, his organization filled to bursting with new members, as Indonesians turned to religion for security and stability. This still happens, an aide told me; when oil prices spike and people cannot afford the fuel they need, new converts appear. Hutasoit's goal was to send his young preachers, some former Muslims, into the 10/40 Window.

One night in 1999, a mob set Hutasoit's seminary on fire. As the students tried to flee, the mob cut them down with machetes. On his laptop, the pastor directed an aide to show me a PowerPoint presentation with photographs used for fund-raising. In one snapshot, a young man named Sariman, a former Muslim, lay dead on the ground, his neck slit open like a fish gill. "We have many martyrs. Sariman is just the tip of the iceberg," the aide said. The attacks had an unintended effect: they attracted converts. "Because we're being persecuted, the more you press us, the bigger our faith becomes," the aide said. Herein lies one of the most striking enigmas about religion: faith grows faster under pressure. In America, for instance, Islam enjoyed a growth spurt after 9/11. The inverse occurred in Indonesia. According to Hutasoit's aide, 9/11 was "a boomerang for Indonesia." Still, Hutasoit felt that the American government had failed Indonesia's Christians—making such an effort at rapprochement with Muslim leaders over the past decade, while having little to do with Christian ones. "For persecution, we get nothing," he said. "All America's money goes to Muslims, because they want to make good relations with them." Hutasoit had recently gone to New York City and visited the Foundation Center, which provides people with information about applying for various grants. He'd counted almost no secular organizations willing to give money to persecuted Christians, but plenty ready to fund different Islamic interests. Although persecution in Indonesia was widespread, much of it took place on a local, not a national level, Hutasoit said, which made it harder to see. One recent case in the Islamic heartland of West Java, with its history of powerful Muslim sultanates dating back to the sixteenth century, had received little international attention outside Christian media. Three female evangelists, Pastor Rebekka Zakaria and her two lay assistants, Ratna Bangun and Eti Pangesti, who belonged to the Christian Church of Camp David, had been charged with running a church out of one woman's home, which was illegal. According to local authorities, they thus had violated the 2002 Child Protection Act, which forbids missionaries from preaching to children. (The act's timing was deliberate: in this new democracy, as religion became more of a political contest, there was growing hysteria about the business of Christians attempting secret conversions, whether or not they actually took place.) The women were serving a three-year sentence at Indramayu State Prison, 120 miles east of Jakarta. Hutasoit, who had attended their trial and was one of their most vocal defenders, sent me to see them.

The hills surrounding the prison had been stepped with the terraces of hanging gardens, earthen ziggurats mostly planted with tea. Teak trees nodded their tufted heads, which looked like something out of Dr. Seuss. Even within its walls, the prison was surprisingly breezy and pleasant. The three women had planted a small garden outside of their cell. They had cleaned the prison's toilets and painted the walls of the cell, where they held church meetings, yellow and blue.[1] Meeting them was surreal at first; these women were in prison *for teaching Sunday school*. Yet despite the gentle atmosphere, they were considered villains among the local Muslims, who saw them as the embodiment of Christianization, a force actively working to erase Indonesia's Islamic identity. Thirty of the forty children who attended their "Happy Sundays" were Muslims, and the local authorities claimed Zakaria and the others had rounded up local kids, fed them, and taught them about Jesus and to sing Bible songs—without their parents' knowledge.

Zakaria, who was about to turn fifty, wore her dark wavy hair sensibly short. She had wispy sideburns and a gentle, jowly face that transformed with righteous anger as she explained that all of the parents knew exactly what was going on at Happy Sundays. "These are children of low intelligence, poor children. Some of their mothers were prostitutes, and we fed them milk," she said. The milk was beyond some parents' means. Happy Sundays came under scrutiny after Muslim teachers at school overheard the children singing Christian songs and greeting each other with "Shalom" instead of "Salam"; the schoolteachers alerted the authorities. The language of a different culture was dangerous. At the trial, the children had to sing the songs Zakaria had taught them, while busloads of protesters shouted her name outside the court. They carried an empty coffin, which they had built for her.

"We must not be afraid of this kind of persecution," Zakaria said. Although Christians from the West had shown support by sending her fifteen thousand letters filled with bubblegum, bookmarks, and currency from America, the United Kingdom, and Israel, Zakaria did not believe that Western Christians really understood the cost of faith here along the edge of the Muslim world.

"They think freedom is free," she said, smiling bitterly.

Zakaria believed that Christianity and Islam were locked in a global contest for souls. Unlike Western Christians, she believed, who could afford to think about God only on Sundays, believers along the tenth parallel did not have the luxury of doubt, or of interpreting scripture as anything but the infallible word of God. "Many people considered us martyrs, but we didn't consider ourselves as such," Zakaria said.

"Because we're close to the tenth parallel we feel more pressure here," she said. The 10/40 Window was a battle map facing all frontline Christians, including herself. As she saw it, the fight playing out in her town was a part of a global battle for this world and the next. Gains on her side, the Christian side, meant more people—more children—in heaven. She said, "We pray for the children, because they're going to hell."

On my return from the prison to Jakarta, I stopped along the highway to visit one of the community elders who had led the fight against Zakaria. Hajji Jamali was sitting in his darkening living room, a walking cane leaning against his leg. It was hard to imagine him helping to lead a violent protest, but he had. He quietly explained that if the Christians were going to impose their beliefs on Muslims, then the Muslims had the right to push back. "She has violated children's rights, human rights, and the child protection law," he said, indignantly emphasizing human rights. The Western concept cut both ways. "She taught these things to Muslim children in the largest Muslim country in the world," Jamali said, explaining that here, due to numbers, Christians were the Muslims' guests. "If a guest is polite to the host, the host is polite. If the guest is impolite, the host can be as rude as he chooses to be," he said. "There will be no more Happy Sundays."

The case of Happy Sundays also deepened a rift within Indonesia's Christian community, which had about twenty-four million members, both Protestants and Catholics. "This extreme evangelical voice is leading to increased violence," said Father Franz Magnis-Suseno, a German-born Catholic priest. The priest, who had worked in Indonesia for nearly fifty of his seventy years, wrote his dissertation on Karl Marx. "Mission now has to be understood as bearing witness, but not trying to convert people." Over the past several decades, the Christian awakening in Indonesia has led to a mushrooming of churches. New congregations kept splitting from old ones, which looked to Muslims like a rapid expansion of Christianity—not like what it was: an increasing number of divisions within the religion.

In the Jakarta courthouse in October 2008, I met with about a dozen members of the Islamic Defenders Force, a militant group that enforces the closure of churches and, on occasion, Christian nightclubs. Clad in all-white fatigues, white berets, and white combat boots, its members looked like storm troopers as they sat in the empty courtroom and ate bag lunches behind the tables for the prosecution and the defense. Up on a platform, a few sat quietly behind the magistrate's desk. One was reading an Indonesian bestseller by Andrea Hirata, *Laskar Pelangi*, or "Rainbow Warrior," about a group of poor kids struggling to go to school.

On this afternoon, the members of the Islamic Defenders Force were awaiting trial for beating up human rights advocates and members of Indonesia's Jaringan Islam Liberal, or "Liberal Islam Network." JIL had been marching to defend Indonesia's religious freedom, including the freedom within Islam to choose different modes of expression. But religious diversity, these members of the Islamic Defenders Front believed, was a hazard to their faith.

Some members also called themselves the Alliance of the Anti-Apostasy Movement, and did a kind of self-styled moral policing, which entailed exacting bribes from business owners in order not to destroy their livelihoods. But they took special pride in shutting down churches, one forty-year-old member named Sunarto told me, since Christianization and Westernization are equally a menace to Islam.

It struck me, as they quietly ate the lunches their lawyers had brought them, how pervasive the Western presence is in places and ways we do not even imagine. Whether it was hymns wafting from a jungle church, or the backbeat of a Britney Spears video, both appeared to these men to be part of the Christian West's effort to spread its influence. "A few years ago, it was food," Sunarto said, referring to the cropping up of fast-food chains, including Kentucky Fried Chicken, which he saw as a plot by the Christian West to tempt Muslims away from religiously sanctioned snacks. In general, their war against Christianization really implied a struggle against globalization—and that was a struggle they were not going to win.

In late May 2006, I went by plane from Jakarta to the central Java city of Yogyakarta to meet with one of Indonesia's most notoriously radical clerics, Irfan Awwas, who was head of the Indonesian Mujahideen Council. Awwas was hostile in general to having Westerners in Indonesia, and demanded a hundred-dollar "donation" and a copy of my passport before we met. That morning, I rose before dawn to climb around Borobudur, one of the world's most ancient Buddhist stupas, a layer cake hewed from stone and dating back to the 800s, with 504 Buddhas tucked into its mossy hollows. It was abandoned in the fourteenth century, when Islam supplanted Buddhism and Hinduism in the region. Even at dawn, it was hot and tiring to circle its three tiers and make the sweaty climb from desire through form to formlessness. Each tier represents a ring of the universe, and by climbing up out of the darkness, I was supposed to be moving toward enlightenment. Unfortunately, the effort of the sacred walk shortened my temper. By the time I arrived at Awwas's office that evening for the long-awaited meeting, I was feeling impatient.

Awwas believed that it was the responsibility of Indonesian Muslims to safeguard this edge of Dar-ul-Islam, the Land of Islam, against incursions from Dar-ul-Harb, the Land of War, which he saw as beginning to the south, in neighboring Australia. Awwas told me that Australian churches were behind the Christian separatists inside Indonesia—those seeking to secede from the Muslim country. In order to penetrate and defeat Islam, the Christians were trying to foment chaos and war in the east, he said, including in places such as Sulawesi and in the Indonesian region of Papua. The practical details of such efforts did not interest Awwas; he, like the leaders of the Islamic Defenders Force, still believed that Christianization and Westernization were one and the same, and had been since the Portuguese invaded five hundred years ago.

"As long as there is imperialism in Indonesia, there will be Christianization," he pronounced. Tired of his monologue, I mistakenly thought this might be the moment to ask about his unorthodox procedure of demanding payment for an interview, which displeased him. He insisted that the practice was nothing out of the ordinary: "Anytime you go to a hospital or school to talk to someone, they will ask you for a donation," he said, ending the interview. As I walked down the driveway an aide came running after me with a hundred-dollar bill. Awwas now wanted to return the cash. "Here is your money," he said. "Now you must say you never met him."

I left town for Malaysia the next morning. Later that day—May 26, 2006—an earthquake struck Yogyakarta, leaving more than five thousand people dead, tens of thousands injured, and more than one million people homeless. Now, only an hour's flight away, there was no way to return. In one of the glimmering high-rise hotels of Kuala Lumpur, I reeled. I picked up the phone to find that everyone I had met had survived, including Awwas. People feared that Borobudur, the Buddhist temple, was going to collapse, but remarkably it was still standing.

23

A WORLD MADE NEW

When the 2004 tsunami struck Indonesia, the province of Aceh—jutting like a thumb into the Indian Ocean a few hundred miles north of the equator—bore the brunt of the tidal wave. One hundred and thirty thousand people lost their lives. Whole families were wiped out, towns disappeared, and a society lay in ruins. Many survivors saw it as a sign of God's vengeance. To them, the tidal wave was God's retribution for their sinful ways, not merely a consequence of an undersea earthquake.

Indonesia lies not only within the storm belt of the intertropical convergence zone but also inside what's known as the Ring of Fire—an upside-down U of seismic activity that stretches for nearly twenty-five thousand miles from America's western coast over the Pacific Ocean to Asia's eastern coast. Although nine of ten of the world's earthquakes take place here, they still seem to many to be signs of God's wrath. This point of view is neither new nor solely Islamic. Long before Noah's flood wiped the sinful earth clean, the narrative of divine wrath and the command to return to a purer, more devout way of life has informed people's responses to countless natural disasters. First, catastrophe destroys; then it offers an opportunity for revival—or renewal. After Hurricane Katrina, some Christian leaders, including Franklin Graham, said they saw a chance for redemption in the storm's aftermath. In Aceh, for many of the tsunami's survivors, only divine will could explain the fact that they were still breathing.

Aceh lies in the Indonesian archipelago's extreme northwest, and the tip of its thumb points directly across the Indian Ocean, east to Somalia. The only landmass lying in between the two is the very southern edge of Sri Lanka. Aceh has been known as the Porch of Mecca since the sixteenth century, when it became a bustling hub of religious scholarship and rebellion against the Portuguese invaders. For more than three decades before the tsunami, the Free Aceh Movement fought for the region's autonomy from the Indonesian government. The tidal wave cracked open the long-isolated province, ushered in the outside world, and finally brought an end to thirty years of civil war between the government and the rebels.

After the disaster, Christian and Muslim relief organizations descended upon Aceh, feeding and clothing survivors, providing medicine, and building shelter. Franklin Graham's organization, Samaritan's Purse, was one of the largest and most effective. At the time, Ken Isaacs—Graham's tough-jawed second-in-command, who'd asked me about my background in Khartoum—headed up USAID's Office of U.S. Foreign Disaster Assistance. This was just one example of the conservative evangelical community's interconnectedness with the Bush administration—on domestic faith-based initiatives and U.S. foreign policy in Sudan and elsewhere. (On my visit to the headquarters of Samaritan's Purse in Boone, North Carolina, in 2003, I had seen a letter from President George W. Bush to Isaacs framed on Isaacs's wall. "We are doing the right things in Iraq and Afghanistan," the president had written.) As Isaacs took the helm of the OFDA, some of his secular counterparts worried that his claims of Christianity's exclusive truth would drive his relief agenda to include proselytizing, and so would alienate Muslims. Yet as they watched Isaacs wrestle deftly with the massive relief effort, they stopped worrying. Indonesia's Islamists did not, however. The Islamic Defenders Front, the same storm-trooper-like group that forcibly closed churches, sent some members by plane to Aceh to bury rotting corpses and ensure that the dead received an Islamic burial. Then they protested against the Christian aid groups, including Samaritan's Purse.

At first, as U.S. troops and aid-bearing Western relief workers arrived in Aceh to rebuild bridges, roads, and homes, the community expressed overwhelming gratitude. Once the shock wore off, however, the deaths of so many people compounded by the influx of Westerners and the abundance of foreign aid money seemed to threaten the fabric of Acehnese society. Relief workers brought with them a new economy—plus bikinis and Chianti. Aid dollars led to massive corruption, as the populace of Aceh watched powerful people skim what seemed to be millions of rupiah off the top of relief projects. Since traditional village leaders were dead, few actual Indonesians could take the lead in the rebuilding of social structures. The only way to rebuild Aceh, its supporters argued, was to implement Islamic law.

"Of course, in the beginning people act as if the sky is falling, that it is barbaric," said Yuni Saba, rector of the State Islamic University. Yet Aceh, he pointed out, has also had Sharia on the books since the fifties. Now, with the place flattened—and under inadvertent cultural siege from the West—the time had arrived to implement it.

"Sharia is about how to mend this torn Aceh. There is a lot of hanky-panky around—illicit sex, gambling, alcohol—but at least let us have a little law." Aceh is the only one of Indonesia's thirty-three provinces to implement Sharia, and although, in theory, Islamic law looked like a solution to reestablishing moral order among the people of Aceh, in practice it has been an inept—and sometimes tragic—affair. The Wilayatul Hisbah, or Way-Hah, as the locals called the "Vice and Virtue Squad," which began its moral policing in 2006, two years after the tsunami struck, has been criticized for targeting women and lower-class citizens, who cannot defend themselves.

"If we're going to jail women for not wearing *jilbabs* [head scarves] it's about identity, not religion," said Shadia Marhaban, a journalist and activist involved in Aceh's long struggle for autonomy. Marhaban had only recently returned to Aceh after fleeing to the United States as a political refugee in 2003. Yet the Aceh she returned to after the tsunami was extremely different. The tidal wave had changed the soil itself, and now the air seemed hotter. An entire society had been leveled by water and war. Yet this opportunity to make the world new in so many more essential ways— including education, welfare, and jobs—was vanishing under the shroud of religion. This turn of events disappointed Marhaban, who had risked so much for a chance to build a new, free Aceh—a chance, paradoxically, that the storm had provided. "We have so much to do," she said. "Why stop boys from chasing girls?"

At eight one Saturday evening in May 2006, in the capital city of Banda Aceh, two young Vice and Virtue officers were playing a fierce game of Ping-Pong before heading out for the night patrol. The table was brand-new, and the office smelled of fresh paint. Both wore dark green uniforms and black baseball hats decorated with gold braid, like a forestry unit on dress parade.

The men smacked the hollow ball across the net. Febbe Orida, my twenty-one-year-old interpreter, usually overbrimming with chatter, looked on in silence. Her full, soft mouth, typically tucked into a grin, had flat-lined; she looked very uncomfortable. The day before, when she I and visited the Way-Hah office to secure our places on this patrol, the officers had scolded Orida for wearing too-tight jeans. I had never seen her balk before; Febbe Orida was ebullient, and also brave. When the tsunami struck, she and her family fled the wall of water, which flattened their vil-lage. In the tidal wave's aftermath, as foreign aid workers and journalists overran Aceh, Orida leaped at the chance to work with Americans. Al-ready fluent in English by virtue of watching American films, Orida be-came a crack interpreter. Punctuated by American slang, her translations could be unusual. The day before, she had lifted her long-sleeve shirt in the privacy of our car to reveal some baby fat on her hips. "I've got to get rid of these muffin tops," she sighed. I had never heard the expression before. A photographer from Southern California had recently taught it to her. (He also taught her to use *bank* for "money," a translation I found perpetually confusing in conversations about aid dollars.)

The officers began to talk to us about the evening's patrol. "We're going to roads where girls don't wear veils and telling them to wear their veils," one officer told Orida. Preventing *khalwat*, or "fraternization between un-married men and women," was their primary objective. "We've seen some squeezing. It gets worse at night. There are a lot of flamers in Aceh," she translated. I stopped her. "Do you mean homosexuals?" I asked. She looked at me impatiently, "Yes, but what he said is 'flamer,' not 'homosex-ual.'" Orida was determined to capture nuance—and prejudice.

Before we left, the squad offered us paper plates of rice. Orida did not want to eat with the police. Something was wrong. "Can we eat in the car?" she asked, eager to escape as soon as possible. Outside police head-quarters, the force's black pickup truck was already thrumming; in its open bed, two park benches were bolted back to back. One of the new officers, a thirty-year-old former kindergarten teacher, Nur Amina, stood in the driveway waiting to climb aboard. She was wearing candy pink lipstick, which seemed incongruous with the task at hand. The police had come under criticism for targeting women, she said, but that was a malicious rumor. "We've heard women say we're against women, but we protect women. Bad things can happen when they're alone with men."

Orida stared at the exposed park benches and pulled me off to the side. "Do we have to go in their car? It's social suicide," she said. ("Social suicide" was another of her newly acquired phrases.) I thought she was simply afraid her friends would see us, but she meant something more. Her anxiety was unusual, so we took Nur Amina along with us to ride in our SUV behind the pickups. As the officers climbed into the truck, men in a nearby barbershop taunted them, calling out *yip yip yip*. Knowing that Nur Amina could not understand English, Orida murmured to me, "It must suck to be Way-Hah. People are laughing at them." Yet Nur Amina had heard the men's taunting as the moral police squad approached. "Most people run from us," she said.

My notes for the night read like the blotter from a bumbling police squad—more Keystone Kops than Taliban Vice and Virtue, but unsettling just the same.

7:00 p.m.: Two housewives wearing slippers and housecoats pump water from an outdoor well. Looking harried from chores, and only outside for a moment to fetch water, they have left their glossy black heads bare in the fading daylight. The Vice and Virtue pickup screeches to a halt before them, and they begin to run. "Stop!" the officers yell. Seven officers clamber down from the park benches, and Nur Amina leaps nimbly out of our car and advances. "Where's your veil?" she shouts at one. The booming voice, coming from her four-and-a-half-foot frame, startles them. "My house is there." An old woman passing by on a bicycle shrieks, "Oh, they're going to cut your hair!"

7:05 p.m.: A young couple astride a motorbike has pulled off the road onto a patch of stubbled grass. The truck stops again. The eight officers march toward the bike's red taillight, winking against the deepening darkness. "Why are you stopped here?" Nur Amina demands. "Only to answer a text message," the boy says, quickly proffering his cellular phone. "And who's he to you?" she asked the sheepish girl. "He's my cousin," the girl answers. "Don't lie; it will make it worse. He's not your husband." The kids fumble in their pockets for their ID cards. Nur Amina jots down their names. Then Vice and Virtue speeds toward the beach—a notorious lovers' lane.

8:00 p.m.: After driving around for a while harassing minor targets, at dusk we arrive at the beach, where couples are gathered. Our gang of eight officers and two reporters wades unstealthily through the deep sand toward couples sitting a little ways from one another. I am beginning to feel ridiculous and mean. So, I'd bet, is Orida, who lags behind and watches waves crest to catch the last bit of orange light. Two young people sit with their heads together facing west, watching the sunset over the Indian Ocean. They don't see us coming until our gang is on top of them, and now it is too late for them to run. "Why are you wearing that shirt?" Officer Amina shouts at the young woman, who is wearing a slightly diaphanous long-sleeve shirt. Orida looks down at the sand as she interprets for me. Then we grimace at each other. The officers—especially Nur Amina—seem always to yell at the women.

"We're newly engaged," the boy answers.

"You think engaged people are allowed to do that? Tell your wife to wear proper clothes. A husband is responsible for his wife."

The last slice of tangerine sun is dropping into the Indian Ocean, and the Vice and Virtue Squad orders the beach cleared, commanding that all couples go pray now at the beachside mosque. It is almost time for *maghrib*, evening prayer. In a moment the muezzin will clear his throat and begin the call. *Maghrib* in Arabic also means "west"—the place of the setting sun—and the western part of Muslim North Africa, including Algeria, Libya, Morocco, Mauritania, and Tunisia. If I were a crow (or, more likely, a cormorant) and took off from the beach to fly west at this latitude, once I reached Africa I would fly straight over Somalia, where, at this hour, the midday heat would be rising in shreds off the desert. If I kept pumping my wings, pushing west against the trade wind's eastward flow, eventually southern Sudan would appear below me, its canopy like a field of broccoli crosshatched with the fresh grids of oil excavation. And if I kept going, the broccoli would thin to pale grassland white-veined with rivers—Nigeria—and I would see the morning breeze ruffling the bur grass.

Instead, I am standing on Banda Aceh's darkening beach, where an officer's mobile phone buzzes as a text message arrives. Orida reads it over his shoulder: "*Salam aleikum, informasi*: there are two foreigners, one white one, one black, with local girls. I think they're prostitutes. They are in a hotel and it's clear they're going to spend the night there."

"For that kind of case, we can't do anything," the officer said. When the patrol ends, and we are finally alone together, Orida tells me that some months earlier she had a run-in with the Vice and Virtue Squad in a nearby town. She had gone to a beach hotel with her boyfriend for the night, and someone pounded on the door. It was the religious police, and the two narrowly escaped arrest. It was just dumb luck they got off, since young people like them were usually made examples of, while the children of government ministers were allowed to do as they pleased. As an activist told me later, "Sharia doesn't apply to anyone with power."

In the next town, Jantho, a poor couple was about to be caned for committing adultery. One Friday that May, Orida and I drove sixty miles east from Banda Aceh to Jantho Prison to try to see them. We arrived just before the Friday midday prayer, the week's most important. The warden had gone, and our driver needed to pray, so he dropped us off at an outdoor café, its blue-and-white-checked tablecloths fluttering in the wind, and went to find the local mosque. The café owner emerged from the cook shack carrying, in one hand, an umbrella to shield herself from the sun, and shooing us out of her café with the other.

"I can't feed you now. I'll get caught by the religious police," she said. For the past five months, a group of girls had been patrolling during Friday prayer to make sure all the men in town were at the mosque. Women were allowed to pray at home, but not to work or conduct business. So, for a couple of sleepy hours each Friday, Jantho became a women's town.

The first caning had taken place a month and a half earlier, the café proprietress said. "People yelled, and it was so exciting," she said, her face contorting, half a grimace, half gleeful. Her interest in the subject, it seemed, outweighed her fear of breaking the law, and she led us to the back of the restaurant, where no one would see us. She and her husband had rebuilt the place since the tsunami, in which she had lost thirteen family members and her husband lost his entire family. "The tsunami happened because Acehnese people are sinners," she said. "It makes sense to me that the ocean would get angry."

In response, she had become a more devout Muslim. "I cover my head even alone in my house," she said. "When I go to the market and see girls in tight clothes laughing too loud, I tell them to be quiet. I like to warn people. I do it every day and I tell them, 'Please don't do this. The tsunami will happen again!'" The girls laughed at her, but she did not care; as she explained, "The world is about to end."

––––––––

After finishing our clandestine chicken-and-rice lunch, we returned to the prison. The guards had decided that it would be no problem to allow us, two women, to speak to the prisoners in the warden's office.

The woman was first. When Anisa, twenty-four—who, like her boyfriend, preferred I use only her first name—was ushered into the office, her pimply face was white as flour. She and her boyfriend, Zulfikar, twenty-eight, had been summoned to the jail the day before, after being granted their freedom for the past few weeks, and then summarily locked up. She'd had no idea the police were going to detain them, so she was clad in embroidered jeans from her date. Then Zulfikar, whey-faced and wearing a yellow-and-blue baseball shirt, appeared at the door. This was Anisa's first glimpse of him since the arrest.

"When will they do it?" she asked him.

"Next Friday," he said.

"Can't we pay anyone? We can pay two million," Anisa pleaded.

Two million rupiah meant two hundred American dollars. The man played with the cellophane on his cigarette pack and said nothing. An L-shaped gash ran across his head and up his scalp, left by the mob that had beaten him. The cigarettes and chocolate bars we had brought as gifts for them now seemed ridiculous, obscene. Neither of them ate the candy; they saved it for their cellmates—Zulfikar kept his for a particularly evil thug who would beat him if he was gone too long from his cell. He kept watching the door, all muscles taut, as if someone might burst through the door and grab him.

"I swear on the Holy Quran nothing happened," Anisa said.

The couple had met about six months earlier, when Anisa took a bus Zulfikar was driving to the capital, from her village twelve hours away. They started to text each other, one thing led to another, and she came for a visit. Zulfikar took Anisa to a friend's house. It got late, then later. His minibike broke down, so they had to spend the night—on opposite sides of the room. Anisa insisted, "I won't deny that he hugged me. I won't deny that he tried to kiss me, but I told him to stop." Before dawn, the door burst open and a mob of villagers armed with knives stormed the room. Zulfikar escaped through a window. "They would have killed him," Anisa said. Instead, the mob shaved Anisa's head, poured "holy" water over her scalp, and made her swear nothing had happened.

"You'll cause another tsunami!" they yelled. The worst part of the social policing wasn't the whipping; it was this kind of mob violence. Interrupting, Zulfikar said, "I have to go. My cellmate will beat me." He filled his pockets with cigarettes and candy so the guards wouldn't see. Once he'd left, Anisa sat forward and began to plead with us: this was her last chance to save herself.

"I am not a virgin," she whispered hoarsely. She had been married before, but her soldier husband had left her and she had never told Zulfikar. Again and again, she asked us questions we could not answer: How soon after the whipping would they be free to marry? Could they marry quickly? Could they pay someone to let them marry that very night? More frightening to her than the pain was the shame. In practical terms, the day's momentary sting was nothing compared to the stigma, which might cast her out of this shining new society forever.

24

THE CLASH WITHIN

To signal a new level of U.S. interest in Southeast Asia and the new president's childhood home, Secretary of State Hillary Clinton traveled to Indonesia in February 2009. After praising the country's more or less successful transition to democracy since the 1998 fall of President Suharto, she told a dinner crowd of Indonesia's academics and activists, "If you want to know if Islam, democracy, modernity, and women's rights can coexist, go to Indonesia."[1]

Clinton was praising a popular form of Indonesian Islam, which Robert W. Hefner, an expert on Indonesian Islam at Boston University, refers to as Civil (or pluralist) Islam. At its heart lies the understanding that Islam and democracy are compatible. The nation's two largest political parties (which are also religious)—Muhammidiyah, with thirty million members, and Nahdatul Ulama, with forty million members—both espouse this point of view, and most Indonesians have no interest in living in a strict Islamic state. The 2009 elections—in which President Susilo Bambang Yudhoyono was reelected to serve until 2014—make this last point exceedingly clear. The conservative Islamist party, the Prosperous Justice Party, lost dismally in its bid to share power.

But parties and elections do not tell the whole story of the state of Islam in the world's most populous Muslim country. As Robin Bush, the Indonesia representative for the Asia Foundation, points out, at the local level poor governance, corruption, and poverty have led many of the country's Muslims to look to religion—instead of civil society—to resolve social questions, including the role of women.[2] And in this regard, Indonesia is not decidedly and suddenly embracing liberalism. Even though Civil Islam is thriving in national politics, and conservative Islamists are losing at the polls, the conservatives still have considerable influence in public life. As Hefner puts it, "Indonesia is a more conservative place than we had imagined it ten to fifteen years ago."

Indonesia is a country of Islams, not Islam, and its public life is animated by conflicts between Muslims and Muslims, not Muslims and Christians. These contests—typically between liberals and conservatives—are not matters of theological principle. They involve practical issues that arise out of questions such as: Is it legal for Muslims to leave the religion? Can some Muslims be declared heretics? What kinds of rights do religious minorities have in a majority Muslim country? Should *Playboy* magazine be allowed to publish in Indonesia? Should Christians be allowed to proselytize and build churches wherever they please, even in Muslim communities? What should the role of women be in modern society, given the tenets laid down for them in the Quran more than a thousand years ago?

The future of such issues in Indonesia, Abdullahi An-Na'im, the liberal Islamic scholar and professor of law at Emory University, believes, will help set the direction of global Islam. An-Na'im argues that, among other factors, Indonesia's location along the religion's geographic border—on the peripheries, where Islam encounters other cultures and worldviews, as he puts it—makes the religion there more fluid than elsewhere. "I look to these peripheries for vigor and change," he told me. These peripheries include Nigeria and Sudan, where he's from, in addition to Indonesia, and An-Na'im thinks that Muslims along this geographic border, which lies largely between the equator and the tenth parallel, will be able to confront the challenges that modern life poses to devotion and practice, in ways that those who live in the conservative Muslim heartland of the Arabian Peninsula, 4,500 miles from Indonesia, will not.

"My sense is that the Middle East is too full of itself in Islamic terms—too arrogant to be willing to ask these hard questions," he said. There is also the matter of numbers, since of the world's 2.6 billion Muslims, only 20 percent live in the Middle East, and the vast majority of the rest live in the Global South. Given the sheer size of such populations, An-Na'im hopes that the more open-minded Muslims on the periphery will gain the power to wrest Islam away from its conservative Arab center. It's quite a hope—a high-stakes, half-billion-player numbers game. Paradoxically, conservative Christian analysts use the swelling numbers of fellow Christians in the same regions as evidence that their faith is moving in a more conservative direction. Numbers do matter, but they are not the sole factor that determines the future of world religions. Christianity and Islam, and others, will continue to shift and splinter in unpredictable ways.

Along these peripheries, as elsewhere, then, exclusive claims on truth tend to call forth their opposites. In Indonesia and neighboring Malaysia, for instance, as conservative Muslims have tried to co-opt the public sphere with their interpretation of Islam, the moderate "silent majority" has begun to pay more attention, and has grown willing to speak out on behalf of the openness it has taken for granted. This may be what happens at some point in a conservative religious reawakening: after a while, the moderates wake up, too. As Zainah Anwar, the founder of Sisters in Islam, a Malaysian NGO that protects women's legal rights, put it, "Moderates can no longer afford to be silent." This is a sentiment one could as easily hear among American Christians, be they Episcopalians, Catholics, or evangelicals.

25

"ALLAHCRACY"

On Sundays in the wealthy Jakarta suburb of Menteng, the streets close, the diesel clouds and horn squawks dissipate, and pick-up violinists gather in a park a few blocks from the Santo Fransiskus Assisi School—the Christian school, named for the twelfth-century Italian saint, that Barack Obama attended when his family moved to Indonesia in the late sixties. In October 2008, Liszt etudes rose, along with the *slap slap* of runners' sneakered feet, into the whorled branches of the mahogany trees that ringed the park. I, too, went for a run that day, to clear my head. I had just arrived after a think tank's meeting on the United States and the Islamic world in neighboring Malaysia. That afternoon I was hoping to see Ibnu Ahmad, the erstwhile warrior with a brain like a broken computer. Two and a half years after I first met him, I wanted to see how burgeoning democracy had affected the relationship between Indonesian Christians and Muslims. I was eager to hear if Ibnu Ahmad and his comrades were still attempting to move beyond jihad, and whether they really could. How, in the long term, could former fighters like him hold on to their millenarian thinking but leave the strife behind; what did the road beyond jihad really look like?

Jakarta is the biggest megacity in Southeast Asia; its population of more than eight and a half million people is slightly larger than New York City's, and just as varied, making it possible for men like Ibnu Ahmad to hide in plain sight. I showered, then met him at the Starbucks in the lobby of my hotel; and a few hours later, in a warren of shanties across town, I followed him into the dark basement of Jemaah Islamiyah's clandestine headquarters. He flicked on the compact overhead fluorescent lights. With the help of Taufik Andrie, a Jakarta-based journalist who was with us that afternoon, it had not been hard to find him. In the more than two years since I had seen him, he had changed: at forty-two, he could now hold a steady eye-to-eye gaze without his focus skipping away. The passage of time had helped him recover from his rough stint in prison, and he once again was a militant accepted by his fellow militants—not a suspected informer fresh out of torture. No longer plugged into earphones or hiding beneath a baseball hat, Ibnu Ahmad had rejoined the world, and he had a new job selling alternative medicine: Islamic cures called *tibbe nabavi*, "the Prophet's medicine."

This new Islamist revival looked a lot like the Mary Kay cosmetics concern: several years earlier, when a handful of veterans of the Afghan war (they called themselves Afghan alumni) needed money, they went to work for Naturaid, the herbal cures company owned by a fellow JI member named Faisal Ishak. Naturaid was run like most door-to-door sales companies. Each agent invested several hundred dollars in the products, and could receive up to 40 percent of the profits from his sales. Hawking these herbal cures also allowed the aging, paunchy jihadis to reach new clients—and prospective recruits—with the message that the world's end was at hand. But jihad was a young man's game. For JI, the times had changed, even if the ideology had not.

Ibnu Ahmad ducked behind the counter of the basement shop, reached into a case, and fished out a plastic vial. He held up the amber liquid; its label read, "100% Cedar." "This is for casting out devils," he said. His JI colleague entered the shop. A fellow Afghan alumnus, he went by the alias "Jibril," or Gabriel, after the angel in both the Bible and the Quran. (It was also the only name he wanted to give.) Wearing a button-down shirt and chinos, Jibril looked like a computer specialist. Running the store and living in JI headquarters above it, he, too, had left jihad life behind. "It is difficult to be a militant if you don't have the money and the training," Jibril confessed. Ibnu Ahmad added proudly, "We fight with our brain, not our muscle." He must have taken this aphorism, like most of his militant one-liners, from someone else. He picked up his cell phone and began to play the game Brick Breaker with his thumbs. Not everything had changed; he was still easily distractible.

The medicine made money and provided a calculated way to do *da'wa*, "missionary outreach," Jibril said. It was their equivalent of a medical mission. It allowed JI to medicate and indoctrinate at the same time, while offering Indonesians something they, like everyone else, wanted: healing. Also, the market for alternative, faith-based cures was exploding in direct competition with the Western ones. But selling the Prophet's medicine had less to do with undermining Western medicine than with ensuring quality medical care for believers.

"It is not really an infidel thing," Jibril said. "This is consumer consciousness. We want people to go back to natural things."

Ibnu Ahmad handed me the amber vial of cedar oil. "Every human is born with more devils than angels," he said. "Only the Prophet Mohammed, peace be upon him, can remove them." When the devils acted up, a person became possessed. A JI member, armed with this oil, could cast them out.

"I have seen it work," Jibril said. "People come to us with their eyes rolling around in their head."

"Like epilepsy," Ibnu Ahmad added.

It probably was epilepsy, I said.

"No, no—you ask, what day of the week, simple things," Jibril explained. Epileptics don't lose their minds, but these sufferers were definitely in the grasp of a devil, or *jinn*. "You put this oil in the mouth, and if they vomit, they were definitely possessed."

"If they vomit, they are cured completely," Ibnu Ahmad said.

He doddered behind the case again and returned with the rest of the Naturaid product line: a blue beauty powder called Zulu, medicinal honey, and, most popular of all, a pill called Power Cleanser. All of them were supposed to contain *habbatusauda*, or "black seed," which, according to the Prophet's sayings, is the holiest medicament in the world. The tenth-century scholar Muhammad ibn Ismail al-Bukhari, the first and most respected of the six Islamic intellectuals who collected the Prophet's sayings, recounts the following story, which one of Mohammed's companions, Khalid bin Sa'd, told:

> We went out and Ghalib bin Abjar was accompanying us. He fell ill on the way and when we arrived at Medina he was still sick. Ibn Abi 'Atiq came to visit him and said to us, "Treat him with black cumin. Take five or seven seeds and crush them (mix the powder with oil) and drop the resulting mixture into both nostrils, for Aisha [the Prophet's wife] has narrated to me that she heard the Prophet saying, 'This black cumin is healing for all diseases except As-Sam.' Aisha said, 'What is As-Sam?' He said, 'Death.'"[1]

This miracle seed goes by a variety of names: black cumin, fennel flower, nutmeg flower, Roman coriander, and black caraway. (Stores on

Brooklyn's Atlantic Avenue advertise the cure-all in English as "black seed.") Cancer, low sperm count, depression, HIV/AIDS—black seed is believed to cure everything but death.

Ibnu Ahmad pocketed a dozen vials; his colleague opened an oversize ledger and noted twelve vials for "Yasir," Ibnu Ahmad's JI alias, which had carried him through the training camps in Afghanistan and through his attempts to blow up the American embassy in Jakarta.

Evening had come, and it was time for the men to pray. They filed outside to a spigot, cuffed their pants and shirtsleeves, and washed their forearms, dirty feet, and legs up to the calf. As they went back inside the shop, I sat on a bench in the alley. Two emaciated cats eyed me warily, flicked their wiry tails, and skulked down the narrow passage Ibnu Ahmad had called JI's "escape route." Through the window's dirty panes, I saw that the men had begun to pray: three shadows lined up and bent forward at the waist, halving themselves. "Allah hears those who praise him," one sang in Arabic as their shadows stretched straight again, then disappeared below the window frame as they knelt and placed their foreheads against the floor.

It was like watching a dance through a scrim; the simple repetitions of their devotions quieted me. In this moment of solitude, it was almost possible to imagine a man like Ibnu Ahmad being ready to give up his fight against Christians. Jihad had cost so much; maybe it was time for him to sell medicine and take care of his family. When he finished praying and came outside again, I posed this idea to him; his face darkened. Although he did not believe in killing fellow Muslims, the fight against Christians was eternal, and everywhere.

His theology needed an opponent—an enemy—to perpetuate itself. This was one of its many weaknesses. Once the "enemy" was vanquished, these fighters would have to administer a state and its functions. They would have to deliver something concrete to their people beyond struggle and the promise of a better afterlife. And building a functional infrastructure in the developing countries along the tenth parallel was much more difficult than calling upon ailing friends to buy the Prophet's medicine.

Later that night, Ibnu Ahmad, Taufik Andrie, and I went to a local mall to see a film called *Laskar Pelangi*, or "Rainbow Warrior." Andrea Hirata's bestselling book was now a film—a musical—and Indonesians were flocking to see this Bollywood version of Indonesian life. The musical followed a small class of poor boys and girls studying the Quran. Sitting in the dark theater, I wondered what Ibnu Ahmad would think: here was revered Quranic scholarship, Western education, singing, and dancing all in one. Never having been to a cinema, he grew too distracted by the video arcade outside and the shopping mall to pay much attention. Afterward, as we rode down the escalator, Ibnu Ahmad stopped before the unguents at the Clinique counter.

"Dunia"—"the world"—he said, pointing sadly. By this, he meant the secular world. He believed that Zulu, the beauty powder he peddled, was sanctioned by God.

Ibnu Ahmad's skepticism reflected a growing mistrust of Western, or infidel, medicine. He'd heard that America was caught trying to sterilize Nigerian Muslims under the guise of vaccinating them against polio. "I don't let my children get vaccinated for polio anymore," he said proudly. I tried in vain to explain that I had actually gone to Nigeria, found the Nigerian doctor who made all the fuss, Dr. Dhetti Mohammed, and heard from the doctor himself that he had changed his position. The vaccine, much of which was now manufactured in Indonesia, a Muslim country, was safe. Ibnu Ahmad narrowed his eyes and pursed his mouth. He did not believe me. It was not that I was lying exactly, but I came from a world he did not believe in. I was a benevolent enemy.

Beyond the Prophet's cure-alls, former fighters, frustrated and broke, were turning to other moneymaking ventures, including publishing. They were doing a brisk business reprinting, translating, and selling the latest militant religious tracts. Most interestingly, Sidney Jones of International Crisis Group, the world's leading authority on Indonesia's militants, pointed out, the tracts revealed a growing debate over what legitimate jihad really meant.

Radical revivals are innately polarizing: those who are not with the radicals are against them; no one is left indifferent. So it was in Indonesia. Some factions spouted ultraviolence in their books; others criticized the tactics of terrorism. The same divisions that had separated Ibnu Ahmad from his younger brother Salahuddin—who was still imprisoned—over whether it was okay to kill fellow Muslims were now being played out across the pages of tracts and magazines.

One of the youngest and hippest of these publishing outfits, Ar-Rahmah, had a high-tech website, www.arrahmah.com; an account on

Friendster; and a blog called Jihadlife, a religious nod to the hip-hop term *thug life*. The company made its money by downloading videos from the Internet and mass-reproducing them. The most popular, a two-disk version of *Escape from Bagram*, was the made-for-DVD tale of Omar al-Faruq, a captured member of Al Qaeda and one of Ibnu Ahmad's colleagues. Al-Faruq had burned down the Sulawesi village of Sepe after Ibnu Ahmad's operation. In 2005, according to the U.S. military, al-Faruq had stacked cardboard boxes against a wall at Bagram Airbase in Afghanistan, and, taking off his shirt like a local workman, he escaped. Afterward, the Iraqi citizen became a folk hero in Indonesia, and the DVD, which featured a dramatic reenactment of his "rescue," became a hit.

Ar-Rahmah had also recently launched a magazine, *JihadMagz*. On its masthead it claimed to have correspondents in Iraq, Afghanistan, Somalia, and the United States, among other places. In reality, the editors downloaded and reprinted accounts from Mujahideen websites. Even Ibnu Ahmad called *JihadMagz* "a cut-and-paste job." Still, it was slick: it had a bimonthly print run of ten thousand, and sold for the equivalent of four dollars per issue.

American slang was splashed across its headlines in pseudoskater font, yet instead of double-page spreads of skateboarders flying along a half-pipe, the issue of *JihadMagz* I saw featured photos of young women fighters posing with Kalashnikovs in the Afghan countryside. *JihadMagz* was a commercial for violence: its glossy features packaged a world in which fighting the West was honorable, and cool. Its slogan, in English, read "Always Making the World Better."

The founder of *JihadMagz*, Mohammed Jibril, ran his publication out of a nondescript stucco prefab in a subdivision at the southern edge of Jakarta. Jibril and his editor, both scruffy twenty-something men wearing low-riding jeans, their hair sticking hiply up, could have been running a startup anywhere—except that the father of global jihad, Sayyid Qutb, graced the cover of the magazines stacked in the corner.

When I arrived unannounced at their office in October 2008, the two young men hopped around nervously, making a batch of sugary orange drink and shuffling papers. They were in the middle of an editorial meeting, and said they had never before had a Westerner in the office, let alone a fellow journalist. Jibril, twenty-six, his baggy, cuffed jeans riding up his calves, lounged cross-legged on the office floor.

"Democracy is bullshit," he said. "We want 'Allahcracy.'" Barefoot, he crossed the tile floor to grab an issue off the pile in the corner, and handed it to me. Inside, in one photograph, an Iraqi insurgent commander sipped tea on a Baghdad street corner. In another, the ravaged faces of Gracia and Martin Burnham—two American missionaries held captive from 2001 to 2002 by the Al Qaeda–linked Abu Sayyaf Group—stared out angrily from the leafy jungle floor of the southern Philippines. Gracia, a fortyish pixie in a head scarf, sat next to a sunburned Martin. About the same age, he was already bald, with a strawberry-blond beard covering most of his hollowed face. The pair seemed solemn, but while Martin looked resigned, Gracia cocked her head at the camera with rage and suspicion. As this 2001 image of dirty, frightened missionaries bounced around the world, it became a harbinger of the West's escalating confrontation with militant Islam.

I'd seen this video still in American magazines, except that where I saw sympathetic victims, the boys of *JihadMagz* saw neo-imperial Christian agents.

Paging through their magazine was like looking through the lens of an old box camera; everything upside down and backward. Our presupposition as to who was winning and losing this war was also diametrically opposed.

On one cover, under the headline "Enemies of Islam," Jibril had reproduced photographs of Salman Rushdie and Sidney Jones of the International Crisis Group. (He was angry with Jones for her revelatory reports on militancy in Indonesia.) Although Rushdie was beyond the reach of the wannabe jihadis who read the magazine, Jones was not. She'd laughed when we'd spoken of the photo, but it was clearly intended as a threat. And in August 2009, a month after coordinated attacks on Jakarta's Ritz-Carlton and J. W. Marriott Hotels left nine people dead, and injured at least fifty more, Jibril was arrested for helping to fund them.[2] From prison, he posted a new Facebook photo. At twenty pounds lighter, he was freshly shaven and shirtless. A digital pinup, he'd listed himself as a fan of Ashton Kutcher, the star of the television show *Punk'd*, and Hizbut Tahrir Indonesia, a radical utopian organization calling for an Islamic state.

Leaving the *JihadMagz* office, I went to meet Ibnu Ahmad for the last time. We were going to visit his brother Salahuddin in prison that afternoon. Word had it that Ahmad's brother—now thirty-two, and still serving time for a 2001 car bombing in downtown Jakarta—was about to be released. I picked Ibnu Ahmad up in a taxi outside a Starbucks in the Menteng suburb; we bought a bag of golden starfruit, some avocados, and a few cellular phone scratch cards, and drove past President Obama's school again on the way to the prison.

To rehabilitate fighters like these two brothers, the Indonesian government was piloting a deprogramming effort, teaching former militants skills such as motorcycle repair, welding, and tailoring. In reality, such skills meant little beyond the promise of a few dollars to their families and a possible job when they got out of prison. According to Ibnu Ahmad, the police could be kind to as many committed young fighters as they wanted, but it was not going to change anyone's thinking about God. "I went through rehabilitation," he scoffed from the taxi's front seat. "We were supposed to get money to start a business, but I did not get it."

Outside the prison, two bored-looking prostitutes sat on a cement culvert. One had a daughter with her; the girl, who looked about ten, lay her head in her mother's lap so her mother could comb her hair before going back to work. It was the most noxious by far of the Indonesian prisons I had visited. The place smelled like carrion; a cart heaped with tangy garbage stood inside the small exercise yard. Men picked through the pile for plastic to recycle. Only the guards wore uniforms. A guard straddling the yard's steel weight bench eyed Ibnu Ahmad. A prisoner sat behind the guard and massaged his back.

When Salahuddin strode into the courtyard—stocky in a Salafi's signature seventh-century pajama—the garbage pickers paid no attention, but the guard did. Salahuddin had done his best to grow a beard, a Fu Manchu affair, long hairs drooping from a pudgy face, just like his brother's. The two men grinned at each other as Ibnu Ahmad handed his little brother the sack of starfruit and avocados.

"No one liked me here at first. They thought I was a terrorist," Salahuddin said, eyes darting around, taking quick stock of our audience. "Now I am their religious teacher."

The thought of Salahuddin teaching the tenets of Islam to his fellow criminals—rapists, robbers, and murderers—was profoundly unsettling. "I follow the thinking of Zawahiri and bin Laden," he continued matter-of-factly and without anger or bluster. Unlike his elder brother, Salahuddin had never been to Afghanistan, nor had he ever received any legitimate religious education. Instead, he belonged to the next generation of jihadis. Coming of age in the nineties after the war against the Soviets in Afghanistan, they ran drills in the jungles of the Philippines, where they learned to fight another dirty, lawless war.

This included the right to call fellow Muslims who opposed them infidels, or *kuffar* (the plural of the Arabic *kafir*), including the members of the Indonesian government. "As long as the *kuffar* do not stop trying to ruin us, we will not retire," Salahuddin said. Jihad was his job; he would protect Islam in Indonesia, just as, in the name of protecting the Land of Islam, their grandfather had fought the Dutch. Their uncle, he said proudly, had also tried to assassinate Indonesia's first president, Sukarno. Now Salahuddin saw the enemy everywhere, even among fellow Muslims. Although locked away for the moment, he completely supported the bombing campaign of his militant colleagues, who belonged to the JI splinter group led by Noordin Top. The group targeted places associated with the West—including the 2003 bombing of the J. W. Marriott Hotel in south Jakarta, the second Bali bombing in 2005, an attack on the Australian embassy in 2004, and the coordinated attacks on Jakarta's Ritz-Carlton and J. W. Marriott Hotels on July 17, 2009, for which Jibril would go to prison. (Two months later, Top would be killed during a police raid in Solo, Central Java, which was Salahuddin and Ibnu Ahmad's hometown.)

In these attacks, which left dozens dead and hundreds more wounded, most of the victims were Indonesians, not Westerners. That fine point did not matter to Salahuddin: a war was a war, and there was no stopping this one until the Islamists had won the whole world. I leaned against the prison yard's concrete-block wall and grew first bored with his rhetoric, then alarmed that this man was soon to be released. I only hoped his inferior training and newfound isolation would neutralize him, since clearly, his thinking had not changed a bit. The former JI leader Nasir Abbas told me that Salahuddin was involved in the deprogramming initiative, but the young man denied it.

Why would he want to sell out? He stole a look at his brother, who was sitting on the prison bench next to him. Apparently, the rift between the brothers had healed enough that Ibnu Ahmad could deliver fruit and phone cards, but had not closed in any ideological sense. Ibnu Ahmad had moved in a middle-aged way beyond jihad, and into selling alternative Mary Kay; his brother had had no such change of heart.

"The people who do not want to keep fighting do not know how bad it is on the front line," Salahuddin said. The front line—where was that mythic division, exactly, that bright, shining divide between good and evil, the Land of Islam and the Land of War? Was it the "Berlin wall" that divided Muslims from Christians on the island of Sulawesi? Or did it hang in the airwaves between the blaring hymn "Jerusalem" and the dueling call to prayer? Or was it dynamic, and running right now between these two brothers standing in the prison yard?

The stench and heat were growing overpowering, and the harder I tried to listen to Salahuddin, the muddier his certainty sounded—thicker with fear and self-defense, as if he knew he was waging a losing battle. To console himself when others, including his brother, dropped away from the cause, Salahuddin found a single verse of the Quran most comforting. It guaranteed him heaven: "Anyone, male or female, who does good deeds and is a believer, will enter Paradise and will not be wronged by as much as the dip in a date stone" (Women 4:124). If there was no justice in this world, he would wait for the next.

MALAYSIA

*Lift up your eyes and look at the fields, for they are already
white for harvest!*
—THE GOSPEL ACCORDING TO JOHN 4:35

*God is my Lord and your Lord, so serve Him:
that is a straight path.*
—THE WORDS OF JESUS, THE QURAN, MARY 19:36

26

THE RACE TO SAVE THE LAST LOST SOULS

Juli Edo, fifty, popped a cassette tape into the deck
of his shuddering Jeep. It was later in the afternoon
of June 4, 2006, than he wanted it to be—late to
start on the hundred-mile drive north from the

gleaming capital of Kuala Lumpur to the jungle outside of Kampar, an old tin-mining boomtown. Edo is an anthropologist; he is also an aborigine, and a leading expert on the last 150,000 of his own indigenous kinsfolk, the Orang Asli, "original people." That afternoon, Edo was headed to his wife's family village for a forest wedding and a long-awaited vacation, along with his wife, Lipah Anjang, his teenage daughter, two younger sons, a six-month-old Chinese baby named Monmon, and me. Rubber trees, which looked like white birches, and dwarf oil palms lined the multilane highway. For miles, each scarred trunk gave way to another of its kind, and another, and another, moving back from the road in perfect diagonals, forming enormous plantations that seemed to have no end. Through the Jeep's scratchy sound system, John Denver sang, "Life is old there, older than the trees."

Edo cursed quietly. Take me home to where, exactly? The jungle in which his people lived was fast disappearing, and since most of the people had no deeds to their land, there was nothing they could do about it. Along the highway, we passed a plantation billboard that read: "WE GREEN THE EARTH."

"It's a lie," Edo snorted. Palm oil plantations, which yield an inexpensive, extra-fatty cooking oil used for deep-frying, are responsible for 80 percent of the deforestation here in the nation of Malaysia, which lies as little as twenty-five miles east of Indonesia, over the South China Sea. Malaysia and Indonesia are being stripped of their jungles and rain forests faster than almost any other tropical countries in the world.[1] Plantations like these are partly responsible. The trees by the roadside—alien species imported from South America—were at most a mere hundred years old. By contrast, Edo's people were descended from Stone Age farmers who first migrated here four thousand years ago. They lived by the sea as fisher folk, until the rise of Islamic sultanates during the fifteenth century. Then, rather than convert to Islam and become ethnic Malays, they fled inland to the jungle to retain their indigenous spiritual practices, based on honoring ancestors and the natural world. As polytheists—*mushrikun*—they were hunted by slave raiders until the 1920s. Now, once again, the dwindling jungle is threatening their survival.

Along with the disappearance of their land, new logging roads snaking through this wilderness are making them the target of Muslim and Christian missionaries, who now have fresh means to reach formerly unreachable areas and communities. In remote jungles and riverine villages, the two are competing over who will convert the Orang Asli, in what one of Edo's colleagues, a Malaysian anthropologist named Colin Nicholas, had called "the race to save the last lost souls."

"It's cultural genocide," Edo said. His brown eyes scanned the paved road as if disappointment lay ahead of us. Tired from a long semester of teaching anthropology at the University of Malaya, he had been looking forward to a week's lazy vacation spent fishing and hunting wild boar when I showed up in his cramped university office at the end of May. Colin Nicholas had sent me to find the Orang Asli anthropologist, since Edo was not only a member of the group but also the definitive authority on their spiritual practices. Pushing my way through a line of frantic students trying to photocopy their final exams, I asked Edo what he knew about this competition for converts among his people, and if I might travel with him to meet the Orang Asli. He eyed me incredulously from between stacks of stapled papers. Their world is a closed one; the aborigines have persevered by keeping strangers out. The Malay government also bans foreigners from visiting their villages, one of many tactics meant to keep Christian missionaries at bay. This was the jungle, he reasoned. It could be dangerous. Was I sure I knew what I was getting into? There would be no doctors and few vehicles, and I would have to eat and drink whatever the aborigines did. "Are you prone to illness?" he asked, squinting across the desk as if to scan my vulnerability to microbes. I tucked my fingernails into the lap of my dirty serge skirt and described the fault line along which I had been traveling. By May 2006, I'd journeyed through Nigeria, Sudan, Indonesia, and the Philippines. Edo nodded sharply, and his weary brown eyes sparkled. At the end of the week, he was going to attend a family wedding at which the Orang Asli bride was marrying an outsider—a Muslim Malay man—and according to law, she would have to convert to Islam. Her father, irate at what he saw as his daughter's desertion of their culture, was threatening to cancel the wedding.

Now, ten days later, all seven of us were squeezed into the Jeep, zipping toward Edo's aunt's home in Kampar and then on to the village. His sons poked at each other; Monmon, the baby, shrieked over the reedy John Denver bootleg. Shouting questions to Edo from the cramped backseat, I feared that I might be about to report on someone's family vacation but had to make the best of it, so I opened to the blank back page of my notebook and taught the boys how to play hangman. Around us, the trees marched out in formation like soldiers staking their claim on a foreign land.

Kuala Lumpur is a glinting forest of steel and glass surrounding the Petronas Twin Towers, two spiky corncobs (taller than the World Trade Center towers) completed in 1998 and named for the state-owned oil and gas company. Prime Minister Mahathir Mohamad, a vocal critic of the West who had served in his post for twenty years, commissioned the towers. The Malaysian government instructed the Argentinean architect César Pelli (who also designed terminals B and C at Reagan Airport in Washington, D.C.) to invoke the Muslim religion in the design. Pelli fashioned the towers using the sacred geometry of Islam's eight-pointed star. Beyond that, he was essentially constructing a national identity—as he has said, "flying blind."[2]

The towers are monuments to Islamic progress—and to wealth. Their interiors are very slick capitalist crypts. In October 2008, between the Prada and Chanel boutiques, the smoothie and wrap stands, I watched a logjam of global identities form. A woman robed and veiled in black followed her husband through a group of chattering Buddhist monks in bright vestments—a cluster of persimmons. Despite the day's monsoon heat, the consumer theme was Christmas.

Petronas has invested $1.45 billion in Sudan; after China, Malaysia is the nation's largest foreign investor.[3] Since the African oil boom in the late nineties, Malaysia has provided military aid to Sudan. Over the past nine years, this relationship has deepened. Khairy Jamaluddin, a thirty-four-year-old investment banker who was head of the youth wing of Malaysia's largest political party and the son-in-law of the former prime minister Abdullah Ahmad Badawi, told me that after the September 11 attacks, Malaysia focused its foreign investments in Iran and Sudan—Muslim countries the West considered pariah states. Malaysia now holds a 30 percent stake in the Greater Nile Petroleum Operating Company, the oil consortium that operates in and around the town of Abyei. Malaysia also provides military aid to the Sudan Armed Forces, the soldiers who drove fifty thousand people off their oil-rich land around Abyei in May 2008, and who orchestrated many of the attacks in Darfur. According to Amnesty International, on February 17, 2004, Malaysia and Sudan signed a formal defense agreement allowing Malaysia to send military hardware to Khartoum. To quell international dissent, then prime minister Badawi visited Darfur on April 18, 2007. Later the same day he traveled on to Khartoum, where he reiterated Malaysia's support for the regime of President Hassan Omar al-Bashir.[4] Unlike China, or the Western oil companies, Malaysia comes under very little scrutiny for its practices in Sudan, partly because of its remoteness and its size, which, at 127,000 square miles, is smaller than Montana.

Malaysia is one of the most technologically sophisticated Muslim countries in the world. (Twenty-three million of its twenty-eight million citizens have cell phones.)[5] It is also, thanks to its oil and gas holdings, one of the most prosperous. With proven oil reserves of 3 billion barrels, Malaysia sends abroad 753,700 barrels a day (nearly double Sudan's output), which makes the country the twenty-seventh-largest oil exporter in the world. The true measure of a nation's oil wealth, however, is not just in billions of barrels; it is in number of barrels per citizen.[6] By this measure, Malaysia has roughly ten times the energy assets of Indonesia.

Nonetheless, Malaysia struggles to exist as a single, diverse nation, one in which religious differences create the greatest divisions and threaten, at times, to pull apart the modern state. Of one hundred Malaysians, sixty are Muslims, twenty are Buddhists, nine are Christians, six are Hindus, and the remaining four follow Chinese beliefs, such as Confucianism or Taoism, or practice their indigenous, spirit-based religion, as do the Orang Asli. This heterogeneity dates back to the 1700s, when colonialists from Britain, which inherited Malaysia from the Portuguese and the Dutch, transported thousands of Indian and Chinese laborers to transform the vast jungles into rubber plantations and tin mines. The Indians worked on the rubber farms. The Chinese mined tin. The ethnic Malay people, who, after the Orang Asli, had been the region's first inhabitants, feared becoming a minority in their own homeland. To protect their interests, they began to coalesce around their shared religion: Islam. In 1946, the British government, bankrupted by World War II, announced that the Malay states would gain their independence and all citizens—regardless of race—would be granted equal rights. The Malay people fought back by forming United Malays National Organisation—still, by a very narrow margin, the leading political party in Malaysia. Thanks to UMNO, when Malaysia gained its independence on August 31, 1957, the constitution enshrined the religious and ethnic superiority of the Malay people. To be

Malaysian meant to be Malay, to be Malay meant to be Muslim, and the Malays were awarded the status of *bumiputra*, a Sanskrit word meaning "sons of the earth."

In 1991, Prime Minister Mahathir Mohamad issued Vision 2020, a fifty-year plan to raise Malaysia's status to that of the West. He modeled this plan for advancement not on the West, but on Islam. The West didn't own prosperity, he argued, and it was time for Malaysia to make its own Great Leap Forward. Drawing on the country's prodigious oil wealth, he began by Islamizing its economic system so that banks, insurance companies, and pawnshops would be compliant with Sharia; usury—or collecting interest—was made illegal. He funded think tanks to wrestle with the question of Islam and development.[7] And in a move toward affirmative action, he made it compulsory for corporate boards to include set quotas of ethnic Malays. Because Malaysia's economy is dominated by Chinese interests, this measure was meant to ensure that the Malays would not lose out to the Chinese in their nation's economic future. As Mahathir put it, "The negative view and attitude of the Muslims toward industry will not only be unprofitable for them, but will in fact be against Islam and its teachings."[8] Islam didn't just sanction industrialization; it was now considered un-Islamic not to industrialize. In 2010, Malaysia is still bidding to become the world's "Halal Hub." This worldwide business of rendering food and other Muslim products religiously permissible—a $635 billion-per-year industry—would make Malaysia a prime location for manufacturing and sanctioning everything from cookies, to handbags, to vaccines.

In Malaysia, for much of the past seven hundred years, Islam has been synonymous with progress. The religion once linked a backwater to a larger global system of trade and culture. Today, in both business and politics, the relationship between Islam and development is remarkably strong. Over the past decade, for instance, the Malaysian government has quietly set up a judicial unit within the state to make sure all its laws are compliant with Islamic law. Many Malaysians fear that bringing religion to bear on secular law marks a step backward. But for those who support the move, this is neither conservative nor reactionary; it is about combating contemporary, secular life with an authentic and sacred moral code. Islamization, a lawyer who served in this Sharia unit told me, has changed in the twenty-first century, and Malaysia must keep up with the times. "The impact of the Iranian Revolution isn't the crucial factor anymore,"

Hassan Abu Bakar, a Malaysian government counsel, said. "Here, global-ization—books from the U.S. and U.K., the Internet—brings Islam into our lives."

Bringing Sharia into all aspects of the law, he and others believed, was the best way to protect Malay Muslims from the onslaught of secular and Christian forces of globalization. Such external forces have made apos-tasy—the act of leaving Islam—such a pressing issue that conservatives recently outlawed it. The most notorious case was that of a forty-six-year-old woman named Lina Joy, who, in July 2007, was not legally allowed to convert from Islam to Christianity. "We view apostasy very seriously," Khairy Jamaluddin, the banker and politician who also holds a degree in philosophy, politics, and economics from Oxford University, told me in 2006. "It is politically one of the biggest concerns and one of the worst forms of sacrilege." For a modern politician to speak of sacrilege can be baffling to those of us in secular democratic societies, and Jamaluddin knew it. "Balancing Islam and the West is not easy, but we live in a one hundred percent Muslim society, which is not easy to manage, either."

In Malaysia, there are other codes that protect Islam's primacy. Chris-tians are not allowed to proselytize to Muslims. And in 2009, the Malay-sian government reinstated a much-disputed ban on the use of the word for God, *Allah*, by Christians. (In December 2009, when the High Court reversed the ban once again, at least nine churches were burned in reac-tion.)[9] The Malaysian home minister, Syed Hamid Albar, said the govern-ment wanted to avoid "confusing" Muslims or allowing clandestine attempts to convert them. In response Malaysian Catholic leaders argued that they have been using the word *Allah* for hundreds of years, and that this was just the latest government attempt to stifle the free exercise of religion in an ever more restrictive society. Moreover, they added, there is no other word for God in the Malay language. In a 2008 editorial in Malaysia's Catholic newspaper, *The Herald*, the editor, Father Lawrence Andrew, asked, "Can't we Christians ask our fellow Christians to pray?"

In this religious struggle over Malaysian identity, the Orang Asli are most often caught in the middle. Since most Orang Asli are neither Chris-tian nor Muslim, but follow their own ancient cosmology, the pressure to convert them—and to usher them into one or the other rival worldview—is fierce. Since the 1970s, as part of a controversial, long-secret program, the Malaysian government has sponsored Islamic teachers to go live in

Orang Asli villages, has built almost three hundred prayer halls (some in villages with few or no Muslims),[10] and has paid Malay Muslims (up to $3,000)[11] to marry Orang Asli women. All of these efforts to do *da'wa*—to proselytize—are intended to ensure the aborigines' conversion to Islam and introduce them to life as modern Malays. The government also grants Orang Asli who convert to Islam better health care, education, housing, and jobs than those who do not.[12] Despite these incentives, the government has had only negligible success among the Orang Asli, who have resisted Islamization for centuries. (In the past thirty years, by unofficial estimates, roughly twenty-five in one hundred have become Muslim; and fifteen of one hundred are now Christian.) "If we go into Islamization, they get a bit sensitive," said Razak Kechik, M.D., a member of ABIM, an Islamic organization founded in 1971 and committed to proselytizing. Kechik worked among the Orang Asli for two decades, not only as a medical doctor preventing malaria but also in supporting income-generating projects, such as sewing collectives. He sees Islam as the only way forward for the aborigines; as he put it, "We teach the ones who want to know about Islam. Of course they need to change."

Much to the government's dismay, Christian missionaries—ranging from local Catholics and Methodists to South Korean Presbyterians— also evangelize the Orang Asli. Many argue that, unlike Islam, which transforms the Orang Asli into Malays, and thus erases their identity, Christianity allows the indigenous people to retain their way of life—to eat what they wish, pray as they like, and marry whom they want—while at the same time facing the reality that a traditional way of life in the jungle is coming to an end, by choice or force of change.

Our cramped band reached Kampar, the colonial tin-mining town, in time for afternoon tea. Its cluttered streets teemed with Chinese food stalls— vats of boiling mee noodles, stir-fried prawns, and chicken biscuits. Wall-eyed river fish dangled from wet twine. Kampar is inhabited mostly by ethnic Chinese, descendants of those whom the British relocated from China to work in the mines more than two hundred years ago. I followed Edo as he fought his way through the market's screaming crowd to play the Chinese lottery, one of his favorite pastimes (we lost), then bought pastries for Edo's auntie, who lived at the edge of Kampar. Before continuing on to the darkening forest, we were going to pay her a visit.

Aunt Sakyah lived alone in a narrow two-story house covered in weathered shingles; hers was the largest to be found among the three hilly streets of macadam that made up a single Orang Asli community. Anyone could see that this paved hummock was not desirable land. Forty years earlier, the Malay government had forcibly resettled the Orang Asli in this concrete version of a village, Edo told me. A Communist rebellion raged in the jungle from 1948 to 1960, and in order to isolate the Orang Asli from the rebels, the British and the Malays trucked tens of thousands of them to internment camps fenced in barbed wire. The move was disastrous. Thousands died.

Sakyah, who looked to be in her sixties, had tea waiting for us on a white tin tray. She opened the greasy white box of our pastries and set them on the linoleum floor among the cups and spoons. We sat on the ground with our backs against a pristine couch and a couple of upholstered chairs that looked like they were rarely used. Monmon, the Chinese baby, crawled around us, and Edo's wife, who told me to call her *Amé*, "Mother," reached for her, clucking absently. It turned out she was babysitting the child as a favor to a neighbor.

"Mostly women work; the men are hopeless drunks," Edo said, explaining that his auntie held down several jobs. She disappeared for a moment, returned with a paper bag, and pulled from it intricately woven squares, which she unfurled against the linoleum. She made them for tourists who used them as placemats. They took a long time to make, she said, squatting and touching their woven edges with an artist's tenderness and frustration.

With Edo's Jeep parked outside, word of his arrival buzzed through the concrete village. Soon two men slouched into the house. One was tall, spare, and serene; the other, elfin and grouchy. The former was the village headman, or chief, named Sam. Being headman was a difficult job, and although Sam was only in his late thirties, he looked closer to fifty. The latter, named Bah Selamat—or "tranquillity"—seemed neither calm nor happy. The father of the bride, he had come to Kampar from the jungle to do some shopping for his daughter's impending nuptials. He wanted to stop the wedding, he said, collapsing at last into one of the scratchy chairs. The issue, he told me, putting his hands on his knees, was Islam.

Paradoxically, the aggressive government proselytizing had pushed him in the other direction. About a decade earlier, with the help of a local Orang Asli minister, he had been baptized as a Methodist. For him, Christianity was a form of common defense, because it allowed him to change as little as possible.

"I converted for freedom," he said. "If you convert to Christianity, it's not a big deal. You're still Orang Asli. But when you convert to Islam, you are Malay." His daughter, Sorya, by contrast, was marrying a Malay man, which meant, legally, she had to become a Muslim. "We didn't want our children converting to Islam. One converts and they all convert." The government push did not target women such as Sorya, he explained, but their children. This was about making the next generation Malay, about using religion to bulk up their numbers, and their claim to the dwindling forest resources.

A car drew up alongside the house and stopped. Edo's auntie crept to the window and peeked out from behind the curtain.

"Missionaries," she said. Next door, two Chinese Christians were visiting some new converts. She let the curtain fall back across the window and sat down to finish her tea.

"Oh, they come here," she said. "I tell them my heart's not open to Christianity. They tell me it's the right path; it's the right thing to do." She bent to refill the cups, but the men were finished with tea.

The faiths compete for converts, Sam, the lanky village head, explained. The men switched to sipping whiskey. We went outside by the laundry line, so Sam could smoke a cigarette. The missionaries' sedan was gone. The Christians were savvier about converting people, because they were subtler about their intentions. "They don't ask us to convert—they give us services, look out for our welfare," Sam said. The Muslims were more direct. "Every Friday, they curse infidels from the mosque." He gestured up the hill to a whitewashed box with a loudspeaker. Community development officers ventured from house to house to persuade people to convert, and the government assigned missionaries to come stay with people in the village.

"The missionaries say, 'We want to give you good values,' but we have better values than they do," Sam said. "If we lose our land, our customs will be lost. If we lose our customs and choose other religions, then we've lost everything."

———

It was almost 10:00 p.m. when we turned off the paved road beyond Kampar and onto the muddy track that led to the village where we were to sleep. Through the Jeep's open window, the ground looked littered with stars where ponds—abandoned tin mines filled with foul water—reflected the obsidian sky. The rough road jostled the Jeep and roused the dozing children. Through the trees ahead, I could see strips of woven light, like huge twig lanterns hanging above the forest floor. Closer, I could see the light was coming through chinks in the bamboo walls of roughly two dozen tree houses, which were standing about five feet off the ground in a leafy clearing. Edo stopped the Jeep, and we climbed the wooden ladder into the tiny, sooty hut where his sister-in-law was stir-frying wild boar in an iron wok on a camp stove on the floor. Sweet smoke from the roasting flesh blew through the open walls, over a bunk bed, a refrigerator, and a computer—only for playing games. Twenty-two of us would be sleeping in a space about the size of three office cubicles.

"Oh, we won't sleep. We'll stay up for the next three days straight," a slight woman with a pageboy haircut and an accent from London's East End said. She had climbed the five-foot wooden ladder into the hut behind me, and stunned me for a second—the hair, the tone, the baby tee—but Lian, who looked to be about forty, was Orang Asli. Another of Edo's sisters-in-law, she had left the village to emigrate to the United Kingdom years earlier, and was currently working in London. She had married a Londoner, and for his sake—and to my relief—the family had installed a porcelain toilet in the outhouse next door.

Blue light flickered over the hut's uneven floorboards, and a pack of feral-looking children, their legs scratched and their hair matted with twigs, sat six inches from a TV screen, entranced by *Bridget Jones's Diary*. At that instant, Renée Zellweger was running down the street in leopard-spotted underpants, but the children did not laugh. Their eyes were dark and glossy—they seemed stoned by the screen's soft light. Next to the TV, a refrigerator hummed; its shelves were lined with beer.

One child stood out from the others. Her brushed hair was braided tightly down her back, and when she turned her head, the TV's light glinted off her braces. Ten years old, L.V. lived in London with her aunt Lian. L.V.'s biological mother, who was cooking boar, could not afford to keep her here. Both women called her "daughter." L.V. had not been back to the village since she was a baby, and remembered nothing of the jungle or its life. In front of the TV, she looked uncomfortable—itchy and glum—

though the world the children were watching, the London world of Bridget Jones, was one only she, among the children, had seen firsthand. When the other children whispered in their language, L.V. threw a tantrum because she could not understand.

As L.V.'s biological mother doled out the boar meat, she tried to quiet L.V. Although they were strangers, each watched the other with a kind of longing—as if on opposite sides of shatterproof glass. "I will tell you the story of the mosquito princess," her village mother said, in hesitant English. Like so many other Orang Asli traditions, their fables were disappearing. "Turn off the TV," she called to the rest of the children, who paid no attention. As L.V. drew close to her, she began:

A mosquito fell in love with a human man. He stayed in a farm near the jungle. He owned a cow and a goat. He was a strong man, and the mosquitoes liked to hover above him and watch him work. One day when the mosquito princess grew up, her father told her to bite him. "Maybe he has good blood." When she went to do her father's bidding, she saw the human's face and felt something in her heart: "I like you," she told him, but he didn't understand, and tried to swat her away. So the princess asked her father if she could become a human. Her father was sad. He knew he would lose his daughter.

He was a good man, though, so he sent her to a powerful shaman. "Yes, you can be a human, but only during the daylight," the shaman told her. "At night you'll turn back into a mosquito. Your whole life must be a secret." The mosquito princess married the human. Everything went fine, until her mosquito parents wanted to meet her husband. One night, when the mosquitoes surrounded him, he did not understand their language, and thought that they were there to bite him. He became so angry, he killed them all.

To my ear, this story seemed to reflect the dangers of overreaching, the hazards of wishing to be someone other than who you are. Later, however, Robert Dentan, an American anthropologist who lived with the Orang Asli for years, told me that although such stories do contain a warning against assimilation,[13] this is only a small part of their significance. Hunted for centuries, and persecuted nearly to the edge of extinction, the Orang Asli also teach their children about the power of collective, familial love, and about the risk of standing outside of that love, which can destroy them.

For the mosquito princess, transforming herself (as when converting to Islam) and marrying a powerful outsider (such as a Malay man) meant destroying her whole family. What good was love like that?

After the story, I went outside to find Edo, but he had disappeared on an all-night boar hunt. The rest of us settled in for a few hours of sleep. I was granted the place of honor: the top bunk. In the night, I awoke urgently needing to pee. Still dozing, I muddled over a floor of prone bodies. Reaching the door hatch, I stepped out into thin air, having forgotten we were five feet off the ground. When I hit the moldering loam with a thud, the house above me erupted in good-natured laughter. For a moment, it sounded like the trees were laughing. Relieved I hadn't broken any bones, I returned to the bunk and waited for Edo, who appeared at dawn, empty-handed, his face pale and his T-shirt filthy. By the time I dared to climb down the ladder, he was sitting outside on a log drinking a beer, watching the children concoct a wild game of badminton. It was difficult to catch him alone and at rest, so I buttonholed the professor there and then. Poor man, I thought, as I took him a cookie from the greasy hotel tin I had brought as a hostess gift.

He waved off the cookie, wearily picked up a stick, and drew a diamond in the sandy soil, an ad hoc blackboard. "This is the world," he said, sketching his people's view of the universe, with the sun at the top of the diamond. "Our universe and our villages have four corners." Within those corners, spirits live in the village's trees, fields, and ponds. "Spirits are good or bad depending on how you treat them," he said. "That's why when we open a rice paddy field, we have to ask permission. We don't kill animals or cut down trees without doing this. We even apologize when we pee anywhere.

"After death, the body transforms into its origin: the earth. The earth where your grandfather died is considered your relative. The blood from your birth is on the ground." As he spoke, I thought of the 1960s environmental theory called the Gaia hypothesis. Its main proponent, James Lovelock, a nonagenarian former NASA scientist, argued that the world is a single living organism—a negative feedback loop that regulates itself like a human body. Although this thinking sounded radically hippie-ish at the time, its innate common sense underlies much of today's environmental science. Many indigenous communities, including some Native Americans, saw the world as a single living—and divine—entity. So, too, it seemed, did the Orang Asli.

"Our connection becomes not to the people but to the whole earth," Edo said. Without land, it was impossible to perform their rituals. Without rituals, their way of life was dying. Deforestation, logging, and development broke the Orang Asli's ties to the land and made it easier—and more necessary—for them to choose a new set of beliefs, a practical how-to guide to modern civilization: Christian or Muslim. This was the choice before them.

THE WEDDING

The smell of roasting chicken wafting uphill from the rubber glade hinted at Bah Selamat's anger. His sulking from the other day had given way to rage. Chicken was cheaper than beef, and his daughter's wedding day feast should have been much more elaborate—and expensive—but he was in a punishing mood.

"I warned my daughter not to marry a Malay," he grumbled. "When they become Muslim, they don't come back." The guests were beginning to arrive, so he rolled up his blue jeans and dragged tree stumps through the clearing to make seats for them. Like most Orang Asli, he had no deed to his land. If the government told him to move tomorrow, he would have to do it. He had no doubt the Orang Asli way of life was vanishing.

"Our culture will die depending on how fast development comes," he said—a predicament that had begun with the building of roads decades earlier. "After the road, a lot of things happened to our community that we didn't want," Bah Selamat explained. "Roads allow us to travel for work outside the village, so this has had a big effect on our families." The road had led his daughter, Sorya, from the safety of her family. The road had led her to Cameron Highlands, the Malaysian resort town where, waiting tables, she met the Muslim busboy who was now her fiancé. A whisper went around the glade that the bride—his prodigal daughter, Sorya—had arrived via overnight bus, along with her fiancé and her future mother-in-law. She was hiding in her brother's hilltop shack, and not planning to appear until her parents and her new Malay family met to haggle over her dowry as a precursor to the wedding ceremony. That event all of us would watch. No one went up to see her, so, along with a zaftig girl cousin of hers, I climbed the hill.

Through the hut's open door, I could see the fiancé's mother collapsed in a yellow chiffon heap on the floor. Sorya, twenty-four, in sweatpants, crouched on the porch—her skin gray as the wall-eyed river fish, her dull black hair bundled sloppily against her neck. She looked as if she'd been up all night studying for finals, but instead she'd been up, sleepless on the rattling bus, dreading this wedding. All of this talk about abandoning her people was a convenient revision of history, she said. Her father had wanted her to get a job—and an income—at the resort. And it wasn't as if some pure ideal of indigenous life was at stake in this village. Sorya explained, "Most people's job here is to spray poison on the paddy fields." She drew her knees up and, receding deeper into herself, looked down the steep slope at the cooking fire's smoke rising from her father's house. With little else to say, I wished her a happy future.

"My future isn't happy at all," she said vacantly. "My father's Christian; I'm marrying a Muslim. I haven't told my father yet, but I've already converted." Her cousin and I looked at each other. "I really don't know very much about Islam because I've been working, so I don't have time to learn. I just went to a one-day seminar. They haven't even taught me how to pray." That was not unusual; as her father had said, for those converting her, this process was more about her children's identity than hers.

Puffy-eyed and blinking, her fiancé, Norsyam, twenty-eight, came out of the hut and plopped down near her. "Today we'll discuss the dowry, and if our parents agree, we'll get married, but I don't think my mother and her father will agree," he said. Sorya blanched. Together, they guessed at the mortifying questions she was about to be asked, such as "Are you sure you want to marry him?" and "When did you convert to Islam?"

"This is the test of my faith," she said. It was a test, all right, but of much more than her newfound faith: it was a test of her and Norsyam's relationship, and of the law, which would soon prevent her from turning back. They gazed at each other with wide, cowed eyes. Then our unenthusiastic procession marched down the hill to the government-built meetinghouse, a cement two-story structure on top of which a Muslim prayer room had been raised. For years, it had seen little use, since Sorya was one of the village's first converts. About a hundred guests sat pressed against the four walls of the large, stuffy room, empty but for two standing fans that only stirred the heat and unease as the entire community awaited the outcome—and lunch. Children, who had been instructed by their parents to stay outside, darkened the windows. In the gloom, I caught the eye of an old man with striking white eyebrows—like hirsute gothic arches—

sitting across the room. Underneath these remarkable brows, his eyes seemed unusually pale. He had that thousand-mile stare that comes after a brush with death or God.

The two families gathered in the room's center, along with a male relative of Norsyam's, an Orang Asli elder, and a wizened man who turned out to be Sorya's grandfather. Bah Selamat, jeans still rolled up, brooded behind his wife. She, in turn, glared at the groom's mother while pointedly avoiding the groom's gaze. Norsyam had combed his hair, donned a fresh polo shirt, and strapped on a fanny pack. Next to him sat Sorya, who had changed out of her sweats and into a shapeless Islamic dress; she picked her nails and didn't dare look up. Edo sat next to me and translated Sorya's mother's harangue: "My daughter came to me and said, 'I want to be married in a month,' so we surrendered to this thing," she began. The onlookers chuckled at her brazen sourness.

"Is it true you want to marry him?" the village elder asked Sorya. "Did he force you? Did you borrow money from him?" Everyone laughed, except the bride and groom.

"We don't want to interrogate further," Sorya's grandfather said. "They talk together; maybe they sleep together." The crowd gasped. "Just finish it. You can settle your Muslim procedures some other time."

Looking unmoored, the groom's mother struggled to cross her legs under the chiffon, and began to massage her feet. Heels had been a poor choice for walking around a rubber glade. She had probably meant to look cheerful, festive, but suddenly she appeared cheap and out of place—a balloon in a morgue. When Sorya's mother demanded one thousand dollars as dowry for her daughter (which Edo said was a large sum, but not an obscene one), Norsyam's mother looked like she might cry.

"If you can't fulfill today, maybe tomorrow?" the village elder asked.

"What about less?" Norsyam's mother countered.

"If you think you can't pay, don't marry my daughter!" Sorya's mother barked. "If you want to get married don't expect it to be cheap!"

"Okay, if that's the case, we accept," Norsyam's mother said.

"Don't cheat us!" Sorya's mother warned. "If this were a buffalo," she indicated her daughter, "we'd hang on to its tether, but since this is a person, we hold on to your promise." She meant essentially that she had no choice but to offer her daughter on credit.

Later, at some unspecified date, Sorya's family would hold a more formal Orang Asli wedding party, or so they said. But for all practical—

conjugal—purposes, the two were now married, and it was time to scrab-ble back down the hill, mope, and eat chicken. As the crowd filed out of the meetinghouse, the man whose pale eyes and arched brows I had spied from across the hall approached me. He introduced himself as Bah Rahu, a Methodist preacher, and the first aboriginal pastor, one who had himself been baptized during the sixties by American missionaries. Having over-heard my earlier questions about religion, he took me for an anthropolo-gist, or a missionary. "I'm neither," I told him, but it did not seem to matter to him who I was. "I am the pioneer of my faith, but we can't talk here," he murmured mysteriously, and asked if I might come to spend a night in his village so we could talk about God.

At the bottom of the hill, the marriage party ground on. The dejected bride stood behind her mother-in-law's chair, waiting to serve her and stealing glances at her own mother. "You see how angry my mother is?" she whispered in English when I approached. "This is not about money; this is about my marrying a Muslim." On this, her wedding day, her father did not speak to her once. When the sun dropped behind a ridge, the glade cooled fast, and the guests began to leave. Bah Selamat started to put the stumps away. "I feel like I've lost my daughter," he said.

28

THE RIVER

By law, every citizen of Malaysia must at all times carry a "biometric smart chip identity card," called MyKad, from the age of twelve onward. (The child's version is called MyKid.) In addition to a microchip that stores the bearer's name, address, fingerprints, blood type, and other information, the card carries the bearer's religion. In contemporary cases of apostasy, like that of the Malay convert Lina Joy, the state would not allow her to change the religion on her MyKad, so she could not officially convert from Islam to Christianity. Sometimes among the Orang Asli, the village chief is the only person to hold such a card, simply because the others have not yet been integrated into the government system. In some cases, his religion determines the religion of the whole village.

Searching for one such village, I stumbled upon word of a recently relocated Orang Asli community. Because a multinational company wanted to build a hydroelectric dam where their village used to be, the entire community had been moved five miles deeper into the wilderness. In June 2006, I attempted to find this new settlement by following a logging road. (Logging roads do more damage to the forest and rivers than logging does.) The silted river ran so thickly with displaced soil, it looked like Willy Wonka's chocolate stream. Few living things can survive in such opaque water. The soil was killing the river.

I happened into a clearing on a shorn ridge built up with around seventy-five small houses. At the edge, on stilts, its bamboo rungs lashed with blue string, was the largest house, which belonged to the village headman, Dero. When I arrived, Dero, who looked to be in his forties, was sprawled out in a pair of Hawaiian shorts on the tree house floor with a younger friend, Ramlan. The only thing they had to do was watch the chickens below them peck at morsels of food that fell between the floor slats. They would have been out fishing, they said, but the mud had changed the river. "We have no more fish," Dero said. They also would have been out harvesting durian—a stinking, delicious fruit—but a chain-link fence now blocked their route to the wild orchard. Plus, what little fruit they were able to harvest they could no longer transport to the market in Kampar. "It's too far," Ramlan said. "The government moved us here, but the road is bad, especially for pregnant women and old people." A young woman who was breast-feeding an infant moved farther back into the hut.

After asking the easier questions about the road, the river, the weather, I inquired about religion. Dero chuckled low in his throat—the sound less a laugh than a kind of confession. He was responsible for converting his entire village to Islam, he said. During the 1980s, a government-sponsored Muslim missionary came to see him. "The missionary persuaded me: 'I'll take you to the right way. We're in the same country, we're in Malaysia, join Islam so we can live in harmony,'" Dero said. "It took a long time for him to convince me, but he told me we could practice loosely." The government gave him twenty-five Malaysian ringgit—less than seven U.S. dollars—to become a Muslim.

Dero fished through a pocket and pulled out his identity card. In the right-hand corner, under his name, it read, "Islam." Now on every major Muslim holiday the government gave them money for new clothing and food. To the Orang Asli, it wasn't so much a holiday as a handout day. "We get paid once a year at Eid [the festival that ends the fasting month of Ramadan]," Dero said. There was a government-built prayer hall here, too. "We don't use it," Dero said. "We don't pray, and we still hunt monkeys with blowpipes." Islam forbids the consumption of monkey meat, as it does pork. These days, the Orang Asli ate less monkey, but only because it was harder to find.

"We don't practice our traditional religion, either," his friend Ramlan added. "Our old people are gone." By old people, he meant shamans. Thanks to the logging road, several Baha'i missionaries had recently visited the village. But the Baha'is did not stay long. Perhaps, Ramlan mused, there had been a problem with the Muslims.

No Christians had come yet, Dero said. "I don't know why. Maybe their missionaries can't come because the road is no good." (In fact, now that the villagers, through their card-carrying chief, were nominally Muslims, it was illegal for Christian missionaries to proselytize among them.

Missionaries caught preaching to Muslims can be sentenced to up to six lashes and fined the equivalent of $2,800.)[1]

"If another religion comes it's going to be trouble," Ramlan warned. "If they all cooperate, it will be no problem, but sometimes with religion, people fight." He laughed again, that same fatalistic guffaw, lined with resignation, and said, "If Christians come, just let them come, as long as they give us money."

29

THE GREATEST STORY EVER TOLD

In June 1930, Nathalie and Paul Means, Methodist missionaries who had met at Oberlin College in Ohio four years earlier, first encountered the Orang Asli. Indisposed to outsiders, the Orang Asli (then called *sakai* by the Malay people, a slur that translates to "slave") did not venture forth to meet the Meanses. Finally, curious to see what a Western woman looked like, one person emerged from the forest. "She was small, dark brown, and wore only a sort of grass skirt that did not serve as much of a cover," Nathalie Means wrote in *And the Seed Grew*, the Meanses' 1981 account of their evangelizing efforts from 1934 to 1939 among the Orang Asli. The title comes from one of St. Paul's jailhouse letters to the Corinthians: "I planted, Apollos watered, but God gave the increase" (1 Corinthians 3:6).

Although Protestant missionaries had come to the Malay Peninsula with the British during the 1800s, ongoing upheavals made it hard for them to put down any real theological roots in the jungle. The Meanses were among the first Protestant missionaries to actually evangelize the Orang Asli. Paul, a Rhodes Scholar from Nebraska and a member of the YMCA's international committee, had traveled to Calcutta and Iraq to study Sanskrit and serve as a language expert during World War I. He arrived in neighboring Indonesia in 1927, along with his new wife, Nathalie, and their newborn son, to serve as the principal of a Methodist boys' school in the province of Medan. Three years later, after promising the local Malay king, a Muslim sultan, that they would baptize no one for ten years, the Meanses began their work among the Orang Asli.

It was not easy. Not only did the Malay government oppose the Meanses' efforts, but the Orang Asli were intensely shy, since they had maintained their identity and escaped slavery through self-seclusion— a trait they still teach their children through stories of violent outsiders. Their most loathed enemies were slave raiders called the Rawa, descendants of immigrants who came from Sumatra. In *Spotted Doves at War*, an epic poem translated by the anthropologist Robert Dentan, the Orang Asli recount the battle against the Rawa slavers: "Oh relatives the Raweys [Rawa] have come up they have given us death remember!"[1]

One evening a few days after the wedding, Edo and I passed through a neighborhood of one-story bungalows around a cul-de-sac in Kampar. "The people who live here are descendants of the Rawa," he said. He was dropping me off to spend the night with Bah Rahu, the Methodist pastor I had met at the wedding, who lived in a village outside of town called Ulu Geruntum; in Malay, "Upriver Geruntum." Most villages are named for rivers, because, until the road was built, the river was the source of everything. Beyond the tract of bungalows, the road, which was tarred to that point, gave way to a bone-jarring dirt track, and we pitched along next to the clean, racing cataract of a river very different from the one along the logging road. Wherever the current eddied and settled, the milk-white water grew glassy and clear. This clarity was partly the influence of the pastor whom I was going to meet, Edo said. Bah Rahu had successfully used religious identity—a Methodist one—to bind his village together and to protect it from outside incursions, be they logging companies or government-run Islamic schools.

We pulled into the pastor's village after true dark—the absolute profundity that occurs only when no city lights bruise the sky plum. He was waiting on the riverbank outside his small house, its windows edged in lace doilies. Heavy-headed marigolds bobbed in the gelid breeze the river made. The churning water seemed phosphorescent; the pastor's white eyebrows and hair seemed to glow against the darkness. The roar filled our ears, and we had to yell over it to make ourselves heard. Somehow, over the noise, Bah Rahu had made out the Jeep's engine coming from miles away. Few vehicles came here, and even fewer strangers. Thanks to the legacy of slavers such as the Rawa, the Orang Asli preferred their solitude.

"My father called them man-eaters," Bah Rahu said, recalling the reason for his people's flight from the coast centuries earlier. "That's why we moved back into the forest." He led me inside the house, where he had hung a print of the Last Supper, not Leonardo's somber depiction but another, more effervescent one, in which a beatific Jesus seemed joyfully resolved to die. We passed a small store where his family sold candy and ramen noodles to supplement their income. The floor was covered with contact paper depicting kittens playing with yarn—poor man's lino-leum the world over. In his closet-size study, a prie-dieu burnished with use held two books, *The Greatest Story Ever Told* and *Seeking the Face of God*.

As the pastor padded barefoot around the house, he told me his ver-sion of how Christianity had saved his community. It was extraordinarily different from the Meanses' version and, I suspect, told from a separate register, in which verifiable fact was a matter of perspective—a modern parable.

"This land used to be a cemetery," he began. The Orang Asli didn't want to move here, but during the Communist rebellion of the 1950s, the government made them relocate to be sure they would not help the rebels by providing them food or guidance through the woods. To live on top of graves was anathema. (The word *anathema* derives from the same root as the Hebrew *herem* and the Arabic *haram*. All three words mean "set apart"—cast out—by God.) Living here, on set-apart land, invites attack by evil spirits. Every evil spirit kills or curses. But the Orang Asli had no choice; the government said they had to move. He went on: "After three months, everyone was sick. Seventy-two people died," so the shamans ordered a series of strictures to appease the spirits. "We made no noise. We had no white things. We spilled no blood, because the spirit didn't like it." Yet the more the shamans worked, the sicker people became. "We were all suffering. Some were crazy. My mother was going crazy. The sha-mans said she was possessed by the spirit of a bird," the pastor, who did not believe in evil spirits, said in disgust. "The shamans wanted us to move, but my father said we're going to have to stay, because if we go, it will cause more problems with the government."

Bah Rahu's father went to visit a newly baptized Orang Asli Christian down the river, and invited the convert to visit his cursed village. It was right before Christmas. On Christmas Eve, according to this tale, three members of the community had portentous dreams. In two, a man came to the village dressed in white and told the villagers he would "clean" this land by the river so they would not have to move. In the third, the spirits came to the village and commanded the Orang Asli to leave. So the village decided to test the man in white to see if he would protect them. Accord-ing to Bah Rahu, they were dreaming of Jesus. "My father said, 'I think we should pray.' We only knew a few hymns. We had no Bible. There were no sermons. So we prayed." Afterward, they did what the shamans forbade in order to see how the spirits would respond. The ground, they decided, had been purified. That marked the end of the curse and the beginning of Christianity in this village. Several years later, in 1960, seven hundred people were baptized in one mass ceremony and the missionaries opened a Methodist school for children, which the present-day pastor attended as a boy. Even so, his parents were afraid of what Christianity would cost them. It could cost them their son, they feared. "I told them I'd love them much more as a Christian," Bah Rahu said.

"We are free now from satanic rules," he said. "We know when we die we'll go to a place promised by God. Now we know what the future holds." The solace of the afterlife—of absolute salvation—was powerful to him. Providence mattered more than anything else.

Although most of the villagers are now Christians, they sometimes ask Bah Rahu to exorcise evil spirits, calling him shaman. "I don't mind, because I'm teaching them about my spirit, which is Jesus Christ," he said. Yet some Christian teachings still elude his flock. "The Orang Asli do not believe in sin, so that's difficult to explain." Communion, with the understanding that the person taking communion eats the body of Christ in the unleavened bread, repulses them: they believe only evil spirits consume human flesh. "It's difficult for my community to understand the meat of Jesus," Bah Rahu said, "so we explain that communion is consuming the power of God." Other teachings come more easily. "The fact that God speaks through Jesus, they have no problem with that, because in our belief, the tiger spirit can speak like a man when he comes into a shaman."

We had finished off the cast-iron frying pan of river fish and peppers. The pastor leaned his back against the woven wall and grew reflective.

"I am the way, the truth, the life. No one comes to the Father except through me," he quoted the Gospel according to John into the now-dark corners of the hut. As a Christian, he told me, he had to set an example for others. "They look closely at your life to see what effect being Christian has had on you." Apparently, the indigenous healers did not like his Christianizing influence. Once, they invited him to dance with them to prove their superior powers could outlast him. "Everyone told me not to go, but I went," he said. "After eight hours of dancing, all of them fell off except for me. They said I couldn't fall because I was a Christian."

It was late. He rose and said, "That's enough for tonight."

His wife led me to a mattress. The river was rushing past about ten feet away, on the other side of the grass wall, and I could feel its chill through the rattan. I crawled under the bug netting, between the Garfield the cat sheets, and opened a book I'd borrowed from the pastor. I skimmed its worn pages until my eye caught this passage: "The first city was Enoch [named for Cain's son]. Cities enable people to live and work near each other. Cities hold a special attraction for evil people." This was a cautionary tale—strangers were dangerous, and so were the places where they congregated. Christians should go forth boldly, but warily. Their faith, it followed, would protect them.

The next morning we drove down the dirt track to the pastor's coral-colored church. "Twice, state security has come to take pictures of the church to see who paid for it," he said. (In other communities, the Malay government has bulldozed churches.) The community paid half the construction costs, and South Korean Methodists paid the other half. South Korea, whose churches now send roughly twelve thousand missionaries abroad a year to evangelize,[2] is second only to the United States, whose churches send an estimated forty-six thousand Protestant missionaries[3] annually on foreign mission.

"In the old days, missionaries handed out things, but that's not helpful," Bah Rahu said. I wondered what he would think of the Indonesian pastor Rebekkah and her Happy Sundays, but did not mention them. "We cherish our land—our language, customs, and rights. People need to help us preserve these things." Christianity, he believed, would protect his people from assimilation by allowing them to retain a more complex identity, allowing them to be Orang Asli and Christians at once. To become a Muslim, he believed, meant to lose everything, to be subsumed by the dominant culture of the Malays. "When we became Christians, the government was very angry," he said. "Their plan was to convert us to Islam, but they found it's not so easy to convert a person. It's hard work. It takes a long time." Bah Rahu knew this from his own efforts. Also, Christianity threatened the government because it was synonymous with the all-powerful and threatening West. And it offered a way to organize around a rival political voice—not those of the popular Muslim political parties. For instance, when the local Malay government failed to provide the Orang Asli here with health care, the community voted together, as Christians, for the multiethnic opposition party.

"I think the policy of the government is to have us disappear," Bah

Rahu said. Converting them to Islam, he believed, and making them de facto Malays, was the easiest way to do that.

Due to centuries of enslavement and marginalization, redemption through suffering was the easiest Christian concept for his people to grasp, he said, returning to our conversation from the night before. "Americans don't care what's happening in other places, do they?" he said, and pondered aloud if need kept people closer to God and God closer to them. "I wonder, is there a place for God's word in the lives of people who have everything?"

He inspected the doorjamb of his simple church. As he saw it, need had turned the Orang Asli to Christianity, and now need was why they'd kept the faith. "Because we're so poor and in need, we take our religion very seriously," he said. The Orang Asli's religious transformation was also proof that Christianity no longer belonged to the West, he added; in fact, it never had.

PHILIPPINES

Then Jesus said to his disciples, "If anyone desires to come after me, let him deny himself, and take up his cross, and follow Me. For whoever desires to save his life will lose it, but whoever loses his life for My sake will find it."
— THE GOSPEL ACCORDING TO MATTHEW 16:24–25

[Prophet], do not think of those who have been killed in God's way as dead. They are alive with their Lord, well provided for, happy with what God has given them of His favor . . .
— THE QURAN, THE FAMILY OF 'IMRAN 3:169–71

30

A KIDNAPPING

Gracia Burnham marched up the ridge at gunpoint behind her husband, Martin. Their captor, Abu

Sulaiman, a top lieutenant of Abu Sayyaf, "Bearer of the Sword," a criminal gang tied to Al Qaeda, had summoned the Burnhams, who were evangelical missionaries, up to his high-ground camp. Night after night in
2001 and 2002 amid wild cinnamon bushes and wet ferns, he tried to
break their absolute and unwavering faith in Jesus Christ. Abu Sayyaf, like
Indonesia's Jemaah Islamiyah, had begun in the nineties with the return
of homegrown jihadis from Afghanistan, where they had gone to fight the
Soviets. The groups are still interwoven through training camps, intermarriage, and violent common purpose.

"We thought that at first the fact we were Christian missionaries would
be held against us, but we found that to not be true at all," Gracia Burnham told me when I met her at a conference in Franklin, Tennessee, in
2007. "In fact, they really admired us, because Martin explained that our
organization, New Tribes, goes into places where people are normally
worshipping rocks and trees, their ancestral spirits. They're not worshipping the one true God, and we tell them who the one true God is. So Abu
Sayyaf felt we were kind of doing the same thing, which shocked me,
because we are as far from Islam as I think you can be."

Before Abu Sayyaf captured the Burnhams in May 2001, the couple
had evangelized in remote regions of the Philippines for seventeen years.
New Tribes focuses on fulfilling the Great Commission by planting
churches among the twenty-five hundred ethnic groups worldwide that
have not yet been reached with the Gospel. These remaining communities are either in remote places or hostile to Christian teachings. Although
their missionaries receive extensive training in language, survival, medicine, and dentistry before going into the field, they still have one of the
highest death rates of any religious organization. Also, their website, www
.ntm.org, has caught the attention of Muslims: it receives twenty thousand hits a day from the Arab world, a New Tribes staff member in the
Philippines told me. After seventeen years in the field, the Burnhams coordinated New Tribes's work all over the roughly seven thousand islands
of the Philippines. Martin, a bush pilot, delivered mail and supplies and
shuttled the sick over the dense jungle; Gracia, a radio operator, home-
schooled their three children, Jeff, Zach, and Mindy, who were fifteen,
thirteen, and eleven at the time of their parents' abduction.

During the 376 days the two Burnhams were held captive, Martin
Burnham and Abu Sulaiman repeatedly debated the nature of God. As
the two men hunkered down on the jungle's spongy floor and spoke into

the night, Gracia said neither wavered. Three times Abu Sulaiman asked Burnham to submit to Islam with the simple profession of the Shahada: "I bear witness to the fact that there is no god but God, and I bear witness to the fact that Mohammed is His messenger." Each time, Burnham refused. "My great-grandfather, my grandfather, and my father were all committed Christians," Gracia heard him say. "I'll die as a believer." Burnham told Sulaiman that only through belief in Jesus Christ would Sulaiman go to heaven. Jihad—the so-called escalator to heaven—would carry him to eternal damnation. The missionary knew such talk could cost him his life: one of their fellow American hostages had been taken down the mountain and beheaded. Yet he believed that his duty as an evangelical Christian was to share Jesus's message—to bear witness—no matter the cost.

Sulaiman excluded Gracia from these debates because she was a woman, which suited her fine. The other women taken uphill at night were raped, or *sobayed*, meaning taken as war booty. Gracia never was. Perhaps Martin's presence protected her; perhaps her white skin did. According to the kidnappers' millennial worldview, Islam would war with anything other than itself until Judgment Day. "Abu Sayyaf thought of themselves as pious and holy," Gracia Burnham told me. "All this lofty chivalry crumbled before our eyes. Anything they wanted or desired, all they had to say was, 'This is jihad and the rules don't apply.'"

On May 27, 2001, masked men had burst into the Burnhams' bungalow at the Dos Palmas resort on Palawan Island. The Philippines, the second-largest archipelago in the world after Indonesia, is divided between a majority Christian north and a minority Muslim south. The island of Palawan lies in the middle of the two, directly on the tenth parallel. It is home to a panoply of odd fauna, among them the bearcat, the mouse deer, and the scaly anteater. World War II made Palawan infamous; on December 14, 1944, before surrendering to the United States, the Japanese army massacred 139 American prisoners of war by setting them on fire here. Yet Palawan's relevance to the Christian West stretches back several hundred years. When the Portuguese first landed on Palawan during the sixteenth century, they unearthed shards of Chinese pots—evidence that travelers had been arriving on these islands from China since the ninth century. But it wasn't until the fourteenth century, when Malay sailors arrived from the nearby western islands of the future Indonesia and Malaysia, that Islam really gained ground here, and Muslim kings began to govern the coasts. On his way to circumnavigating the world, Ferdinand Magellan, a Spanish Catholic, conquered the islands with the express purpose of converting their people and christening the country in the name of King Philip II of Spain. On April 21, 1521, Magellan planted a huge iron cross on the island of Cebu, also on the tenth parallel, to celebrate the mass Catholic baptism of a Muslim king and hundreds of his followers. Subsequently, the Muslims rose up against the Catholic invaders. And despite Portuguese and, later, Spanish efforts to conquer and subdue Islamic rebels—whom the invaders named Moros, after their North African enemies the Moors—the southern Muslims held their ground into the nineteenth century.

In 1898, the United States claimed victory over Spain in the Spanish-American War, and bought the Philippines for $20 million. The Moros hoped America would grant them an independent homeland in the Muslim south. President William McKinley, a devout Methodist who'd planned to become a pastor early in his life, had other plans. Baffled, at first, with what to do with the islands, one night he had the notion that America would establish something like a Christian civilization. He told a Methodist delegation visiting the White House that it was the United States' duty "to educate the Filipinos, and uplift and civilize and Christianize them, and by God's grace do the best we could by them, as our fellow-men for whom Christ died."[1] This story, largely lost to history, is but one instance of the role Christianity has had in American foreign policy.

Today, the Philippines is Asia's only Christian country—nine out of ten of its nearly ninety-six million citizens are Christians (80 percent are Roman Catholics; 11 percent are Christians from other traditions, including Evangelicals and Pentecostals; 5 percent are Muslims). Since independence, along with the military, the Roman Catholic Church and various Catholic religious orders have taken a strong hand in the running of the country. The Muslim south has continued to rebel against the north's Christian-led government, over time forming regular armies to fight (unsuccessfully, so far) for an autonomous Islamic homeland.

In some ways, this conflict resembles Sudan's in that the southern Philippines is also a source for raw materials, left undeveloped while the more powerful north thrived. In the Philippines, however, the north belonged to the Christians, and the country's five million Muslims lived in the south. In much the same way that Christianity served as a vehicle of liberation for Sudanese Christians, Islam provided a means of self-determination for Filipino Muslims—a source of power in opposition to the Christian-supported government. For the Muslims, Islam harks back to a time when they held power. Today, they find inspiration in this history, much as Sudan's Christians look back to their ancient Christian kingdoms of Nubia. The armies of the Muslim south and the government of the Christian north first attempted to make peace in 2003, but that deal, and subsequent efforts—brokered by Malaysia—failed.

Abu Sayyaf was born out of this cycle of endless, fruitless rebellion. When the group's founder, Abdurajak Abubakar Janjalani, an eloquent young Filipino teacher, returned from Afghanistan in the early nineties, he split from other, older Islamic groups fighting for independence in the Philippines' Muslim south. Claiming that the other groups were not Islamic enough, Janjalani preached the merits of martyrdom: the Moros had to be willing to die for their cause. In 1991, his splinter group launched its first attack, targeting a Christian missionary ship called the MV *Doulos*. (The ship, christened the SS *Medina* in 1914, belongs to the German organization Good Books for All, and contains between three and five thousand Christian books. It is the largest floating library in the world.) As Abu Sayyaf saw it, all Christians were their enemies. The group was an example of global jihad gone awry, even by Al Qaeda's standards. Their stealing, kidnapping, and killing earned them such a bad reputation that eventually one of their benefactors, Osama bin Laden's brother-in-law Jamal Khalifa (who'd moved to the Philippines in the 1990s and married a Filipina), told them to clean up their act. Still, they continued filling their militant coffers by crime—the most lucrative of which was kidnapping for ransom, especially nabbing foreigners vacationing at expensive resorts.

On Palawan, the Burnhams had splurged on a night of relaxation for their eighteenth wedding anniversary. They were lying in bed half-dressed when their bungalow's flimsy door burst open. Their kidnappers shoved them onto a waiting speedboat, where, in the ocean's darkness, they counted more than a dozen other sleepy and scared hostages. As the boat sped away from the island, their captors shouted, *"Allahu Akbar!"* One kidnapper handed Martin Burnham a satellite phone and told him to call the authorities. "Tell them you've been taken by bin Laden's group." Martin didn't know what that meant and, at that point, early in 2001, neither did most of the world.

"The country had fallen off our radar screen," a U.S. intelligence officer told me in the Philippine capital, Manila, in 2006. The September 11 attacks exposed the relationship between Al Qaeda, the kidnappers, and their American missionary hostages. U.S. aid to the Philippines government shot up from $14.5 million to more than $245 million.[2] An elite team of 120 U.S. Special Forces traveled to the southern Philippines. Yet due to a Visiting Forces Agreement between the United States and the Philippines, the Special Forces could only advise and watch a series of sixteen botched rescue attempts as the Philippine army alternated between colluding with Abu Sayyaf and blindly shooting their way into the Burnhams' camp.

Abu Sayyaf kept the Burnhams on the move and near starving;[3] they slept on mosquito-infested ground and hiked for hours in circles. The rescue attempts were the worst: the Filipino soldiers shot at anything that moved. It got to the point where Gracia wished the soldiers would stop trying to save them. When the Filipino television crew hiked into the jungle and shot the famous footage I'd seen reprinted in the Indonesian outfit *JihadMagz*, the injustice of their visit seemed unbearable. How could a TV crew talk to ASG, hike in, film the Burnhams sick and wasting away, and leave the weakening couple to their fate? Gracia believed God was testing her, and she wasn't pleased with what she was observing. "The worst part was seeing who I really was," she said. She coveted food sent into the jungle for them, which Abu Sayyaf refused to share. "There were times when I really hated those Muslims," she said, so she and Martin prayed for a way to love their captors. "We never forgot they were the bad guys, but they were also our family for more than a year."

Tired of praying to "a God who sometimes seemed to have forgotten us," Gracia would say to Martin, "You know scripture says these words: 'If you will ask anything in my name, I will do it.' In my situation, that verse is not true, so why is that in there?" There was no room in their faith for doubt, sweet-tempered Martin told her. "You believe it all, or you don't believe it at all."

Burnham prayed without ceasing for her and her husband's release.

Since God did not seem to hear her, or to listen, she tried a new prayer: instead of asking for their release, she prayed for a hamburger. There was no way God could deliver the hamburger to the remote Philippine jungle, she figured. If He was going to answer, He would have to free them first.

Toward the end of their captivity, when it looked like the Burnhams might be released, Abu Sayyaf bustled them closer to civilization. One night for dinner, their captors delivered hamburgers and French fries from a nearby fast-food chain, Jollibee. Awestruck, Gracia believed that God was teaching her a lesson: she had to submit to His will. Not long after, on June 7, 2002, for the seventeenth time in more than a year, Filipino soldiers blasted into the camp in an attempted rescue. By the time she dropped from her hammock to the ground, Gracia had been shot in the leg and Martin lay dead beside her.

31

FROM TWO THOUSAND FEET

The Sulu Sea's Chinese blue waters glistening below us formed a jihadi highway. On fishing boats, amid the stink of sunbaked bonefish, an alphabet stew of fighters—JI, ASG, RSM, and so on—skipped from Indonesia to Malaysia to the Philippines training henchmen, smuggling weapons, and simply hiding out. The Indonesian fighters Ibnu Ahmad and his brother Salahuddin had traveled these routes before Salahuddin went to jail and Ibnu Ahmad started peddling beauty powders. The captive Burnhams had crisscrossed the same waters in the stern of a speedboat.

On July 26, 2006, I hovered two thousand feet above the crystalline water in a U.S. helicopter, with Colonel James Linder, commander of the U.S. forces in the Philippines, as he explained what had gone awry with the Burnhams' rescue. When the U.S. Special Forces arrived in the Philippines after September 11 to free the Burnhams, many came from the jungles of Central America, where they were well trained in rescuing kidnap victims. Global jihad, however, was totally foreign to them.

"What began as a rescue attempt quickly became a classic counterinsurgency," Linder shouted into his headset microphone over the *thwup thwup* of the helicopter's blades. Over the past twenty years, Linder, a forty-five-year-old South Carolina native with remnants of a southern drawl, had led operations in the Middle East, Central and South America, and East Africa, and now he was fighting the "gee-watt"—the GWOT, the Global War on Terror. By 2006, the United States was trying something new in Southeast Asia: proportional response. If a large military footprint created a large-scale insurgency, as it had in Iraq, then the United States was gambling that a softened approach in the Philippines would result in a less explosive reaction. Linder, for instance, was wearing a green felt beret, not a combat helmet. His elite soldiers spoke the language and learned the culture, and many saw their mission more as an armed Peace

Corps than a counterterrorism force. The less visible the U.S. military, the less militant the Moros would become, the argument went, and in 2006 it seemed to be working.

Through the helicopter's open door, Linder pointed proudly as we passed a brand-new Jollibee fast-food franchise on a neighboring island. The accessibility of fast food, he seemed to think, meant that America had scored a point in the culture war. Maybe he was right; people here welcomed any hint of development, which Jollibee certainly provided.

In 2006 (and still through the end of 2009), if there were a thumbtack stuck in the geographic center of militant hideouts in Southeast Asia, it would have been pushed into the tiny island of Jolo (HO-lo.) As a reporter working for an American magazine, I had asked Linder to take me there so that I could observe the softened U.S. military approach firsthand. Below us, limestone reefs surrounded its 345 square miles. Slightly larger than New York City, this volcanic burp in the middle of the Sulu Archipelago jutted out of a North Pacific basin more than 18,000 feet deep, and rose to a series of steep, bottle green ridges. Among them, some of the world's most wanted terrorists were hiding. Almost every large-scale terrorist attack has been planned in Southeast Asia, including 9/11, which was born out of Operation Bojinka—"explosion" in Serbo-Croat—named by Al Qaeda fighters on Balkan battlefields. It was in the Philippines during the nineties that Al Qaeda's Khalid Sheikh Mohammed dreamed up the scheme to hijack twelve airplanes and fly them into CIA headquarters. Until it proved easier to hijack them in Boston and Newark, the planes were supposed to come from the Philippines, among other Southeast Asian nations.

Linder's helicopter buzzed above a tiny U.S. base in a clearing, and the rotor wash sent three American soldiers scrambling and grabbing at their floppy green hats. The mechanized wind flipped the palm fronds and flattened the blades of sword grass. Nearby, solders were lifting solar panels, which glinted like chewing gum wrappers, onto the roof of a new school, where they would power the school's modem—the island's first Internet connection. Since World War II, largely because of corrupt officials, most notably President Ferdinand Marcos, the Philippines has gone from being one of the richest countries in Asia to one of the poorest, and its population is among the fastest growing on the continent. Before the Americans arrived on Jolo, its people had no electricity, little fresh water, and no roads. Since the Moros had no relationship to the Filipino Christian–led government, being a Filipino meant very little, if anything at all. It was Islam that held Moro society together.

The soldiers had clear-cut ribbons of red earth into the jungle. Along these rude roads, the ethnic Tausug people—a Moro subgroup of nearly a million—could carry their cows and papayas from their farms to a brand-new market courtesy of U.S. largesse. Roads and roads and roads—in Sudan, it was oil companies; in Malaysia, logging companies; and in the Philippines, it was the American military. The contours of each road signi-fied its use: logging and market roads meandered around rivers and rocky outcroppings; the oil roads were thousand-mile grids blasted straight through whatever stood in their way.

Watching in real time, we spluttered above as the last vestiges of Jolo's rain forest wilderness were connected to the outside world for the first time in history. Some of these incursions extended far beyond Jolo, thanks to the solar-powered Internet. If globalization had introduced the Philip-pines to the radical theology of Afghanistan's jihad, then the Americans could use a competing version to their advantage. Globalization was part of the American strategy: give these isolated children a look at the wider world, and extremism would seem a less attractive career path. In a counter-version of *JihadMagz*, the Americans were about to distribute a comic book—the story of a Tausug man who leaves home for the Merchant Ma-rine. (The Tausugs are sailors, their name roughly translating to "men of the current.") Returning to find that pimply faced thugs have taken over his island, the hero battles the "backward" gang and defeats them, restor-ing the island's honor. Comic books, solar panels, computers, schools, and farm-to-market roads: all were part of America's counterterrorism effort in the Philippines. Colonel Linder did not believe that religion had anything to do with the conflict playing out beneath us, and he hated the expres-sion "hearts and minds." "We're not trying to change anyone's culture, or religion, or mind," he said.

The colonel was right, to a point. These problems were rooted in pov-erty, not extremism—one reason the United States was succeeding in the jungles below us. This was a campaign of hearts and stomachs, and for the moment, on Jolo, it was going well. "The enemy is an idea of intolerance and subjugation," he went on. "We are freedom-loving people looking for the opposite." Yet his freedom agenda, like Christianity, was also an ideology, and although the Tausug people cheered when they accepted their new tractors, talk about freedom was not relevant.

"It's not about how many people we shoot in the face," Linder added. "It's about how many we get off the battlefield." This involved building an economy that could create jobs other than kidnapping. The question was whether that economy was sustainable in the long term without a U.S. presence. As long as America was willing to pay for vaccinations and tractors that made farming profitable, great. But what about when the few smiling soldiers went home, the tractors rusted out, and the cows grew too sick to give milk? What ideology would dissatisfaction and disappointment breed then?

We landed to visit one of the new American solar-powered schools, where Butch Izquierdo, the local mayor, was waiting to meet us. He shook my hand vigorously. All Americans were welcome here, he told us. "We thought at first the Americans wanted to build a base, or dig up Yamashita's gold," he said, referring to the legendary Japanese treasure from World War II. But America had proven it wasn't out to take anything from Jolo; to the contrary, both the military and USAID, which provided $29.7 million[1] and $69.9 million,[2] respectively, in 2006, had been very generous. Gifts guaranteed no commitment, he hastened to add: "This island is like a beautiful woman. You can love her, but you cannot marry her." We continued on to the U-shaped elementary school—its new tin roof was the first the school had had. At recess, children ran through the courtyard, still piled with dirt from construction. Teachers ventured out, too, where a pleased Linder shook hand after hand.

After a few more meetings with local farmers, and other photo opportunities, it was time to go. We took off from outlying Jolo to fly one hundred miles back to Mindanao, the main island of the Muslim south. On our way, the helicopter headed for one of Jolo's defunct volcanoes. The blown-off top had left a crater so deep that what looked like a jeweled pool of water in its center was actually a pocket of trees. On the slope of this volcano one hundred years ago, American forces confronted Islamic fighters for the first time in history. The United States saw the Moros as the Native Americans of the Philippines: uncivilized, brazen, and in need of taming. On March 7, 1906, fearing that American schools would make their children into Christians, two kinds of Islamic fighter revolted against the forces of Captain John "Black Jack" Pershing, a veteran of America's campaigns against its own natives, the Indian wars. Juramentados, suicidal fighters, launched attacks against the U.S. soldiers. Amoks went homicidally berserk on the battlefield. (Our word *amok* memorializes them.)[3]

"Captain Pershing chased a bunch of Moros up that old volcano and killed them," Linder said, pointing down at the tree-lined crater where more than a thousand men, women, and children fought and died. "It was commonly referred to as a massacre," he said. Then, as the island shrank behind us, he repeated something I'd heard him say several times, like a mantra: "We'll spill American blood on Jolo." I took this as the kind of hard-talking overstatement designed to impress a listener with his men's courage, which turned out to be wrong. On September 29, 2009, two U.S. soldiers, Christopher D. Shaw, thirty-seven, and Jack M. Martin III, twenty-six, were killed, along with a Filipino marine, Private First Class Estrada. They died in a coconut grove when their Humvee hit a landmine Abu Sayyaf had planted on the road leading to a solar-powered school.

The current conflict in the Philippines is less a product of terrorism, or any ideological clash between Catholics and Muslims, than the result of American involvement during the early twentieth century. The United States employed a policy of shipping Filipino Christians from the Catholic north to the Muslim south. The United States believed that Christian farmers—rather than Muslims—would better safeguard American rubber, banana, and pineapple plantations and secure foreign business interests. To further break the Moro ancestral land rights, the United States pushed forward laws stipulating that only individuals and corporations—such as Dole, B. F. Goodrich, Del Monte, Weyerhaeuser, and Goodyear—could own land, not Moro tribes or clans.[4] A few years before independence on July 4, 1946, more than one hundred Moro leaders wrote President Franklin Roosevelt to ask for their right to form a government. "Our religion should not be curtailed in any way," they wrote the American president. "Once our religion is no more our lives are no more."[5]

Nevertheless, Washington ceded the south to the Catholic north, and the newly independent Christian-led government stepped up its policy of relocating Christians to what had been traditionally Muslim land. The Moros began to form armies to fight for their land: first, in the early seventies, the Moro National Liberation Front, then, in 1977, the more conservative splinter group, the Moro Islamic Liberation Front, which is still at war with the Filipino government today, in a conflict that has claimed up to two hundred thousand lives. On the other side, the Christians settlers became foot soldiers for the new state. Given weapons bought through the military and financial support of the government from the 1970s onward, the Christians protected their new farms from the Muslims fighting to reclaim them. Some formed Catholic gangs called Ilaga, which means "rat." These militias were paramilitaries doing the government's dirty work while perpetrating horrific violence in the name of Christianity. This is the legacy of the conquistadores in a former Spanish colony: a dark skein of Christianity bound up with violence and oppression. The southern Philippines now seethes as a gangland rain forest, where religion legitimizes a conflict over resources and political hegemony.

In 2006, as the peace deal between the Muslim south and Catholic north looked likely to fail once again, a new Ilaga was forming on the southern island of Mindanao. Domos, a farming village not far from the northern town of Marawi (also known as "the Islamic City of Marawi"), is located within the 1,085 square miles the Moros claim as their authentic homeland, the Autonomous Region in Muslim Mindanao. One July morning, I paid a visit to a family of Catholic farmers who belonged to a Christian militia. To defend their land against the Muslims, the police, fellow Catholics, had provided about a week's training to militia members, they told me. Their son, Bernard Joval, twenty-five, had died weeks earlier, shot to death on the night of June 30 while guarding his farmland against a Muslim splinter group called the Pentagon Gang (the name a typical twist of Filipino black humor). Next to a hammock in the living room, the family had erected a shrine to Joval, whom they called "little Jesus."

On an altar next to photos of Joval stood an icon of Jesus with His heart aflame; another of the Virgin Mary marbled with votive candle wax; and a line of pinkie-size paper scrolls. After the family granted permission, I unrolled one talisman and read its nonsense verse: *HINIT PINIT PICA HINT AGRAMEUM EGU SOME PER DEUM MATAR.* As much as I could puzzle out this higgledy-piggledy Latin, it said something about a farm, I am for God, and kill.

The scroll said more than the family could. Joval's brothers, fellow members of this resurgent Ilaga, had little to add, beyond that their religion allowed them the right to shed blood. They were more eager to pose for snapshots in front of their shrines with their homemade shotguns—as if they possessed a divine kind of muscle.

The leading authority on the Ilaga death squads was a Catholic priest named Peter Geremia, a seventy-one-year-old motorcycle-riding, bandana-wearing member of the Pontifical Institute of Foreign Missions, which has sent missionaries into non-Christian lands for more than a century. A few days after meeting the Christian farmers, I went to visit him at the Lady of Guadalupe House, a Catholic refuge in the Diocese of Kida-pawan, located in the district of Cotabato, about seventy-five miles to the south of Marawi and outside the designated Moro ancestral land. In the classroom where we met, the blackboard was chalked with arrows and tiny cars: the priests, who have been outspoken critics of the government since the days of Ferdinand Marcos, were learning how to escape assas-sins. A month earlier—on June 19, 2006—George and Maricel Vigo, two married journalists and parents to five children, had been gunned down while leaving the sanctuary after meeting with Geremia. I came to meet Geremia to learn about the Ilaga, but also because George Vigo was sup-posed to have been my interpreter on Mindanao. *Interpreter* doesn't quite cover it; he was to be my fixer, a term reporters use for the local person who knows everything, sets up meetings, guarantees safety—does every-thing but report the story, and sometimes even that. I'd corresponded with Vigo, known among friends and reporters as intelligent and kind, but never met him, and I found out that he and his wife had been killed just before I left New York for the Philippines. The Vigos were casualties of another war: between Communist rebels called the New People's Army and the northern government. From what I'd heard from the Moro Islamic Liberation Front, on occasion they shared training camps with the Com-munists, but not usually. The United States had designated the Commu-nists as "terrorists," which made it possible for the Philippine government to use American funds to fight against them. The Vigos had been report-ing on this conflict when they were gunned down by right-wing parami-li-taries. Geremia's life was currently under threat, too, but he was used to it. In some ways, he was an anti–Colonel Linder: a lefty, organic rice farmer who could not be less interested in establishing American-style order. He was eager to expose injustice and corruption in the name of the people—and God—whenever the need arose. When Geremia first spoke against the Ilaga, almost thirty years earlier, the Christian gang sent an assassin—a man named Manero—to kill him. (Manero, however, murdered the wrong priest on a motorcycle, a young Italian colleague of Geremia's, Father Tullio Favali.) Afterward, Geremia learned all he could about Manero, who had reportedly once cooked and eaten an Islamic teacher. "If you take the name of God to kill, you become fear," Geremia said. "The more atrocities you commit, the more power you have." He led me outside to Father Favali's grave. Behind the wooden cross was the old, rusted red motorcycle overgrown with vines. It looked like a bush of abandoned tomatoes. The old priest knelt in the dirt and prayed.

Manero, who would soon be let out of prison, had converted from Christianity to Islam and back again. The killer had recently written to Geremia to ask the priest for the Catholic Church's permission to make a movie of his life story. Reluctantly, Geremia had said yes, hoping the film would spread a peaceful message. But how that could possibly be was hard to see. Geremia, who was born at the end of World War II in Italy, wanted to be a different kind of missionary. Having come of age during the heady, liberal years of Catholic reform in the sixties and seventies, he believed in the Gospel of social justice: that being a Christian is about empowering the weak to defend themselves against the strong in the feudal Philippines. He did not agree with Pope Benedict XVI's recent criticisms of Islam's propensity to advance itself through violence. Nor did he believe that salvation was the exclusive purview of Christians. To him, bearing witness meant speaking out against injustice, not trying to save souls. As the gap between liberal and conservative Catholics widened, Geremia, though no radical, had found himself positioned farther and farther to the left. The fight, he argued, raged between power and powerlessness, not Christianity and Islam.

According to Father Geremia, America's recent infusion of more than $100 million in security aid had escalated the local conflict simply by making higher-caliber hardware readily available. Who wanted a bowie knife when it was possible to procure an M16 with a brand-new night-vision scope, made in the U.S.A.? American money paid for the motorbikes and weapons used to fight the Philippine government's dirty war, and to kill those who spoke out against it, including the Vigos. "This isn't a climate of freedom and democracy," the priest added. "If this is what the war on terror is, then it is about terrorizing the people."

32

REVERSION

In the Philippines, a group of former Christians have embraced Islam with particular verve. They call themselves reverts—not converts—to signify both the historical fact that Islam reached these islands before Christianity did, and the belief among some Muslims that, according to the Quran, all human beings are born as members of Islam. Over the past several decades, as Islam has come under increasing pressure as a local minority and a global threat, more than two hundred thousand Filipino Christians have left their churches to "return" to Islam. Part of this phenomenon can be attributed to economic migration: 8.7 million Filipinos (almost a tenth of the population) have left the country for work over the last several decades. And many go to the Persian Gulf, where Muslims frequently get better jobs—with higher pay—than Christians, and this disparity creates an incentive for "reversion."

This, however, was not the case for the fifty former evangelical pastors I met on a July morning in 2006 not far from Geremia's monastery. This gathering took place in a school that had been a Protestant mission until several years earlier. (The American mission pastor with watery blue eyes whom I met in a nearby town had left in disgrace. It turned out he'd fathered a dozen illegitimate children among this rural tribe—a transgression uncovered when the brown-eyed mothers gave birth to blue-eyed babies.) Now, with financial help from the World Assembly of Muslim Youth (WAMY), a Saudi Arabian nonprofit organization that specializes in converting non-Muslims to Islam, the former Filipino pastors were renting the errant missionary's compound for their local chapter of Balik Islam, or "Return to Islam." A poster on the wall read, "Ishmael . . . I Will Make Him a Great Nation" (Genesis 17:20). This biblical verse, the members of Balik Islam believed, foreshadowed the birth of a great Islamic nation, one that would eventually encompass the entire world. Around the ring of school desks in the former mission classroom, forty-odd men—most former Pentecostal preachers—had squeezed themselves. "We don't know where to look!" one shouted as I took a seat among them. They'd recently learned that as Muslims, they were not supposed to meet a woman's eye, so they gazed at their hands and fiddled with their stiff new prayer caps. They'd agreed to meet with me to defend themselves against charges of being terrorists. It was true that at the extreme fringe of the movement, a few of their members had joined militant Muslim groups. This was a new trend in jihad: the recruitment of converts who would not raise suspicions among a crowd of Christians, and could carry out attacks. Willing to undertake more dangerous missions than "born" Muslims, reverts seemed eager to prove their zeal. Yet reverting to Islam had nothing to do with violence, these members of Balik Islam wanted to assure me.

"We are like newborn babies," one of the movement's leaders, Brother Abdul Latif Jongay, an ex-pastor at Jesus Is Lord Church, a Pentecostal outfit started by Californian missionaries, told me. Now in his late forties, he wore his beard uncut, as Mohammed's companions, the Salafs, are said to have done.

"We are born-again Muslims!" he added. Their new religion governed every aspect of life—clothing, daily schedule, diet. Many members of Balik Islam were searching for a code of total certainty, or what they called "universal guidance."

"Have you met Cat Stevens?" another former preacher asked. The folk singer had "reverted" to Islam years earlier. "Cat Stevens, the most famous Balik Islam in the world!" Stevens, aka Yusuf Islam, had visited the Philippines several years before and they assumed that I would know him personally, and were disappointed that I did not. Latif hushed their sighs as he told his life story as a case study of this revivalist movement. Raised a Catholic and a Christian settler fighting for his family's land, Latif grew up hating Muslims. "We were forced to leave the area we thought we'd inherited," he said. "On the grounds of that, from the radio and the TV, we thought that Muslims thought they go to heaven if they kill people." About a decade earlier, Brother Latif met a group of American missionaries from Faith Bible College in San Jose, California, who converted him from Catholicism to Pentecostalism. He became a Pentecostal pastor and wanted to preach to Muslims, but the American missionaries forbade it. "They told me the Muslims would kill me." As a preacher, Latif spoke in tongues, and when filled with the Holy Spirit, he fainted. Both, he confessed, were a sham, just part of a desire to feel connected to God. "Our listeners wanted to feel something." Latif had doubts about Christianity. There were twenty-three thousand sects, he claimed, an ever-expanding figure— so many fissures—how could they all be right? I'd heard this argument many times: Christianity, especially in the fast-growing Pentecostal churches, was subject to so many schisms, and the groups were always battling and starting new churches just down the road from each other. To those Muslims who did not understand the splintering of identity, as I had seen in Indonesia, these splits looked like a rapid and threatening proliferation of the rival faith. The core tenets of Islam were so universal, they told me, that true Muslims did not fight one another. As new Muslims, they firmly believed there would be nothing about which to argue.

What's more, the evangelical practice of praying to Jesus, instead of God the Father, seemed suspect to Latif now. How could there be two Gods, God the Father and God the Son, let alone three, if you threw in the Holy Spirit? It was the nonfamiliar issue of the Trinity, which sounds to outsiders like polytheism. Curious about these questions, Latif asked a friend to take him to a conference on Islam. As soon as he heard the words "God: there is no god but Him, the Ever Living, the Ever Watchful" (The Family of 'Imran 3:2), which sounds a lot like "I am the way, the truth, and the life" (John 14:6), Latif decided to revert. Islam offered him a more absolute way of life and, ultimately, God's certain favor. Now he believed that Islam, not Christianity, was the exclusive doorway to everlasting freedom. His personal conversion had political connotations, too. Latif saw the Philippines in terms of a larger struggle for dominance between Islam and the West. Whoever had more members would win. When it came to religion, believers were pawns in a zero-sum game. He called this the "plus/minus factor": a plus for one side was a minus for the other. "The conflict here and in the rest of the world isn't just political," he said. "It's economic, social, everything a person needs." Islam, for him, was essentially a means of liberation—a way to be free of the oppressive West, which was ruled by the United States.

"America is interested in economic power. We can't stop America. They need to dominate us economically in order to survive," he went on. "But we can't separate out the universality of our religion. Economic repression is a spiritual repression." Their responsibility, as Muslims, was to resist. "We Balik Islam play a different role than warriors." *Da'wa* drove their mission, in much the same way as evangelizing had when they were

Pentecostal preachers. The only difference was that they were Muslims now. "We fight and defend by conveying the message to unbelievers, and that's our war. This is our jihad."

About six hundred miles north of Mindanao, in the seamy capital of Manila, the most notorious member of Balik Islam, Ahmed Santos, was awaiting trial in the Philippine version of Cuba's Guantánamo Bay, the Special Intensive Care Area of Taguig Prison. During a recent riot at Camp New Horizons—another optimistic handle for the place—the militants successfully seized control of the prison. Twenty-two inmates were killed and five policemen were injured. Among the dead was the prisoner accused of beheading the American hostage held captive alongside the Burnhams.[1] I tried to visit Camp New Horizons many times and was turned away, until I secured the support of a Filipino congressman. Finally, reluctantly eyeing the congressman's faxed permission letter, the warden agreed to admit me to the prison camp, but he doubted the three-hundred-odd men, most of whom had been found guilty of terrorism, would speak to an American woman. We marched down the dirt track to the entryway of the cavernous warehouse. Inside a three-story chimney of open-air blocks—a multitiered Guantánamo—long-bearded men in tangerine jumpsuits peered down at me.

Hesitantly, I stepped up to the bars and called out in English to a skinny, bearded teenager walking around freely outside some of the open cells. "I'd like to talk to Ahmed Santos," I said. The teenager shuffled off, and soon returned followed by a reed-thin man in his mid-thirties wearing rimless glasses and sporting a T-shirt with the spiky corncobs of Malaysia's twin towers. I had prepared my case to persuade Santos to speak to me, but he did not need to hear it. "I'll talk to you," he said.

According to U.S. intelligence officers, Santos was the leader of the Rajah Solaiman Movement, a radical splinter group of Muslim converts he'd started in 1991, which was now linked to both Abu Sayyaf and the Indonesian group Jemaah Islamiyah. RSM was supposedly named for a sixteenth-century Muslim prince who revolted against the Catholicism of the Portuguese invaders. Before dawn one morning in October 2005, Santos was arrested with weapons, explosives, and maps, all allegedly intended for use in attacks in predominantly Christian areas. By his name alone, Ahmed Santos represented a double helix of religious identity inextricably bound. *Ahmed* means "worthy of praise" in Arabic; *Santos* means "saints" in Spanish. Born a Catholic, Santos converted to Islam in the nineties, while working for a computer company in Saudi Arabia. The reversion, he stressed, had nothing to do with any kind of financial incentive he might have had to become a Muslim. It was a purely spiritual decision, he argued. Santos seemed like so many people at once: a bookish rebel, a preacher, and an intellectual who angered easily when he felt his intelligence was insulted. It was easy to see him in another context, wearing a Che Guevara T-shirt in the hills of Colombia, rather than one depicting Malaysia's Twin Towers.

He had ended up working as a journalist in the southern Philippines, where he interviewed Muslim separatists on the radio. According to American intelligence sources, Santos migrated from journalism to starting RSM through friendships with members of Abu Sayyaf. After a $500,000 bounty was placed on his head as part of the American Rewards for Justice program, which offers cash to those who identify suspected terrorists, someone turned him in. The U.S. embassy touted his arrest as a victory in the "war against terrorism."

At a red picnic table outside the cellblock bars, Santos was willing to confess that he had advocated holy war against the enemies of Islam. Yet he denied any practical role in violence. "I don't consider this a case about terrorism," he said. "This is about religion." He believed that the West was at war with Islam. He put his elbows on the table and rolled up his sleeves to reveal charred circles on his forearms, each about the size of a fingertip: cigarette burns. He claimed that the Filipino security officers branded them into his arms during interrogations. They were nothing, however, next to his certainty that he would be assassinated. Although the bounty on his head had already been paid once, that didn't really matter to most Filipinos. Due to the overwhelming poverty of his country, he was certain he would be killed when he left the prison. "In this country a man can kill a man for a pack of cigarettes. How much can five hundred thousand dollars do?" he asked, not expecting an answer. "The Americans already bought me."

33

VICTORY OR MARTYRDOM

The long wooden boat pulled out into the open water beyond the ramshackle red-and-white ferries. The boat was chugging toward a destination only the boatman knew. The island of Mindanao, just south of the tenth parallel, is the Moro Muslim homeland. It is also still feudal, a place where, for centuries, Filipino landowners have controlled vast plantations worked by tenant farmers. The river, the Rio Grande de Mindanao—a relic of the Spanish conquest—used to be the road in the southern Philippines until roads became the roads. Now the ferryboats rot on their moorings. In the water beneath us, mangrove roots swayed like the matted hair of a drowned woman. We were traveling along the reedy tributaries of the Liguasan Marsh, 850 square wetland miles veined in rice patties and mangroves. A local Muslim leader, a hereditary lord called a *datu*, was feuding with the Christian government over who controlled the rights to potential reserves of oil and natural gas in the marsh's watery labyrinth.

In some ways these skirmishes resembled those six thousand miles away in Sudan, yet the Philippines has much less oil. With 138.5 million barrels of proven reserves, the Philippines exports only 23,910 barrels a day, ranking it an unimpressive seventy-first in the world. These figures, however, don't stop locals from vying to control the marsh's future. If Sudan was a scrap of parched earth where fishermen waded in shallow puddles made by the oil companies, then the Philippines was its opposite. Everything—the mangroves, my fingers, and the boat's worn green gunwales—swelled in the humidity. When it comes to prospecting, Sudan is a place of aftermath, and the Philippines one of "not yet." Along the bank jungle leaves rot. Flat, low, wet, and hot—it is a place of intrigues. All manner of rebels and criminal gangs have found safe haven by terrorizing villagers and building training camps in the marshland along inaccessible rivers. Islam, and Islamic rebellion, like its Christian counterpart, meant whatever anyone wanted it to, and could be manipulated accordingly. I had seen this in Nigeria, Somalia, Indonesia, Malaysia, and Sudan: religious identity as a way to guarantee and control resources. But religion meant other things, too.

"In the Philippines, Islam is feudal," Amirah Ali Lidasan, a Muslim human rights worker on Mindanao, told me. Liberal activists such as Lidasan were attempting to reclaim the religion, to argue that Islam could function as the basis of a moral society, a set of shared principles—such as equality and social justice—that could be used to protect people against a rapacious government. This was not so different from Father Geremia's view of Christianity, which was supposed to guarantee the rights of the poor and powerless.

That July morning in 2006, following instructions from a rebel go-between, I had driven to a rural bodega. Inside, a heavyset shopkeeper wearing a black *abeya* barked, "Move to the back of the store quickly and stay out of sight." It was disorienting. Too many strains of the world intermingled at once—Latin America and Islam, as odd and improbable as a dry goods store in El Salvador run by a devout Yemeni woman. In the back of the shop, a large door in the storeroom opened unexpectedly onto the river, where a boat was waiting to take me to visit a man in hiding, the most powerful commander of the Moro Islamic Liberation Front. Although the MILF has harbored Abu Sayyaf and other militants, it signed a cease-fire with the central government in 2001, and denounced terrorism in 2003, to stay out of America's crosshairs. More recently, the MILF has been vying for control of oil prospecting in the deposits that underlie their land.

Pakila Datu Zaid, the MILF commander I was hoping to meet, was recuperating somewhere along this river after a bloody battle with a local governor over control of a swath of potentially oil-rich swampland. Weeks earlier, sixteen thousand people had fled their homes, the MILF commander vanished, and a $100,000 bounty was placed on his head. To punish the escaped commander, government toughs had shot his wife dead while she was on her way to the mall on July 5. The wreck of her car sat on the wharf outside the bodega. In this war, wives and family members were frequent targets. Word had it that the commander had spirited her body away up the river to be buried at his hideout, and when he heard that I had been asking around about her death, he got in touch through a MILF spokesman and invited me to come meet him.

I hadn't expected an entourage, but five or six veiled women climbed into the boat after me, including the heavyset shopkeeper. All were relatives of the murdered woman, and this was their first chance to visit her grave. We passed small villages along the water: clusters of shacks on stilts surrounded by groves of coconut seedlings and jackfruit trees. A few children bathed in the river; they didn't look up as we passed. We were chugging southward toward the equator: deeper into the heart of Moro land. A fifty-three-year-old bespectacled schoolteacher named Rhuyaga Daud, sitting beside me, explained that no government troops would dare come onto this land. This was MILF territory, she said, and everyone who lived here, the farmers and fishermen, supported the rebels' cause.

"We want an Islamic state," Daud said, frankly. These days the rebels were rarely this forthright as they tried to soft-pedal their attachment to Islam in order to convince America they posed no security threat. To my surprise, the schoolteacher had recently traveled to Washington, D.C., as part of a delegation of Muslim teachers trying to convince the U.S. government that the MILF are not terrorists. This war was as much about freedom as it was religion, Ghansali Jaafar, the MILF vice-chairman for political affairs, explained to me. The Moro struggle was more like the Vietnam War than the Iranian Revolution.

"We admire the Iranians' courage," Jaafar said, "but we are a free people trying to regain our independence." As one Moro professor told me, the Communist state that Marx outlines in *Das Kapital* could serve virtually the same need as the Islamic state does for his people. "The problem here is liberating our homeland from a colonial power."

An hour passed, then most of another, before Ms. Daud, the schoolteacher, leaned forward and said, "We're almost there." We rounded a bend, and suddenly more than a hundred soldiers in camouflage were smiling and waving from the riverbank. As we grew closer, I could see that all of them carried assault rifles. Several carried two rocket-propelled grenade launchers at once—slung like bandoliers over each shoulder. Some were children. I had never seen so much military hardware in my life. With the weaponry by that river, they could have taken a city.

The soldiers helped us out of the boat as a good-looking fortysomething man in a gray T-shirt emerged from among them: Pakila Datu Zaid. He led us straight to his wife's grave: just a simple stone set in a dirt patch at the edge of the compound. It would have been un-Islamic to build an ornate grave. "I spoke to her on the phone twenty minutes before she was killed," he said, looking dazed. The women wept.

His hideout consisted of an unused mosque, a basketball court, and a farmhouse in which he himself was cooking a lunch of curried chicken. A charismatic chef, he spooned the chicken onto plates and said something to his soldiers, who disappeared. A few minutes later, they returned and placed three brand-new American-made M16s with night-vision sights on the kitchen table. He'd bought them from Filipino soldiers after joint military exercises with the American troops called "shoulder to shoulder," or *balikatan*. The infusion of high-powered American weaponry on all sides meant that more and more people were dying.

Behind me, a young soldier, his hair stiff with gel, leaned against the kitchen counter, cradling an assault rifle. His name was Ibrahim Daud; he was Pakila Datu Zaid's nephew.

"How old are you?" I asked.

"I'm fifteen but was fourteen when I joined. We have eight-year-olds who are in weapons training." The room was silent but for the clanking of forks against plates. To change the subject, Zaid asked me to come outside into the now-glaring sun. Concerned about the child-soldier revelation, Ms. Daud approached me again to make sure I understood the members of MILF were indeed fighting jihad for a cause. Islam was about justice for the poor.

"They are fighting because the government stole their land," she told me as the men lounged around us on hammocks, rocking themselves by pressing their rifle butts in the dirt. Few spoke English, so I asked her to translate the question: Would everyone who had lost their land to the government please raise their hands?

No hands went up. Maybe they didn't understand, I thought. As I asked her to repeat my question, Zaid leaned over and interrupted.

"No," he said, slowly, as if I were missing a very basic point. "The land the government has taken is mine."

"*All* of it?" I asked.

He nodded: 2,500 acres. These "Islamic rebels" were simply his private army. The soldiers were serfs; Zaid was a very rich landowner. "So let me get this straight," I said. "If you weren't at war right now, would these men be workers in your fields?"

He beamed. *Exactly.* To these serfs, jihad meant little more than the patch on their jackets, which read, in English, "Victory or Martyrdom." The patches, like the camouflage uniforms, were simply a way to legitimize war and guarantee that their death would give them a way to reach heaven. And by the way, Zaid asked, pulling me aside as we headed back to the pirogue tethered to the bank, did I know of any American company interested in prospecting for oil and natural gas on his marshland? He was ready to make a great deal.

Islam here could mean whatever one wanted it to; it could hold a link to the past or forge a vision for the future. It could reinforce a family's feudal power or promise liberation from colonial oppression. This is today's splintered Islamic rebellion, I thought to myself. Its leaders are more concerned with oil than either justice or jihad. The Moro people caught in the middle were dying for it: martyred not even for money, but for the prospect of oil.

34

TO WITNESS

Martyrdom today may seem like a strictly Muslim phenomenon, but when Martin Burnham was shot to death in the jungle, he became, for many Christians, a modern-day martyr. The two kinds of martyrdom are related; the Arabic word *shaheed* and the Greek word *martus* both mean "bearer of witness." And before Mohammed died, he is said to have counseled his followers to be prepared to die for their beliefs, just as Jesus's did, according to the following Hadith: "Do as the apostles of Isa ibn Maryam [Jesus the son of Mary], they were cut by saw and hung upon wood. Being killed in obedience to Allah is better than a life of sin."[1]

Since Jesus's death, more than seventy million people have been killed for their Christian faith, according to one of the leading sources of Christian statistics, *World Christian Trends*. Its authors estimate that there are currently around two hundred million Christians living under persecution and four hundred million at risk. And for many Christians today, especially those minority populations in divided communities along the tenth parallel, living and dying for their beliefs is a necessary element of faith.

"People are used to the Joan of Arc type of martyrdom, an individual on trial," Todd Johnson, one of the world's most prominent Christian demographers and coeditor of *World Christian Trends*, told me in the fall of 2007. We'd met that day in a Cambridge, Massachusetts, coffee shop. Johnson is working on cataloging every Christian martyr from the inception of the faith to the present day. "Martin isn't in here yet, but he will be," he said, flipping through the pages of *World Christian Trends*. In one chart, the causes of death are listed alphabetically: roasted alive, sawed in two, thrown from airplane. Some of the statistics are suspect—too high to be believed. For instance, it's hard to imagine that between one hundred thousand and five hundred thousand Christians have been thrown to sharks. Still, much of the data is factual and gruesome. To make sense of such staggering numbers, Johnson cited the mass killings of Christian men, women, and children in Idi Amin's Uganda, since the dictator feared their religious commitment threatened his omnipotence. These types of large-scale targeted killings perpetrated by Amin, Stalin, Pol Pot, and Omar al-Bashir, Johnson contends, explain why 60 percent of all Christian martyrs have been killed since the beginning of the twentieth century. Such numbers help to explain how the issues of persecution and religious freedom are now a top priority among human rights activists.

I first met Gracia Burnham in April 2007. It was 6:30 in the morning and she was eating dry cereal in front of the early morning news at the Comfort Inn in Franklin, Tennessee. Now forty-eight and six years out of the jungle, her once-pinched face had softened and filled out. She turned from the TV and looked up at me with earnest violet eyes that almost swallowed her face. On this morning, she had not needed an alarm clock. "God woke me up," she said.

After returning from the Philippines in the fall of 2006, I'd gotten in touch with Gracia to ask her for her thoughts on martyrdom. She'd invited me to come with her to this conference, which was hosted by the Voice of the Martyrs, an evangelical nonprofit organization founded in 1967 by Pastor Richard Wurmbrand, who'd been tortured in Romanian prisons for fourteen years. Begun during Billy Graham's worldwide crusade to rescue Christians behind the Iron Curtain, the Voice of the Martyrs informs fellow believers about contemporary persecution and martyrdom. I had seen its efforts firsthand in Nigeria's Middle Belt town of Yelwa, where, according to the town's pastor, Sunday Wuyep, the Voice of the Martyrs had contributed $40,000 to rebuild the church.

By the time Burnham's book about her time as a prisoner of Abu Sayyaf, *In the Presence of My Enemies*, made it to the *New York Times* bestseller list in May 2003, she had already become an evangelical superstar. Born in Cairo, Illinois, the daughter of a pastor, she had decided from an early age that she would give her life to Christ and become an evangelical Christian, much as her parents before her had. When I met her, only her worn, square hands betrayed the harshness of the life she had led in jungles as a missionary and a captive. Thanks to the generosity of fellow believers—and the success of her books—she and her three children had made a new home in Rose Hill, Kansas.

At the Christ Community Church in Franklin that morning, I mixed with a crowd of more than three hundred other attendees, some of whom had driven for hundreds of miles to meet Gracia Burnham. Tables were set up selling literature and jewelry, including Lance Armstrong–inspired rubber bracelets—just like the pink one that Noviana Malewa wore in Indonesia, which read, "HE IS ALIVE!" These, however, were black-and-gray interlocking rubber handcuffs that read, "Remember them that are in bonds, as bound with them; and them which suffer adversity" (Hebrews 13:3). Green T-shirts silk-screened with lions' eyes—"It Didn't End with the Coliseum"—were also for sale.

On another table was a stack of what looked like orange kitchen bags printed in Korean. The words were Bible verses, and the bags were balloons, millions of which had been released over the North Korean border by the Voice of the Martyrs since the 1960s. The North Korean government reportedly orders anyone who finds these balloons to deliver them to a police station.

Robert Brock, a mission representative for the Voice of the Martyrs, took the stage, and began the conference with prayers for North Korea's president Kim Jong Il and Iran's president Mahmoud Ahmadinejad. "We work mainly in the 10/40 Window, the bastion of communism, Islam, and Hinduism," he said. "It's the hardest place to work, my friends. It could cost you your life."

Not all martyrdom happens so far away. Tom Zurowski, a baby-faced preacher in his thirties from Albion, New York, with downy blond hair and eyebrows to match, looks like a newly hatched chick. When I'd met him that morning at breakfast, he'd given off an air of clear-hearted innocence—a wide-eyed certainty I envied. He told me that one night, when he was nineteen, he sat at the end of his bed with a hunting knife, contemplating suicide. Christ had saved his life. A recovering alcoholic and drug addict, Zurowski started Global Response Network, an organization like the Voice of the Martyrs, that "aids suffering Christians as they take up their cross and follow Jesus." He'd had his first encounter with martyrdom more than a decade earlier when a Christian asked him if he would die to save the life of an unborn child. He had no answer. Not long after, during a protest outside an abortion clinic, he found himself on his knees, nose to bumper with an angry motorist. Zurowski knew, then, that he was not going to move, and that he had the answer to his friend's question: he was willing to die to stop abortion. Now Zurowski had made more than forty trips overseas. From the stage, he told the story of one teenage boy he met in southern Sudan—an escaped slave. As a seven-year-old, the boy had sneaked out of his master's house to go to church. When he came home, the irate master nailed the child's knees together and his feet to a board, telling him to "be like your Jesus." Zurowski showed the audience a photograph of the boy: his maimed legs looked hinged like a stork's.

I, too, had heard such stories in Sudan, when traveling with Franklin Graham in 2003, and along the north-south border in 2008. I didn't doubt the story, and yet the boy's suffering—Christian or not—was one aspect of a war in which race, oil, and power played as large a role as religion. Zurowski wasn't wrong by definition; he was telling the story as he saw it, and was teaching others to see the war through the same absolute lenses of good versus evil, Christian versus Muslim.

The most incendiary speaker was the Reverend Mujahid el-Masih—or "warrior for Christ" in Arabic. A former Muslim, he had fled Pakistan after converting other Muslims to evangelical Christianity. But the threats on his life had followed him here to America. Two weeks earlier, while speaking in Sioux Falls, South Dakota, he had received anonymous letters warning that if he preached, he would be murdered and the church would be bombed. He ignored the ultimatum.

"Allah is not the same God as the God of the Bible," he said. "We don't need bombs to destroy terrorism, we need Bibles." Mujahid el-Masih was echoing what I'd heard time and again from Christian leaders in Nigeria, Sudan, Indonesia, Malaysia, and the Philippines: Islam was out to dominate the world. Shortly, they warned, the confrontations along the tenth parallel would find their way to America, as they were already exploding in Europe. And they believed that in a war Muslims were waging by demographics—by having multiple wives and many children—they would inevitably turn our democracies against us.

"Love Muslims," al-Masih said, "but don't trust them."

The crowd laughed. The crux of his rousing diatribe, however, was not the fight against Islam. It was the fight against liberalism, especially liberal, or nominal, Christianity: any form that did not espouse faith in Jesus Christ as the only path to salvation. While Muslims wandered blindly in the dark, he argued, liberals knew the truth and turned against it anyway. They were the real hypocrites, refusing to acknowledge the battle at hand,

and weakening the faith with their moral relativism. This was the struggle within Christianity over who had the right to negotiate the faith. "Political correctness is more evil than Osama bin Laden!" he shouted.

He was talking about me, an opposing member of the unfolding culture wars, although he had no idea that the enemy was sitting in the audience. Gracia knew, however, that I was not a born-again Christian, but she did not flinch, so neither did I. I looked down at my clenched hands—their nails hard-bitten and ragged—then at Gracia's weathered ones, calm in her lap beside me, and I recalled a phrase from childhood: "Hands to work, hearts to God." In my parents' house—the rectory of a parish priest and his wife—this meant "be of unending service." That's how my mother lived it. And her hands looked like Gracia's—tools of devotion building homes in Honduras, ladling chili in a North Philadelphia soup kitchen, making eighty cream puff swans by herself for a ladies' summer luncheon while the ladies sat waiting in the garden.

Mine looked like the hands of a judge nibbling away at the cuticles while the brain churned in assessment. I, too, have found solace by living in motion. Since kneeling with Franklin Graham on a Persian rug in Khartoum five years earlier, I had stood among throngs of swaying Christians in an Indonesian Chinese restaurant, said grace in the Malaysian jungle with an aboriginal priest, observed jihadis pray in a Jakarta vitamin shop, danced awkwardly with Sufis to an electronic steel drum in a Nigerian slum, and been serenaded by a fakir in a Mogadishu refugee camp. Worship often took the form of celebration, and for all I had seen of religion's divisive power, for most people, their faith was, above all, about finding joy. Even in the midst of war and catastrophe, I had watched time and again how people were able to undertake the extraordinary tasks of daily life—to keep going—based on their absolute belief in God's Divine Plan.

When Gracia Burnham climbed onto the church stage, she seemed untouched by the provocative rhetoric of the previous speakers. "People have called Martin a martyr," she said. "That has always bothered me." The three-hundred-odd nodding heads before her stopped nodding, but she continued. For Gracia, losing Martin in the jungle was not about heroic martyrdom. His death was merely something all Christians need to be prepared to do: to "give up everything for the Lord and be willing to die for him if need be," she said. "There's no safe or easy way to be a follower of Christ."

She had survived her tribulation, in part by loving her captors and herself enough to forgive both their petty mortal failings. She'd focused on their shared humanity.

At the break, three teenage Mennonite girls approached Gracia, who was signing copies of her books. The girls wore matching gingham dresses with puffy sleeves and three-button vests. Mercy Grace, fifteen, also wore a small white veil, her dishwater blond hair pulled tightly back under it. When she was twelve, Mercy Grace had read Elisabeth Elliot's book *Shadow of the Almighty*, which tells the story of her husband, Jim, one of the most famous twentieth-century martyrs, killed by the Auca people when he went to Ecuador as a missionary. (I'd first heard of Elliot and seen an Auca spear in Franklin Graham's Boone, North Carolina, home. Graham's wife, Jane Austin, told me the story.) Mercy Grace had been so moved by Elliot's book that she decided to become a missionary. Now she'd fallen in love with Gracia and her account, too. So her family had piled into their car and driven from Bagdad, Kentucky, five hours away, so that Mercy Grace could attend the conference and meet Gracia. As a missionary, Mercy Grace didn't know yet where she'd be called. "I'd like her to go to a closed Muslim country," her mother said, "because people have the idea that Muslims are a lost cause." Mercy Grace did not fear martyrdom. "It would be neat!" she said, grinning widely enough to show her braces. Her mother nudged her, and she closed her mouth. "It would be a privilege," she corrected herself.

The next morning, Gracia taught a senior citizen Bible study class at the First Baptist Church in Mount Juliet, Tennessee. Fifteen well-coiffed ladies, some wearing sweaters decorated with hollyhocks, watched Gracia open a white plastic Voice of the Martyrs shopping bag and pull out a piece of stiff batik fabric. Using her teeth, Gracia showed the class how she'd wrapped the fabric around her waist to make a changing room, and a bathroom. "The first few times I made a mess of it and had to wait until I got to the next river to wash it," she said. The women looked stunned. "You've washed it since then," one said. Gracia shook her head no. "If I did, it would fall apart," she said, then demonstrated how the fabric served as a blanket, a backpack, and even, on one occasion, a stretcher for one of her captors, a fourteen-year-old Abu Sayyaf member named Ahmed who had been injured in a firefight. They carried him wounded through the jungle in this fabric, called a *malong*. She told how she had loathed Ahmed before he was injured for hoarding food when she had none, and for throwing stones at her while she bathed—fully clothed—in the river. But she had prayed to find a way to love him, even as she and Martin slowly starved.

The last time Gracia saw Ahmed, his mind had gone mad from infection, or simply pain. He was tied by the hands and feet to the walls of a hut, and someone had stuffed a sock in his mouth to keep him from screaming. She wondered aloud to the Bible study class where Ahmed was now—still crazy, perhaps, or pushing another hostage up another steep mountain path. Or, most likely, he had died and gone to hell.

When we left the classroom together, she seemed more subdued, as if her bubbliness had been a mode of translation, a physical dialect that allowed the women listening to actually hear her. She could hold up her soiled *malong*, talk about blood and shit with a smile, force them to listen to the story of a boy with a gangrenous body chained to a bed. In the hallway, she told me that two of her former captors had been baptized as born-again Christians. This heartened her. Maybe Martin's bearing witness had made the difference in saving their souls for eternal life. When I brought up the fact that several days earlier, Abu Sayyaf had beheaded seven more hostages, Christian construction workers on the island of Jolo, Gracia's shoulders rounded forward and her violet eyes dulled. She hadn't heard.

"Everyone told me Abu Sayyaf was dying out, but I knew they were wrong, because the economy in that area is so bad. There's nothing else for the Muslims to do." She understood the economic realities of life in the Torrid Zone's jungles. Jihad was a "career move," she said. The only other job besides kidnapping was fishing. And fishing required a boat.

"If they couldn't die in jihad, their next choice was to go to America and get a good job," she said. The gap between the poverty she had lived through with the Muslim Filipinos and the relative wealth of the women in the First Baptist Church classroom seemed difficult for Burnham to accept, as if she didn't want to be here among the SUVs and hollyhock sweaters. Gracia kept returning to where small things mattered more, and had even traveled to the Philippines, in disguise. She missed the place that much. Yet her duty was to fulfill the Great Commission, and there were a multitude of souls to save here in America, she said, tactfully implying that mine was one of them. "You know, I don't believe that only Abu Sayyaf is going to hell." I nodded, feeling no resentment. Perhaps this was the tender way in which she approached those young thugs, witnessing to them in vulnerable moments when they had shed the bandanas tied over their faces, shaking from a bout of bad diarrhea, homesick.

If Franklin Graham is a warrior for his faith, then Gracia Burnham is the very thing she refused to call her husband: a martyr. She is alive, but the life she had loved the most was lost to her, and so was her husband. Wounded, she came home, accepted the suburban house and the mini-van. She wrote her books, drove the carpool, let the kids' fast-food wrappers pile up in the backseat's foot well. In this paler, tempered version of her once-Technicolor life, she spent her days bearing witness in a carpeted church hallway to people like me. A soul is a soul, as she saw it, and each deserved a chance at heaven.

EPILOGUE

This is what I see: my muddy green flip-flops and, a few steps ahead along the slippery hedgerow, a pair of darker-skinned feet in leather sandals. The man in front is speaking to me, but his French is hard to understand. He talks as if there's gravel in his mouth. As we trudge along the raised dirt hump that marks the edge of a cornfield, I run my eyes along his narrow back, clad in a white robe. A nylon backpack swings awkwardly from his prominent shoulder blades. He calls himself Reverend Abdu. I don't know how old he is—he could be forty or sixty—and neither does he.

I am dragging myself along the tenth parallel in Nigeria, and I am nearly asleep on my sore, crusty feet. One village has begun to bleed into another, thanks to the steep angle of the light, a grueling gray light that is the same from here to Sudan to Indonesia to the Philippines. The air is so humid it's impossible to tell where the moisture ends and my neck's sweat begins. The crickets drone, a tone lower than that of the endless trudge of our feet, as we go to meet people who do not want to be met—people who have left the road behind on purpose.

A child's cry of horror goes up from within the cornstalks, and Reverend Abdu stops walking and turns to me. The child cried out when he spotted me, the reverend explains: the people we are going to see have never seen a white person before. "They think you are the devil, because their devil is white," he says. "They are afraid you will curse them and turn them white, too."

Reverend Abdu lives only a few miles away from these fields, but he is an outsider, a native of the northern, French-speaking country of Niger. Born in a village called Adunu, he began his life as Abdullah Ahmadu, a Muslim nomad. When he was a small child—perhaps five years old, he thinks—the village was visited by evangelical Christians from the Sudan

Interior Mission (founded a century earlier to bring the Gospel to "the 60 million souls of the Soudan"). As he tells it, after hearing the message that Jesus had come to redeem the world, the villagers decided to convert en masse to Christianity, and he was born again. The notion of describing the childhood experience makes no sense to him. "I met Jesus and he saved me," is all he will say. In 1981 he left Niger and came south to Nigeria to teach his former kinsmen, ethnic Fulani Muslim herders, about salvation through Jesus Christ. At some point he began introducing himself as Reverend Abdu, consecrating himself with the name.

Reverend Abdu's name, like those of so many other people I had met—Ahmed Santos, the Muslim revert in the Philippines' version of Guantánamo Bay; or Mujahid Masih, the warrior for Christ at the Voice of the Martyrs conference in Franklin, Tennessee—held together a complicated identity. Abdu was a cowless Fulani herder, a citizen of Niger, a former Muslim. It mattered most to him that he was a Christian, and yet he wouldn't say why he was a Christian, other than that he had met Jesus and, in his own fashion, followed Him.

I had first met Reverend Abdu by following a signboard for a mission outpost—a square of white wood reading, "The Great Commission," with an outline of Nigeria split by a cross, the crossbar running along the tenth parallel. I'd first seen this sign a year earlier, while driving around the hilly Middle Belt capital of Jos in the gold minivan I'd borrowed from Pastor James Wuye and the imam Nurayn Ashafa. I hadn't had time on that trip to visit the offices of the Great Commission, so when I returned to Jos the next summer, I went looking for the signboard. But the governor had ordered all such signs taken down, lest they contribute to the ongoing religious violence. With Haruna Yakubu, the minivan's savvy driver, I spent hours pulling off the road and peering behind locked gates, until I spied the displaced sign leaning against a compound's high wall. We found the gatekeeper of the place, who let us in, and there I met Reverend Abdu for the first time.

He had just completed a training course at the Great Commission compound, learning how to evangelize Muslims from an American missionary who had translated the New Testament into Fulani. He was about to hitchhike home—to a shanty a five-hour drive northwest of Jos. I offered him a ride, and he took me along to watch him in action, evangelizing among the nomads.

We had set out long before dawn. At daybreak, somewhere on the road northwest of Jos, we left the minivan by the roadside and headed on foot into the six-foot-high cornfields, searching for nomads' cattle camps. Now, as we hiked along the ordered grids of other people's crops, the sugary scent of sweet corn gave way to the muskier smell of livestock. Then we spied their dull coats in a wallow off to the right: thirty cows moving tightly around one another like a school of hungry fish waiting for food to drop from the sky. The reverend turned left and cut through the bush, and I followed him. Within minutes we had broken into a clearing of pounded earth large enough to hold two grassy igloos. A bicycle was propped against one, and a man, a woman, and a girl of maybe ten, the last holding a baby, crawled out of a low doorway to greet us.

The father eyed the reverend narrowly. He looked to be in his forties. He was broad and thick-muscled, and did not seem thrilled at the arrival of visitors. His name, he told us, was Mallam Ibrahim. (*Mallam*, like *mullah*, is a general term for "Islamic teacher" or "scholar.") His was a family of nomads, he said. "We don't have our own land." It was too dry for them to stay among their own people in the northeast of Nigeria, and drought had driven them, twenty members in all, to these trammeled cornfields, where they hoped to go unnoticed. That was impossible. Even I could see that the cows had already flattened someone's harvest. The situation would not remain peaceful for long.

The last thing these nomads needed was attention from a freestyle Fulani evangelist and a white Western reporter. To try to ease the tension, I asked Ibrahim how many cows he had, a question that Reverend Abdu translated into a mixture of French and Fulani, indicating that this group had likely made it as far as neighboring Chad, or Niger, both former French-speaking colonies. He didn't want to answer—I had misjudged the question, thinking it was as harmless as discussing weather. As it turned out, asking these herders about their cows was akin to asking how much money they had, since the cows were all the wealth they had in the world. "It's a secret," Mallam Ibrahim said, his eyes thinning to slits, as if I were trying to take the cows from him.

The reverend pulled a portable solar-powered DVD player from his backpack and set it up on a stump. "Who is Jesus?" he asked Ibrahim, translating the questions and answers for me as he posed them.

"I don't know," Mallam Ibrahim said.

"Who is Mohammad?"

"A Muslim."

The mother tried to tell me something, and the reverend translated. "She says that I have come here once before to show this." She did not look pleased. He searched in his backpack for the Jesus film—the two-hour 1979 film that its promoters at the Jesus Film Project claim has been shown to six billion viewers.[1] When Reverend Abdu opened the DVD cover, however, it turned out he'd brought a disc of Christian music videos by mistake. He slid it into the machine anyway. Singing and dancing people appeared on the screen for a few seconds, and then the screen went blank.

"I forgot to charge it," Reverend Abdu said sheepishly. The American at the Great Commission compound had given him this high-tech machine, he said, but in order to make it work here in the bush, he had to leave it in the sun for several hours beforehand, and this he had forgotten to do. In the sticky silence, he turned to Ibrahim and asked, "Will you accept Jesus?"

"No," Ibrahim answered. "It will unsettle our Muslim prayers. I like the way I pray, and I am not changing it."

There was silence but for the crickets rubbing their legs together and the cows swishing their fly-and-shit-covered tails. There wasn't much else for the reverend to say. He changed the subject, telling me, "These children do not go to school. Their father refused to let them go."

"I'm not afraid of school," Ibrahim said. "But if the children go to school, they may not come back."

It turned out that Ibrahim had more pressing concerns. "The cows are sick," he told us. "Their livers are swollen. Do you have any medicine for them? Do you have any food?"

The reverend said nothing and began to pack up the DVD player.

"How did you come here?" the mother asked.

"Why did you come here?" Ibrahim asked.

Reverend Abdu did not answer these questions. He crooned goodbye, and we left the clearing; he seemed torn, as if he were taking leave of his own family for a long journey.

We plodded through the cornfields, found the minivan, and drove off. And a few minutes later we were at the reverend's cement-block home— an isolated two-room shack that stood atop a mild rise. In a tiny enclosed courtyard, his daughter, who looked about ten, was washing china teacups in a metal bucket. The reverend showed us into the narrow room that served as everything but the bathroom. And we sat on his only chairs, in front of a poster of Noah's ark he had nailed to one wall. "They always ask me for medicine and food for the cows," he said, subdued.

I thought at first that he was embarrassed at how badly the mission had gone. The Jesus Film Project claims that two hundred million people have accepted Jesus Christ as a direct result of watching the film—a claim I found incredible. Was it the film itself that was supposed to impress the would-be convert? Was it the DVD player? I looked around the reverend's shanty. The device in his backpack cost at least two hundred times as much as the teakettle, the wash bucket, and his wooden chairs. The reverend saw no personal gain from working for the Great Commission; he had no interest in the prosperity gospel, or in improving people's material lives, including his own. To him, numbers were about souls in heaven, not the conquest of earth. I asked him what made days like this day worth it. "People ask me why I left my heritage," he said, pausing. "Jesus is the only way." He had nothing else to say; faith couldn't be explained, or wrapped in a tidy life story, or cast aside as an inconvenience on a hot, embarrassing day.

When his daughter finished washing the cups, Abdu lit the burner on a camp stove and set the kettle to boil. He crouched over the flame protectively, as a nomad would guard his fire from the wind, although he had left the open air of his own cattle camp behind decades earlier for the shelter of the zinc roof above us. At last, he handed me the cup of steaming tea, which, in this stifling outpost along the tenth parallel, I dreaded drinking. To be polite, I took a sip, and the tea's immediate effect surprised me—somehow its warmth branching out in my chest offered relief from the day's heat, another paradox. I slumped against the hard chair. I had reached a limit of interpretation, and drank the tea down without trying to read every object, every gesture, for its significance. Here I was on the tenth parallel with a man who had once been a Muslim and now was a Christian, who had spent his life preaching to his former kinsmen driven south by the need for water. Set against these simple facts, explanation failed. So much history and theology had been grafted onto the people of the tenth parallel over the centuries: the dramatic images of clashing civilizations and competing fundamentalisms; the demographics and big-picture analyses of the roles played by oil, weather, war, colonial interest, and clan conviction. All of these sought to explain Reverend Abdu and his like, and yet here he was before me, sheltering the gas flame and defying explanation—a man who believed what he believed for reasons that were mysterious even to him. He was not a foot soldier in a fundamentalist army or a statistic in some relief agency's annual report; he was not in revolt against his government, nor was he waging a one-man protest against Western hegemony. He was a walking, talking hierophany, and he embodied the space where the horizontal, secular axis of the everyday intersected with the vertical, sacred world of God.

I had met many believers like him—those whose religious convictions were emphatic and elusive—and every time I thought I had them classified, they slipped out of my easy distinctions. That such people could accommodate conflicting worldly labels (evangelist, nomad, Muslim, and Christian in Reverend Abdu's case) was a talent of postcolonial life, evidence of adaptation by people who have had many different categories foisted on them by outsiders. But it was also born out of nearly fifteen hundred years of religious coexistence, of Christians and Muslims living together, and it had moved far beyond the binary divisions between Saved and Damned, Good and Evil, Us and Them.

Religious strife where Christians and Muslims meet is real, and grim, but the long history of everyday encounter, of believers of different kinds shouldering all things together, even as they follow different faiths, is no less real. It follows that their lives bear witness to the coexistence of the two religions—and of the complicated bids for power inside them—more than to the conflicts between them.

Reverend Abdu bore his several identities, and all their contradictions, in a single skin. It wasn't relativism; his convictions went deeper than that. His was the experience of true religion, which is dynamic because it is alive. Such labels seemed ultimately unimportant to him because he did not belong to himself, or to this world, at all; he belonged to God. The identities that mattered to him told him not simply where he came from, but where, with God's help, he was going.

NOTES

BIBLIOGRAPHY

ACKNOWLEDGMENTS

INDEX

NOTES

PROLOGUE

1. For further reading on the noble spiritual beliefs, see Francis Deng, *The Dinka People of Sudan*, and Wendy James, *The Listening Ebony: Moral Knowledge, Religion, and Power Among the Uduk of Sudan*.
2. www.vatican.va.
3. African trypanosomiasis infects between fifty thousand and seventy thousand people each year, and leads to about forty-eight thousand deaths, according to the not-for-profit R&D organization Drugs for Neglected Diseases Initiative.
4. National Hurricane Center, National Oceanic and Atmospheric Administration
5. www.worldchristiandatabase.org.
6. These statistics on population growth are United Nations figures. Unless otherwise noted, aggregate population and religious statistics are from *The CIA World Factbook 2009*.

NIGERIA

1. All further citations of the Bible taken from the New King James Version. Copyright © 1982 by Thomas Nelson, Inc. Used by permission. All rights reserved.

I. THE ROCK: ONE

1. Sola Odunfa, "Nigeria's Counting Controversy," BBC News, March 21, 2006, at news.bbc.co.uk.
2. U.S. Department of State, Washington, D.C., August 11, 2009.
3. "Corruption, Godfatherism, and the Funding of Political Violence," *Human Rights Watch*, October 11, 2007.
4. The Hadith, collected centuries after Mohammed's death, fall into different categories, some considered more accurate than others.
5. Sahih al-Bukhari, volume 9, book 84, number 63.
6. All further citations of the Quran come from *The Qur'an: A New Translation* by M.A.S. Abdel Haleem (New York: Oxford University Press, 2004).

7. Pew Forum on Religion and Public Life, "Historical Overview of Pentecostalism in Nigeria," December 22, 2006, at www.pewforum.org.

2. THE ROCK: TWO

1. The term was coined by the nineteenth-century British evangelist John Spencer Trimingham. His popular book, *The Christian Approach to Islam in the Sudan* (London: Oxford University Press, 1948), cast Islam as a threat against religion and empire, and had a major influence on colonial thinking.

2. Pew Forum on Religion and Public Life, "Historical Overview of Pentecostalism in Nigeria."

3. For further reading, see Dana L. Robert's excellent biography, *Occupy Until I Come: A. T. Pierson and the Evangelization of the World* (Grand Rapids, Mich.: Eerdmans Publishing, 2003).

4. Luther H. Gulick, "What the Triangle Means," *Young Men's Era*, January 18, 1894.

5. John Mott, *The Decisive Hour of Christian Missions* (New York: Young People's Missionary Movement of the United States and Canada, 1910), pp. 60–61.

6. For many evangelicals, the distinction of denomination is irrelevant, since it is linked to man-made hierarchies and rites, and not a direct experience of Jesus Christ.

7. Peter Spartalis, *Karl Kumm: Last of the Livingstones—Pioneer Missionary Statesman* (Bonn: Verlag Für Kultur und Wissenscheaft, 1994), p. 34.

8. Sudan United Mission Archives, Lamont Library, Harvard University.

9. Hermann Karl Wilhelm Kumm, *From Hausaland to Egypt Through the Sudan* (London: Constable and Co., 1910), p. 227.

10. The pastor's name has been omitted for his safety.

11. "Nigeria: Jos, a City Torn Apart," *Human Rights Watch*, December 18, 2001.

12. Mark Noll, *A History of Christianity in the United States and Canada* (Grand Rapids, Mich.: Eerdmans Publishing, 1992), p. 380.

13. Although this chapter, "The Bee," speaks about the healing properties of honey, most chapter titles in the Quran may appear somewhat random to non-Muslims. Like the verses themselves, Muslims consider them to be divine revelation.

3. THE FLOOD

1. Malaria, which, according to the World Health Organization, is the world's foremost killer of children, leads to the deaths of an annual average of one million people, the majority under five years old, in sub-Saharan Africa.

2. "Lost in Limbo," *Economist*, August 27, 2009.

3. See George Ochoa, Jennifer Hoffman, Tina Tin, *Climate: The Force That Shapes Our World and the Future of Life on Earth* (London: Rodale Books International, 2005), p. 142, and Alexandra Olson, "U.N. Forum: Deserts Advancing Faster Than Development Funding for Poor Nations," Associated Press, February 20, 2002.

4. Ernest Zebrowski, Jr., *Perils of a Restless Planet: Scientific Perspectives on Natural Disasters* (Cambridge, UK: Cambridge University Press, 1997), p. 21.

5. *IOM Policy Brief: Migration, Climate Change and the Environment* (International Organization for Migration, May 2009).

6. Norman Myers and Jennifer Kent, *Environmental Exodus: An Emergent Crisis in the Global Arena* (Washington, D.C.: Climate Institute, 1995); and Norman Myers, "Environmental Refugees: Our Latest Understanding," *Philosophical Transactions of the Royal Society* B:356:16.1–16.5, 2001.

7. "In Search of Shelter: Mapping the Effects of Climate Change on Human Migration and Displacement."

4. DROUGHT

1. Amin, Al Amin, *Almajiri and the Quranic Education* (Kaduna: Rishab Printing Press, 2001).

5. THE TRIBULATION

1. "Nigeria Cartoon Protests Kill 16," BBC News, February 19, 2006, at news.bbc.co.uk.

2. "Revenge in the Name of Religion," *Human Rights Watch*, May 25, 2005.

3. "African Divide over Gay Bishop," BBC News, September 8, 2003, at news.bbc.co.uk.

6. MODERN SAINTS AND MARTYRS

1. In a letter to *The Independent on Sunday*, Cox claimed to have redeemed 2,281 slaves on eight visits to Sudan. ("This is no scam. The slaves are real," *Independent on Sunday*, March 3, 2002.)

SUDAN

1. In the Quran, the original Arabic word *islam* can be interpreted in different ways. Some translators simply use the word *submission* or *devotion to God* to imply that all those who submit to God, including Jews and Christians (fellow people of the Book), are considered legitimate believers. Others translate *islam* to mean only Mohammed's followers. The debate over *islam's* true meaning indicates one of the growing fissures between liberals and conservatives within the religion today.

9. IN THE BEGINNING

1. For further discussion of the problems of longitude, see Dava Sobel's book *Longitude: The True Story of a Lone Genius Who Solved the Greatest Scientific Problem of His Time* (New York: Penguin Books, 1995).

2. Aristotle, *Meteorologica*, translated by E. W. Webster (Oxford: Clarendon Press, 1923), book 2, part 5.

3. Abū I-Walīd Muhammad ibn Ahmad. Muhammad Ibn Rushd was born in al-Andalus, contemporary Spain, in 1126.

4. Nicolas Wey-Gomez, *Tropics of Empire: Why Columbus Sailed South to the Indies* (Cambridge, Mass.: MIT Press, 2008), p. 70.

5. Maps Division, Library of Congress, Washington, D.C.

6. Ovid, *Metamorphoses,* translated by Mary M. Innes (London: Penguin Books, 1955) book 2, ll. 218–57.

7. Maps Division, Library of Congress, Washington, D.C.

8. Oliver Dunne and James E. Kelley, eds., *The Diario of Christopher Colombus's First Voyage to America* (Norman, Okla.: University of Oklahoma Press, 1989), p. 19.

9. Wey-Gomez, *The Tropics of Empire*, pp. 88–89.

10. Giovanni Vantini, *Christianity in Sudan* (Bologna, Italy: EMI, 1981), p. 33.

11. Ibid., p. 34.

12. The Prophet Mohammed's early biographers first compiled accounts of his life from the eighth to the tenth century. For further reading, see Muhammad Husayn Haykal's *The Life of Muhammad* (Indianapolis, Ind.: North American Trust Publications, 1967).

13. Richard Lobban, "The Slow Arrival of Islam in Christian Nubia." Institute for the Study of Islamic Thought in Africa Program of African Studies, at Northwestern University, May 23–25, 2003.

14. Vantini, *Christianity in Sudan*, p. 24.

15. Ibid., p. 207.

16. The cross, too, was influenced by the religions that predated Christianity in Sudan; it was a version of the ancient Egyptian ankh ☥.

17. "Railroads in Africa," *New York Times*, August 23, 1891.

18. Mansour Khalid, *War and Peace in Sudan* (London: Kegan Paul, 2003), p. 7.

19. "General Act" of February 26, 1885.

IO. FAITH AND FOREIGN POLICY

1. www.charitynavigator.org.

2. Samaritan's Purse Annual Report 2006.

3. "Christian Right Might Inflame War, Observes Fear," *Africanews* 63, May 2001.

4. Jemera Rone of Human Rights Watch was trying to get the word out on this then little-known spree of massacres in the region of Darfur.

5. Giles Fraser, "The Evangelicals Who Like to Giftwrap Islamophobia: The World's Largest Children's Christmas Project Has a Toxic Agenda," *Guardian*, November 10, 2003.

6. The Communist persecution of Christians was real and awful. Inside the Soviet Union, Christians who would not recant their beliefs were bound to crosses and laid on prison floors, and then fellow prisoners were forced to relieve themselves on the victims' faces, according to one witness, Richard Wurmbrand, a Romanian evangelical pastor imprisoned in Romania for fourteen years, who testified before Congress in 1966. In his book, *Tortured for Christ* (London: Hodder & Stoughton, 1967), Wurmbrand also recalled seeing another prisoner forced to serve human excrement as Com-

munion; another, fed to hungry rats; another, forced to watch his son beaten to death.

7. Franklin Graham, *Rebel with a Cause* (Nashville, Tenn.: Thomas Nelson, 1995), p. 74.

8. Ibid., p. 239.

9. Amit A. Pandya, "Faith, Justice and Violence," Stimson Center Report (Washington, D.C.: Henry L. Stimson Center, 2009), p. 34.

10. *Wall Street Journal*, July 5, 1995.

11. For a thorough discussion of the politics of the International Religious Freedom Act (IRFA), see Allen D. Hertzke's 2004 book, *Freeing God's Children*.

12. Other recent campaigns include anti–human trafficking and sanctions against North Korea.

13. William F. Schulz, ed., *The Future of Human Rights: U.S. Policy for a New Era* (Philadelphia: University of Pennsylvania Press, 2008), p. 200.

14. *New York Times*, March 21, 2001, and *Middle East Report*, March 29, 2001.

15. William Martin, "The Christian Right and American Foreign Policy," *Foreign Policy* 114, Spring 1999, 66–79.

16. www.1040window.org.

17. Elizabeth Kendal, "Cote D'Ivoire on Fire: West African Church at Risk," *World Evangelical Alliance*, April 8, 2004.

18. Amir Abdullah, "The 10/40 Window," *Nida'ul Islam*, no. 20, September–October 1997.

19. Graham, *Rebel with a Cause*, p. 187.

20. www.foxnews.com, February 22, 2007.

II. "MISSIONARY MAYONNAISE"

1. Darfur was an independent sultanate of the Fur people roughly the size of France until 1899, when the British incorporated the territory into their colonial landholdings.

2. Peter Martell, "Dancing Bashir Scoffs at Darfur Warrant," BBC News, March 5, 2009, at news.bbc.co.uk.

3. Khalid, *War and Peace in Sudan*, p. 65.

4. Fergus Nicoll, *The Sword of the Prophet: The Mahdi of Sudan and the Death of General Gordon* (Sutton, UK: Sutton Publishing, 2004), p. 194.

5. *Times* (London), December 31, 1898.

6. Nicoll, *Sword of the Prophet*, p. 9.

7. H.D.S. Greenway, "A Case for Doctor Watson," *Boston Globe*, April 3, 2007.

8. M. W. Daly, *Empire on the Nile: The Anglo-Egyptian Sudan 1898–1934* (New York: Cambridge University Press, 1986), p. 6.

9. Robert O. Collins, *British in the Sudan* (London: Macmillan, 1984), p. 173.

10. Tennyson crafted this epitaph for the Westminster Abbey gravestone of Charles Gordon, and it was published without the poet's permission in *The Times* of London on May 7, 1885.

11. Daly, *Empire on the Nile*, p. 253.

12. Mansour Khalid, *War and Peace in Sudan* (New York: Columbia University Press, 2003), p. 34, note 76.

13. Robert O. Collins, *Civil Wars and Revolution in the Sudan: Essays on the Sudan, Southern Sudan, and Darfur* (Hollywood, Calif.: Tsehai Publishers, 2005), p. 297.

14. On November 25, 2007, Gillian Gibbons, a teacher at Unity High School—founded by Gwynne—was deported from Sudan for allowing her students to name their class teddy bear Mohammed.

15. Collins, *British in the Sudan*, p. 195.

16. August 29, 1911, and May 17, 1911 (dates of correspondence).

17. Collins, *British in the Sudan*, p. 199.

18. Spartalis, *Karl Kumm: Last of the Livingstones*, p. 84.

19. Lilian Passmore Sanderson and Neville Sanderson, *Education, Religion and Politics in Southern Sudan, 1899–1964* (London: Ithaca Press, 1981), p. 1.

20. Heather Sharkey, "Christians Among Muslims: The Church Missionary Society in the Northern Sudan," *Journal of African History* 43 (2002): 57.

21. John Burton, "Christians, Colonists, and Conversion: A View from the Nilotic Sudan," *Journal of Modern African Studies* 23, no. 2 (June 1985): 361.

22. Niels Katfelt, ed., *Religion and African Wars* (London: C. Hurst, 2005), p. 14.

23. Collins, *Civil Wars and Revolution in the Sudan*, p. 300.

24. Khalid, *War and Peace in Sudan*, p. 58.

12. JUSTICE

1. Alex de Waal, *Islamism and Its Enemies on the Horn of Africa* (Indianapolis: Indiana University Press, 2004), p. 65.

2. Heather Sharkey, "Christians Among Muslims: The Church Missionary Society in the Northern Sudan," *Journal of African History* 33, no. 1 (2002).

3. Some militant leaders quietly kept their children in the "imperialist" Christian schools they denounced, and their successors still do today.

4. Benjamin Soares, ed., *Muslim-Christian Encounters in Africa* (Leiden; Boston: Brill, 2006), p. 71.

5. For further reading on America's use of Islam in Europe during the cold war, see Ian Johnson's 2010 book, *A Mosque in Munich*.

6. Copeland outlines his so-called "Search for the Muslim Billy Graham" in his memoir, *The Game Player: Confessions of the CIA's Original Political Operative* (London: Aurum Press, 1989).

7. Ibid., p. 133.

8. Thomas Joscelyn, "The Pope of Terrorism," *Weekly Standard*, July 25, 2005.

9. Rudyard Kipling, "The White Man's Burden," *McClatchy's*, 1899.

13. CHOOSE

1. The missionaries' names have been omitted to protect their safety.

14. SPOILING THE WORLD

1. Francis Deng, *The Dinka People of Sudan* (Long Grove, Ill.: Waveland Press, 1984), p. 150.
2. In 2009, the land dispute went to the Permanent Court of Arbitration—a UN-backed court at The Hague—which, on July 22 of that year, granted the north the rights to Heglig (that is most of the oil) and the south the land up to 10'10". Whether this deal will hold remains an open question.

SOMALIA

15. "THE REAL SUPERPOWER"

1. "Trip Report of Arlen Specter," September 30, 2002, on specter.senate.gov.
2. Ken Menkhaus, *Somalia: A Country in Peril, a Policy Nightmare*, ENOUGH, September 3, 2008.
3. Alex de Waal, *Islamism and Its Enemies to the Horn of Africa*, p. 254.
4. "Zawahiri Calls for Attacks on Ethiopian Forces in Somalia," Globalsecurity.org, January 5, 2007.
5. For a fascinating if somewhat fanciful account of Ethiopia's early religious history, see Graham Hancock's account of the Ark of the Covenant in *Sign and the Seal: The Quest for the Lost Ark of the Covenant* (New York: Simon & Schuster, 1992).

16. "THEY'LL KILL YOU"

1. In 2010, Jeffrey Gettleman and Neil MacFarquhar exposed the controversial diversion of food aid. See "Somalia Food Aid Bypasses Needy, UN Study Says," *New York Times*, March 9, 2010.

17. PROXY

1. Sunan Abu Dawood, book 37, number 4288.

18. "GATHER YE MEN OF TOMORROW"

1. John Miller, "A Conversation with the Most Dangerous Man in the World," *Esquire*, February 1, 1999.

INDONESIA

20. NOVIANA AND THE FIRING SQUAD

1. www.oikumene.org.
2. "Vatican Deeply Saddened over Indonesia Executions," *Ansara News*, September 23, 2006.

3. Andrew Causey, *Hard Bargaining in Sumatra: Western Travelers and Toba Bataks in the Marketplace* (Honolulu: University of Hawaii Press, 2003), p. 80.

21. BEGINNING ON THE WIND

1. Gerry Van Klinken, "Ethnicity in Indonesia," in Colin Mackerras, ed., *Ethnicity in Asia* (London: Routledge Curzon, 2003), p. 69.
2. Karel A. Steenbrink, *Dutch Colonialism and Indonesian Islam: Contacts and Conflicts 1596–1950* (New York: Rodopi, 2006), p. 69.
3. Ibid., p. 71.
4. Martin Van Bruinessen, "Global and Local in Indonesian Islam," *Southeast Asian Studies* 37, no. 2 (1999): p. 57.
5. www.shell.com.
6. Ibid.
7. Theodore Friend, *Indonesian Destinies* (Cambridge, Mass.: Belknap/Harvard University Press, 2003), p. 113.
8. For further reading on this history, see Robert W. Hefner's *Civil Islam: Muslims and Democratization in Indonesia* (Princeton, N.J.: Princeton University Press, 2000).
9. Lorraine V. Aragon, *Fields of the Lord: Animism, Christian Minorities, and State Development in Indonesia* (Honolulu: University of Hawaii Press, 2000), p. 314.
10. Ibid., p. 60.

22. "NO MORE HAPPY SUNDAYS"

1. Open Doors UK, "Sunday School Teachers Freed," August 6, 2007, at www.opendoorsuk.org.uk.

24. THE CLASH WITHIN

1. Mark Landler, "Clinton Praises Indonesian Democracy," *New York Times*, February 18, 2009.
2. Robin Bush, *Expressing Islam: Religious Life and Politics in Indonesia* (Singapore: Institute of Southeast Asian Studies, 2008).

25. "ALLAHCRACY"

1. www.thejakartaglobe.com/home/police-arrest-jakarta-bomb-finance-suspect-muhammad-jibril/326126.
2. Alvin Darlanika Soedarjo, "'Prince of Jihad' Arrested in Indonesia: Police," Agence Presse-France, August 25, 2009.

MALAYSIA

26. THE RACE TO SAVE THE LAST LOST SOULS

1. "Indonesia's Dwindling Rainforests," *Economist*, September 10, 2009.

2. Clifford A. Pearson, "Petronas Towers," *Architectural Record* (1999): 95.

3. "Sudan: Whose Oil? Write a Letter to China," *Fatal Transactions*, newsletter, January, 2, 2008, at www.fataltransactions.org.

4. Reuters, April 18, 2007.

5. *The CIA World Factbook 2007*.

6. For a discussion on the global politics of oil, see Peter Maass's 2009 book, *Crude World*.

7. A. B. Shamsul, "Identity Construction, Nation Formation, and Islamic Revivalism in Malaysia," in Robert W. Hefner and Patricia Horvatich, eds., *Islam in an Era of Nation-States: Politics and Religious Renewal in Muslim Southeast Asia* (Honolulu: University of Hawaii Press, 1997), p. 218.

8. Mahathir Mohamad, *Islam and the Muslim Ummah: Selected Speeches of Dr. Mahathir Mohamad, Prime Minister of Malaysia* (Putrajaya, Malaysia: Pelanduk Publications, 2001), pp. 267–68.

9. Rachel Harvey, "Malaysia Church Attacks Continue in Use of 'Allah' Row," BBC News, January 11, 2010, at news.bbc.co.uk.

10. Robert Dentan, "Ambivalences in Child Training by the Semai of Peninsular Malaysia and Other Peoples," *Crossroads: An Interdisciplinary Journal of Southeast Asian Studies* 15, no. 1 (2001): 96.

11. Chow Kum Hor, "Are They Losing Their Cultural Heritage?" *New Straits Times*, July 5, 2006.

12. Robert Dentan, *Malaysia and the "Original People": A Case Study of the Impact of Development on Indigenous Peoples* (Boston, Mass.: Allyn and Bacon, 1997), p. 144.

13. Dentan, "Ambivalences in Child Training," p. 102.

28. THE RIVER

1. "Malaysian State Stiffens Penalties to Stifle Muslim Conversions," Associated Press, June 27, 2002.

29. THE GREATEST STORY EVER TOLD

1. "Spotted Doves at War: The Praak Sangkiil," *Asian Folklore Studies* 58, no. 2 (1999): 407.

2. Charles Scanlon, "South Korea's Zealous Mid-East Missionaries," BBC News, May 6, 2004, at news.bbc.co.uk.

3. Norimitsu Onishi, "Korean Missionaries Carry Word to Hard-to-Sway Places," *New York Times*, November 1, 2004.

PHILIPPINES

30. A KIDNAPPING

1. Mark A. Noll, *A History of Christianity in the United States and Canada* (Grand Rapids, Mich.: Eerdmans Publishing, 1992), p. 293.
2. Sarah Fort, "Collateral Damage: Human Rights and U.S. Military Aid After 9/11," *Center for Public Integrity*, May 31, 2007.
3. Gracia Burnham, *In the Presence of My Enemies* (Carol Stream, Ill.: Tyndale House, 2003), pp. 218–19.

31. FROM TWO THOUSAND FEET

1. www.state.gov/t/pm/ppa/sat/c14560.htm.
2. www.usaid.gov/policy/budget/cbj2007/ane/ph.html.
3. From the *Shorter Oxford English Dictionary*, sixth edition, p. 70.
4. Hilario Gomez, Jr., *The Moro Rebellion and the Search for Peace: A Study on Christian-Muslim Relations in the Philippines* (Zamboanga City, Philippines: Silsah Publications, 2000), pp. 96–97.
5. Astrid Tuminez, "The Past Is Always Present: The Moros of Mindanao and the Quest for Peace," Southeast Asia Research Centre (of City University of Hong Kong), Working Paper Series No. 99, May 2008.

32. REVERSION

1. Maria Russa, "Twenty-two Die as Police Storm Manila Jail," CNN, March 15, 2005.

34. TO WITNESS

1. This was recorded by a tenth-century Islamic scholar, Sulaiman bin Ahmad al-Tabarani, three centuries after Mohammed's death.

EPILOGUE

1. Unlike many other evangelical groups, the Jesus Film Project explicitly says that they measure their success not on how many people see the film but on how many dedicate their lives to Christ as a result.

BIBLIOGRAPHY

In addition to conducting interviews, I used archives at Harvard University, the Library of Congress, the New York Public Library, and the University of Durham in northern England, as well as research materials from the BBC, *The New York Times*, *The Wall Street Journal*, the Associated Press, Reuters, hundreds of local newspapers, radio broadcasts, and human rights reports by secular and religious groups. Below, grouped according to country, is a partial list of other sources for further reading. For a complete list of sources, see www.thetenthparallel.com.

NIGERIA

Amin, Al-Amin. Almajiri Directorate National Council for the Welfare of the Destitute. *Almajiri and the Quranic Education*. Kaduna, Nigeria: Rishab Printing Press, 2001.

Ashafa, Ustaz Muhammad Nurayn, and Evang. James Movel Wuye. *The Pastor and the Imam: Responding to Conflict*. Lagos, Nigeria: Ibrash Publications, 1999.

Berger, Peter. "Secularization Falsified." *First Things* (February 2008).

Berger, Peter, et al. *The Desecularization of the World: Resurgent Religion and World Politics*. Grand Rapids, Mich.: Eerdmans Publishing, 1999.

Cooper, Barbara. *Evangelical Christians in the Muslim Sahel*. Bloomington: Indiana University Press, 2006.

Cox, Caroline, and Catherine Butcher. *Cox's Book of Modern Saints and Martyrs*. London: Continuum, 2006.

Falola, Toyin. *Violence in Nigeria: The Crisis of Religious Politics and Secular Ideologies*. Rochester, N.Y.: University of Rochester Press, 1998.

Freston, Paul. *Evangelicals and Politics in Asia, Africa, and Latin America*. New York: Cambridge University Press, 2001.

Fyfe, Christopher, and Andrew Walls, eds. *Christianity in Africa in the 1990s*. Edinburgh: Centre of African Studies, University of Edinburgh, 1996.

Haynes, Jeff. "Religion, Secularisation, and Politics: A Postmodern Conspectus." *Third World Quarterly* 18, no. 4 (1997): 709–28.

Jenkins, Philip. *The Next Christendom: The Coming of Global Christianity*. New York: Oxford University Press, 2002.

———. *The New Faces of Christianity: Believing the Bible in the Global South*. New York: Oxford University Press, 2006.

Johnson, Todd M., and Sun Young Chung. "Tracking Global Christianity's Statistical Centre of Gravity, AD 33–AD 2100." *International Review of Mission* 93, no. 369 (April 2004): 166–80.

Kastfelt, Niels. *Scriptural Politics: The Bible and the Koran as Political Models in the Middle East and Africa*. London: Hurst and Co., 2004.

———. *Religion and Africa's Civil Wars* (New York: Palgrave/Macmillan, 2005).

Kukah, Matthew Hassan. *Religion, Politics, and Power in Northern Nigeria*. Ibadan, Nigeria: Spectrum Books, 1993.

Kumm, Karl W. *From Hausaland to Egypt, Through the Sudan*. London: Constable and Co., 1910.

Küng, Hans, and David Tracy. *Paradigm Change in Theology: A Symposium for the Future*. New York: Crossroad Publishing Co., 1989.

Larson, Erik. *Isaac's Storm: A Man, a Time, and the Deadliest Hurricane in History*. New York: Random House, 1999.

Levtzion, Nehemia, and Randall L. Pouwels. *The History of Islam in Africa*. Athens: Ohio University Press, 2000.

Maass, Peter. *Crude World: The Violent Twilight of Oil*. New York: Random House, 2009.

Maier, Karl. *This House Has Fallen: Nigeria in Crisis*. Cambridge, Mass.: Westview Press, 2000.

Ranger, Terence. *Evangelical Christianity and Democracy in Africa*. New York: Oxford University Press, 2008.

Roy, Oliver. *Globalized Islam: The Search for a New Ummah*. New York: Columbia University Press, 2004.

Sanneh, Lamin. *Whose Religion Is Christianity? The Gospel Behind the West*. Grand Rapids, Mich.: Eerdmans Publishing, 2003.

Voll, John. "African Muslims and Christians in World History: The Irrelevance of the 'Clash of Civilizations.'" *Journal of Islamic Studies* 18, no. 3 (2007): 436–39.

SUDAN

Abdullah, Dr. Amir. "Christian Missionaries in the Muslim World: Manufacturing Kufr." *Nida'ul Islam* 20 (September 1997), available at www.islam.org.

An-Na'im, Abdullahi Ahmed. *Proselytization and Communal Self-Determination in Africa*. New York: Orbis Books, 1999.

———. *Islam and the Secular State: Negotiating the Future of Shari'a*. Cambridge, Mass., and London: Harvard University Press, 2008.

Burton, John. "Christians, Colonists, and Conversion: A View from the Nilotic Sudan." *Journal of Modern African Studies* 23, no. 2 (June 1985): 349–69.

Bush, Luis. "Opening the 10/40 Window." *Frontlines* 2, no. 2 (Fall 1995), available at www.heartofgod.com.

———. "The 10/40 Window Overhead Transparency Map Set." Global Mapping International website, April 1996, at www.gmi.org.

Coll, Steven. *Ghost Wars: The Secret History of the CIA, Afghanistan, and bin Laden, from the Soviet Invasion to September 10th, 2001.* New York: Penguin Press, 2004.

Collins, Robert O. *Civil Wars and Revolution in the Sudan: Essays on the Sudan, Southern Sudan, and Darfur, 1962–2004.* Hollywood, Calif.: Tsehai Publishers, 2005.

Collins, Robert O., and Francis M. Deng. *The British in the Sudan, 1898–1956.* London: Macmillan Press, 1984.

Copeland, Miles. *The Game Player: Confessions of the CIA's Original Political Operative.* London: Aurum Press, 1989.

Deng, Francis Mading. *The Dinka People of the Sudan.* Illinois: Waveland Press, 1984.

———. *War of Visions: Conflict of Identities in the Sudan.* Washington, D.C.: Brookings Institution, 1995.

De Waal, Alex. *Islamism and Its Enemies in the Horn of Africa.* Bloomington: Indiana University Press, 2004.

Eliade, Mircea. *The Sacred and the Profane.* Translated by Willard R. Trask. New York: Harcourt, Brace, 1959.

Haykal, Muhammad Husayn. *The Life of Muhammad.* USA: American Trust Publications, 1976.

Hertzke, Allen D. *Freeing God's Children: The Unlikely Alliance for Global Human Rights.* New York: Rowman and Littlefield Publishers, 2004.

James, Wendy. *The Listening Ebony: Moral Knowledge, Religion, and Power Among the Uduk of Sudan.* New York: Oxford University Press, 1988.

Jenkins, Philip. *Jesus Wars: How Four Patriarchs, Three Queens, and Two Emperors Decided What Christians Would Believe for the Next 1,500 Years.* New York: HarperOne, 2010.

Johnson, Douglas. *The Root Causes of Sudan's Civil Wars.* Bloomington: Indiana University Press, 2003.

———. "Why Abyei Matters: The Breaking Point of Sudan's Comprehensive Peace Agreement." *African Affairs* 107, no. 426 (2008): 1–19.

Johnson, Ian. *A Mosque in Munich: Nazis, the CIA, and the Rise of the Muslim Brotherhood in the West.* New York: Houghton Mifflin Harcourt, 2010.

Khalid, Mansour. *War and Peace in Sudan.* London: Kegan Paul, 2003.

Lobban, Richard. "The Slow Arrival of Islam in Christian Nubia." Paper presented at Institute for the Study of Islamic Thought in Africa (ISITA), May 23–25, 2003.

Lobban, Richard A., et al. *Historical Dictionary of the Sudan.* Lanham, Md.: Scarecrow Press, 2002.

Marty, Martin E., and R. Scott Appleby. *Fundamentalisms Observed.* Chicago: University of Chicago Press, 1991.

Nanji, Azim, and Malise Ruthven. *Historical Atlas of Islam.* Cambridge, Mass.: Harvard University Press, 2004.

Nicoll, Fergus. *The Sword of the Prophet: The Mahdi of Sudan and the Death of General Gordon.* Stroud, UK: Sutton Publishing, 2004.

Robert, Dana L. "The First Globalization: The Internationalization of the Protestant Missionary Movement Between World Wars." *International Bulletin of Missionary Research,* Overseas Ministry Study Center, April 2002.

———. *Occupy Until I Come: A. T. Pierson and the Evangelization of the World*. Grand Rapids, Mich.: Eerdmans Publishing, 2003.

Sanderson, Lilian Passmore. "The Sudan Interior Mission and the Condominium Sudan, 1937–1955." *Journal of Religion in Africa* 8, no. 1 (1976): 13–40.

Sanderson, Lilian Passmore, and Neville Sanderson. *Education, Religion and Politics in Southern Sudan 1899–1964*. London and Khartoum: Ithaca Press/Khartoum University Press, 1981.

Sharkey, Heather. "Christians Among Muslims: The Church Missionary Society in the Northern Sudan." *Journal of African History* 43, no. 1 (2002): 51–75, available at www .jstor.org/stable/4100426.

———. "Arabic Anti-missionary Treatises: Muslim Response to Christian Evangelism in the Modern Middle East." *International Bulletin of Missionary Research* 28, no. 3 (July 2004): 1–10.

———. "Arab Identity and Ideology in Sudan: The Politics of Language, Ethnicity, and Race." *African Affairs* 107, no. 426 (2008): 21–43.

Vantini, Giovanni. *Christianity in the Sudan*. Bologna, Italy: EMI, 1981.

Wey Gomez, Nicolas. *The Tropics of Empire: Why Columbus Sailed South to the Indies*. Cambridge, Mass.: MIT Press, 2008.

SOMALIA

Menkhaus, Ken. *Somalia: A Country in Peril, a Policy Nightmare*. ENOUGH, September 3, 2008.

———. "The Crisis in Somalia: A Tragedy in Five Acts." *African Affairs* 106, no. 424 (2007): 357–90.

INDONESIA

Aragon, Lorraine V. *Fields of the Lord: Animism, Christian Minorities, and State Development in Indonesia*. Honolulu: University of Hawaii Press, 2000.

———. "Communal Violence in Poso, Central Sulawesi: Where People Eat Fish and Fish Eat People." *Indonesia*, October 31, 2001, p. 72.

Bertrand, Jacques. *Nationalism and Ethnic Conflict in Indonesia*. New York: Cambridge University Press, 2004.

Bush, Robin. "Regional Sharia Regulations in Indonesia: Anomaly or Symptom?" In Greg Fealy and Sally White, eds. *Expressing Islam: Religious Life and Politics in Indonesia* (Singapore: Institute of Southeast Asian Studies, 2008), pp. 174–91.

Conboy, Ken. *The Second Front: Inside Asia's Most Dangerous Terrorist Network*. Jakarta, Indonesia: Equinox Publishing, 2006.

Friend, Theodore. *Indonesian Destinies*. Cambridge, Mass.: Belknap Press of Harvard University Press, 2003.

Hefner, Robert W. *The Politics of Multiculturalism: Pluralism and Citizenship in Malaysia, Singapore, and Indonesia*. Honolulu: University of Honolulu Press, 2001.

Hefner, Robert, and Patricia Horvatich. *Islam in an Era of Nation States*. Honolulu: University of Honolulu Press, 1997.

Hooker, M. B. *Indonesian Islam: Social Change Through Contemporary* Fatawa. Honolulu: University of Hawaii Press, 2003.

Husein, Fatimah. *Muslim-Christian Relations in the New Order Indonesia: The Exclusivist and Inclusivist Muslims' Perspectives*. Jakarta: Mizan Media Utama, 2005.

Lumsdaine, David. *Evangelical Christianity and Democracy in Asia*. New York: Oxford University Press, 2009.

Ricklefs, M. C. *Mystic Synthesis in Java: A History of Islamization from the Fourteenth to the Early Nineteenth Centuries*. Norwalk, Conn.: Signature Books, 2006.

Stauth, Georg. *Politics and Cultures of Islamization in Southeast Asia: Indonesia and Malaysia in the Nineteen-Nineties*. New Brunswick, N.J.: Transaction Publishers, 2002.

Wilson, Christopher. *Overcoming Violent Conflict: Vol. 5: Peace and Development Analysis in Indonesia*. Jakarta: Indonesian Printers, 2005.

MALAYSIA

Andaya, Barbara, and Leonard Andaya. *A History of Malaysia*. Honolulu: University of Honolulu Press, 2001.

Cheng, Tun-Jen, and Deborah Brown. *Religious Organizations and Democratization: Case Studies from Contemporary Asia*. New York: East Gate Books, 2006.

Dentan, Robert. *Malaysia and the "Original People": A Case Study of the Impact of Development on Indigenous Peoples*. Boston, Mass.: Allyn and Bacon, 1996.

———. "Spotted Doves at War: The Praak Sangkiil." *Asian Folklore Studies* 58, no. 2 (1999): 397–434.

———. "Ambivalences in Child Training by the Semai of Peninsular Malaysia and Other People." *Crossroads: An Interdisciplinary Journal of Southeast Asian Studies* 15, no. 1 (2001): 89–129.

Duncan, Christopher. *Civilizing the Margins: Southeast Asian Government Policies for the Development of Minorities*. Ithaca, N.Y.: Cornell University Press, 2004.

Mahathir, Dr. Mohamad. *Islam and the Muslim Ummah*. Selangor, Malaysia: Pelanduk Publications, 2001.

Means, Natalie, and Paul Means. *And the Seed Grew*. Singapore: n.p., n.d. (1981).

Nicholas, Colin. *The Orang Asli and the Contest for Resources: Indigenous Politics, Development and Identity in Peninsular Malaysia*. Denmark: International Work Group for Indigenous Affairs, 2000.

Noor, Farish. *Islam Embedded: The Historical Development of the Pan-Malaysian Islamic Party, PAS (1951–2003)*. Kuala Lumpur: Malaysian Sociological Research Institute, 2004.

Winzeler, Robert. *Indigenous Peoples and the State: Politics, Land, and Ethnicity in the Malayan Peninsula and Borneo*. New Haven, Conn.: Monograph 46/Yale University Southeast Asia Studies, 1997.

PHILIPPINES

Barrett, David, et al. *World Christian Encyclopedia*, 2nd ed. 2 vols. New York: Oxford University Press, 2001.

Burnham, Gracia, with Dean Merrill. *In the Presence of My Enemies*. Wheaton, Ill.: Tyndale House Publishers, 2003.

———. *To Fly Again: Surviving the Tailspins of Life*. Wheaton, Ill.: Tyndale House Publishers, 2005.

Hsu, Becky, et al. "Estimating the Religious Composition of All Nations: An Empirical Assessment of the World Christian Database." *Journal for the Scientific Study of Religion* (December 2008).

McCoy, Alfred. *Policing America's Empire: The United States, the Philippines, and the Rise of the Surveillance State*. Madison: University of Wisconsin Press, 2009.

O'Brien, Joanne, and Martin Palmer. *The Atlas of Religion*. Berkeley: University of California Press, 2007.

Vitug, Marites Danguilan, and Glenda Gloria. *Under the Crescent Moon: Rebellion in Mindanao*. Quezon City, Philippines: Ateneo Center for Social Policy and Public Affairs, 2000.

ACKNOWLEDGMENTS

Grateful acknowledgment to the New America Foundation, the American Academy in Rome, the Nieman Foundation for Journalism at Harvard University, the Woodrow Wilson International Center for Scholars, and the Corporation of Yaddo.

I am indebted to Jonathan Galassi for his patience, guidance, and inestimable friendship; to Paul Elie, for his keen mind and prodigious faith—without both, this book would not exist; to my dearest friend and agent, Bill Clegg, and to Sloan Harris, for shepherding this idea into the world.

In addition, I'd like to thank those without whom this reporting and research would have been impossible, beginning with the crack investigative work of Rachel Nolan and Annabel Hogg. In alphabetical order: The United States: Reza Aslan, Wah-Ming Chang, Jenna Dolan, Ian Douglas, John R. Hebert, the late John Hyde, Sophie Fels, Dexter Filkins, Philip Jenkins, Todd M. Johnson, Karen Maine, John McGhee, Walter Russell Meade, Kate Peters, Tim Shah; Nigeria: Reverend Abdu, Chris Albin-Lackey, Imam Nurayn Ashafa, Archbishop Josiah Fearon, Archbishop Benjamin Kwashi, Alex Last, Murray Last, Pastor James Wuye, Haruna Yakubu; Sudan: J. Carrier, Francis Deng, Alex De Waal, Brian D'Silva, Carolyn Fleuhr-Lobban, Ivan Giesbrecht, Franklin Graham, Ken Isaacs, Douglas H. Johnson, Chief Kwol Deng Kwol, Richard Lobban, Jason Matus, Chief Nyol Paduot, John Prendergast, John Ryle, Heather Sharkey, Roger Winter; Somalia: Ali Musa Abdi, Dr. Hawa Abdi, Peter Bergen, Matthew Bryden, Jose Cendon, Charles Ehrhart, Roland Marchal, Ken Menkhaus, Dr. Deqo Waqaf, Bashir Yusef Osman; Indonesia: Taufik Andrie, Andreas Harsono, Robert Hefner, Sidney Jones, Jacqueline Koch, John MacDougall, Dave McCrae, Zamira Loebis, Febbe Orida; Malaysia: Farish Ahmad-Noor, Robert K. Dentan, Dr. Juli Edo, Nora Murat, Sam Zia-Zarifi; Philippines: Gracia Burnham, Father Peter Geremiah, Orlando de Guzman, Bong Sarmiento, Jose Torres, the late Maricel and George Vigo, Marites D. Vitug.

I am so grateful to those who read and reread this book, including Vijay Balakrishnan, Victoria Churchville, Steve Coll, Meredith Davenport, Tim Golden, Dana Goodyear, Susanna McFadden, David Siegel, and Amy Waldman. To mentors Susan Cheever, John Guare, Richard Holbrooke, Paige Kelly, Kati Marton, Julia Murphy, Seamus Murphy, and my parents, Phoebe and Frank Griswold.

To my sister, Hannah, and her family, who allow me to orbit around them.

INDEX